Three Lions Versus the World

England's World Cup Stories from
the Men Who Were There

Mark Pougatch

**MAINSTREAM
PUBLISHING**

EDINBURGH AND LONDON

First published in Great Britain in 2010 by
MAINSTREAM PUBLISHING COMPANY
(EDINBURGH) LTD
7 Albany Street
Edinburgh EH1 3UG

ISBN 9781845965563

A catalogue record for this book is available
from the British Library

Typeset in Adobe Caslon and Franklin Gothic

Printed and bound in Great Britain by
CPI Mackays, Chatham ME5 8TD

1 3 5 7 9 10 8 6 4 2

To Victoria, Sam, Isobel and Saskia, with all my love.
And in loving memory of my father, who used to wear the West Ham
badge I gave him on his dressing gown.

ACKNOWLEDGEMENTS

I am enormously grateful to a large number of people for all their help, encouragement and cooperation with this book.

It was a great pleasure to speak to so many players and managers who kindly gave up their time. I would like to thank Sir Tom Finney, Roy Bentley, Bert Williams, the late Gil Merrick, Ivor Broadis, Bryan Douglas, Don Howe, Bill Slater, Jimmy Armfield, Ron Flowers, George Cohen, Martin Peters, Roger Hunt, Alan Mullery, Terry Cooper, Paul Mariner, Phil Thompson, Sir Trevor Brooking, Terry Butcher, Gary Lineker, Peter Reid, Chris Waddle, Des Walker, Glenn Hoddle, Graeme Le Saux, Tony Adams, Michael Owen, Trevor Sinclair, Danny Mills, Nicky Butt, Paul Robinson and Peter Crouch. It was also wonderful to speak to the doyen of football journalists, Brian Glanville, who kindly shared his memories of World Cups past.

There were many people who helped pave the way for these interviews. I would like to place on record my appreciation and gratitude to Jimmy and Anne Armfield, Brian Finney, Rachael Flint, Johnny Whitmore, Rhodri Burgess, Barbara Slater, Mark Cooper, Rick Glanvill, Rob Mason, Neil Duncanson, Ian Payne, Pete Stevens, Peter Kay of Sporting Chance, Mark Hannen of Newcastle United FC, Simon Felstein and Richard Hubbard of Tottenham Hotspur FC and the team at BBC Radio WM sport.

Working in a busy sports room, I was never going to be short of advice – not all of it helpful, of course – from my friends and colleagues at BBC Radio 5 Live. It's a wonderful place to work, and I am particularly grateful to Ian Dennis, Mark Clemmit, Nigel Adderley, Steve Houghton, Mark Bright, Juliette Ferrington, Caroline Short and Matthew Allen for their contacts and suggestions.

It is a privilege to have Fabio Capello write the foreword, and I thank him, Adrian Bevington and Stuart Mawhinney at the FA very much indeed.

Nick Canham and Iain McGregor were midwives at the book's birth, and although they both left home soon after, I hope they are pleased with the way the baby has grown up.

At Mainstream Publishing, Bill Campbell put his faith in me to write the book, Alex Hepworth was my hugely efficient editor, Graeme Blaikie was the editorial coordinator and Fiona Atherton was in charge of the PR. Thank you to the whole team.

My friend Gavin White kindly provided me with the perfect quiet bolt-hole in which to write in London, when I needed it. Thank you, Gav, and I hope this goes some way to make up for Liverpool's season.

This project simply would not have happened without the hard work and dedication of my agent, Michael Cohen at MPC Entertainment. Michael – and Ian and Liga – I thank you and look forward to many more years together.

But, most of all, I owe an enormous debt to my wonderful wife, Victoria. Her love, her unswerving support, her sense of humour and her advice have sustained me throughout this project and my whole career. It is a debt I am lucky to have. My love and gratitude are hers.

CONTENTS

FOREWORD

For as long as I can remember, it has been my dream to manage the England team. It came true for me more than two years ago, and right from that moment all my focus has been on the World Cup. As a club manager, I took my teams into important finals, important tournaments, but even with the likes of AC Milan and Real Madrid we were representing just one city. With a country it is different: you carry the expectation of an entire nation with you. It is a big responsibility, but it is an even bigger honour and something to make you very proud.

I have been made to feel very welcome in England since the first moment I came here. I have travelled to watch games up and down the country, and the people I meet are fantastic. My life in football and away from my job has been perfect. The affection I have for this country and everyone I have met here will stay with me once we are at the World Cup. You have to keep in your mind those who are supporting you, who follow you everywhere you go.

I am looking forward to South Africa, when we will have the chance to have the team together for a long period, like a club environment. It will be a big challenge but one I will relish, having waited such a long time to have this opportunity.

My recollection of taking part in the World Cup is not a good one, and I hope to change that. I was part of the Italy squad that travelled to West Germany in 1974, and we went out in the first round. It should have been the ultimate sporting moment for me, but it was one of the lowest points. I hope to create new memories with England. This new chapter – perhaps it could be lucky number 13.

Enjoy reading this document of England at the World Cup, and I will do all that I can to create a new story in South Africa with my staff and the players. Mark is a respected journalist who has spoken to the people who lived these stories, who are part of history, and it is an important record of England's World Cup story.

Fabio Capello
February 2010

1

||||||||||||||||||||||||||||||||||||||||||||||||||||||||||||||||||||||||||||||||||||||||||||||||||||||||||||||||||||||||||||||||||||||||||||

BRAZIL 1950

I had just been asked to write this book when I ran into Mick in the village post office. He is a Wolves fanatic, a seasoned football fan and a walking encyclopaedia on the game. He was adamant about who I should interview: 'Tom Finney. You must go and see Tom Finney. The greatest player this country's ever produced.' I promised Mick I would go and see him first – not just to avoid one of Mick's lengthy monologues on the England goalkeeping situation, the lack of English players at Arsenal or who should replace Andrew Flintoff but because I knew Sir Tom was in a unique position to give me an insight into the early days. He is the last man remaining to have played in England's first three World Cups. A couple of weeks later, I drove to see him at his home in Preston.

Sir Tom was born in the street next to Preston's home ground of Deepdale. He was a frail boy and not even 5 ft tall by the age of 14. When Preston offered him terms, his father insisted he still completed his apprenticeship at the family's plumbing business, and he continued to work in the trade for some time after the war to supplement his weekly wage from football. Inevitably, he became known as the 'Preston Plumber'. He stayed at this same club throughout his football career, and such is his status in the town that there are a Sir Tom Finney Stand and a Sir Tom Finney statue at Deepdale; they held a Sir Tom Finney Day in March 2009 in his honour; and, to reach his house, I drove up Sir Tom Finney Way.

Sir Tom, now 88, sat contentedly in his chair, surrounded by photographs of his family and from his days in football, as his son and grandson led me into his sitting room. I asked him about playing in the 1950 tournament: 'It was very strange being asked to play for England in the World Cup.

It had never happened before. It wasn't the strongest squad that went to Brazil. In those days the members of the FA Board didn't really meet that often, and I felt sometimes they left better players out.' That quote alone says so much about the way football was run in this country in the post-war period. Despite being the so-called 'home of football', England had not yet played in the World Cup, and, in stark contrast to the way the game is today, the power then was totally with the administrators and the clubs – and certainly not the players.

England had missed the first three tournaments, held between 1930 and 1938, because they had withdrawn from FIFA over an argument regarding the status and treatment of amateurs and professionals. In the run-up to the 1928 Olympics football tournament, FIFA ruled that 'broken-time payments' had to be paid to cover the expenses of the amateurs involved. The four Home Nations regarded this as unacceptable interference from the game's global governing body and resigned from FIFA. They rejoined in 1946, and the World Cup Committee responded by generously designating the British Championship a qualifying zone not just for the winners but for the runners-up as well.

Both England and Scotland won their first two games to secure the two spots on offer ahead of their meeting at Hampden, but, far from embracing the World Cup Committee's gesture, the Scottish FA truculently decided they would accept the invitation only if they travelled to Brazil as British Champions. The clash at Hampden suddenly assumed far greater importance. Chelsea's Roy Bentley scored the only goal of the game for England, Bert Williams had a blinder in goal, Scotland hit the bar and the Scottish FA obstinately refused to budge, despite protestations from their own players.

Walter Winterbottom had become England's first full-time national manager in 1946, but he never had official responsibility for picking the team. That fell to a group of selectors who were club chairmen or directors, and it often felt as if these selectors would press for their own players even if others were in better form or if the team suffered from a lack of continuity as a result. Hence what Sir Tom meant when he suspected better players were sometimes left out.

The clubs held all the cards. Players were tied to them by what was known as the 'retain and transfer' system. Clubs could keep a player's registration – and so prevent him from moving – while refusing to pay him if he asked for a transfer. Even if they did get a move, all players were subject to the maximum wage, which had been enshrined in the game since the previous century. No player, whether at the bottom of the game's pyramid in the Third Division South or North, or a regular international like Tom Finney, could earn more than £12 a week in the 1950–51 season. Win bonuses and international match fees (£20 for the 1950 World Cup) would top that up, but in the 1950s professional footballers' earnings were very much on a par with the average working wage. Only a few players earned enough to buy a car or a house, and most lived in property owned by the club and travelled to training by bus. They weren't quite serfs, but they simply were not permitted the chance to earn anything like the sum commensurate with their ability – and they played through an era when the game was enormously popular. Attendances rocketed to a record of just over 41 million in the 1948–49 League season as a war-weary and indebted nation, which was still subject to rationing, looked for some cheap entertainment at the weekend.

These enormous crowds were certainly not watching football that was the result of sophisticated training methods. Training consisted mainly of lapping the pitch, to keep or get fit, and many clubs never even got a ball out during the week, working on the bizarre principle that it would make the players want it more and look after it better on a Saturday: a sort of absence-makes-the-heart-grow-fonder approach for the 1950s footballer. Tactically, England knew what they liked and stuck to it, because more often than not it worked. They lined up in what was known as the 'WM' formation. Three defenders and two half-backs, or wing-halves, made up the 'M', and five in attack the 'W': outside-left, inside-left, centre-forward, inside-right and outside-right.

England travelled to South America as one of the hot favourites, and yet to some extent they were in a state of flux. The core of the team, which had existed since the end of the Second World War, had gone. Goalkeeper Frank Swift had retired; Laurie Scott's broken leg virtually finished his career; George Hardwick was injured, and struggled for form from then on; and Tommy Lawton dropped down to the Third Division with Notts County. Raich Carter had retired in 1947, his best years being lost to the war.

However, England's results were impressive, with just four defeats in twenty-nine matches following the resumption of international football.

Dubbed the 'Kings of Football' by the Brazilian press, they were led by the fair-haired Billy Wright at wing-half and had some fine players to choose from up front. The great Stanley Matthews was thirty-five but still a top-class player, and with him on the right wing and the marvellously two-footed Finney on the left, there was a stream of chances created for the other forwards, chiefly Stan Mortensen and Wilf Mannion. Tom Finney had made his England debut in 1946 and had been a fixture in the side ever since.

The reason Sir Tom was, and is, held in such regard by everyone, from Mick in my post office to the great former Liverpool manager Bill Shankly, was because of his ability to play in so many of the different forward positions they used in the '50s. Shankly was a teammate of Finney's at Preston and said of him, 'He would have been great in any team, in any match and in any age . . . even if he had been wearing an overcoat.' Equally at home on the right wing, the left wing or even as centre-forward, Sir Tom remembers his rivalry with the great Stanley Matthews as a friendly one, and when Finney was switched to the left to accommodate Matthews down the right, the upshot was a 10–0 win against Portugal in Lisbon in May 1947 and a 4–0 humbling of the still World Champions Italy in Turin a year later.

The FA clearly still regarded this international jamboree as a bit of a gimmick, and just to underline how seriously they were – or were not – taking the World Cup, they arranged a goodwill tour of Canada to overlap with the start of the tournament. Seen through the prism of today's World Cup and all the hoopla that goes with it, it is a decision that seems barely believable, but the FA really felt the only decent football was played at home – and they were only going to Brazil very reluctantly. The trip to Canada included England's most valuable blue-chip commodity, Stanley Matthews, who, as a result, arrived in Brazil just three days before the opening game, after the slog of a 28-hour journey from Canada via New York and Trinidad. Manchester United had also organised a trip to the US and requested that none of their players should go to the World Cup, a request the FA did not turn down flat – as might have been expected – but prevaricated over before saying the United players were wanted in Brazil.

Just before the squad left, the issue of the maximum wage came back to bite England hard on the backside. The Stoke centre-half Neil Franklin had accepted a lucrative offer from the Colombian club Santa Fe. Stoke held his registration, so the move was against FIFA regulations and Franklin became ineligible for the England team. An outstanding centre-half, fast and strong, he had missed only two England matches since 1946, forming the valuable partnership in midfield with Billy Wright that had served England so well. Now, with the World Cup imminent, that partnership was being broken, and England went into the tournament with a new and inexperienced defensive unit. Billy Wright was annoyed but sympathised with his teammate's motives, as he outlined in Norman Giller's book, *Billy Wright: A Hero for All Seasons*:

> It was a complete shock, because Neil was a close friend, but he had kept everything secret even from me . . . Now we had lost our linchpin with the World Cup just weeks away. I was fond of Neil and understood his motives for taking the offer to go to Bogotá. We were so poorly paid in England, and he wanted to put his wife and children first. But I could have kicked him for his timing.

The goalkeeper in Brazil, Bert Williams, is now a sprightly 90, and he is England's oldest surviving World Cup player. His memories of this time are very sharp. I went to see him at his home in Shifnal in Shropshire, where he has one whole room dedicated to his career – full of photographs, sketches, newspaper cuttings and mementos. Bert, who won the League and the FA Cup with Wolves, said that Franklin regretted the move almost immediately: 'Had Neil played, I'm sure we would have gone on to win the World Cup. He told me later that as soon as he got to Bogotá he realised he had made a mistake and phoned the FA and told them, but they said it was too late. He got a £750 signing-on fee in Colombia.'

Bert's hair was quite long in those days, and he used a bootlace to keep it out of his eyes and always played in a flat cap, thanks to some paternal influence. 'I played for Walsall reserves against West Brom reserves, and my father told me to put the cap on to keep the sun out of my eyes,' said Bert. '"Then," he said, "if by chance they get a penalty, take your hat off and nonchalantly throw it into the back of the net to show confidence." Well, they got a penalty, and if I had have stopped it, it would have killed me! I said to Dad when I came off, "Dad, I don't think the idea of the cap's going to help me any more!" But I wore it out of respect for him.'

As England prepared for the World Cup, the Scottish players had to deal with the frustration of being barred by their own administrators, and they were not the only ones. Argentina argued with the Brazilian Federation and refused to play a World Cup in their own backyard; Czechoslovakia and Turkey wouldn't compete, meaning the French received a call-up, but, after two defeats in warm-up matches, they took one look at their schedule, which compelled them to play group matches two thousand miles apart, and threatened to pull out if it wasn't changed. The Brazilian Federation refused, and so France ducked out. Germany were still excluded from FIFA following the war, Austria thought their team too inexperienced, Hungary and Russia were locked behind the Iron Curtain and Portugal declined to take Scotland's place.

The upshot was that the qualifying sections in Brazil had a ludicrously lopsided look. There were two groups of four, one of three and Uruguay had to beat only the hapless Bolivians to advance to the final pool, from which the eventual World Champions would emerge. There would be no 'final' as such, although, serendipitously for the organisers, the last pool game turned out to be the dramatic, showpiece occasion everybody wanted in the chase for the renamed Jules Rimet Trophy. It was fitting that the World Cup was now named after the French lawyer and FIFA president who had done so much to establish the competition and who had kept the trophy hidden under his bed, from the Germans, during the war years.

England were drawn in one of the groups of four, along with Chile, Spain and the US. The Bristolian Roy Bentley had made his international debut away to Sweden the year before, where he seemed more taken aback by the locals than the football: 'We went into this shoe shop, and, my God, they were all size 14. The men were so tall, all well over 6 ft!' Bentley was fighting for a place in a front line full of goalscorers but had timed his run in to the side well with his first international strike in only his second appearance in that vital win at Hampden in April 1950. He was captain of the Chelsea team who went on to win the League in 1955, and, aged 86, he still goes to Stamford Bridge today from his flat in Reading.

England endured a torturous journey to Rio de Janeiro, a 31-hour marathon that took in Paris, Lisbon, Dakar and Recife. They arrived jet-lagged and exhausted, but Bert Williams remembers that initially they were not allowed off the plane: 'These three blokes came on with huge gas masks and bottles on their backs and sprayed us all because they feared we would bring some bugs in with us. So that was a good start! We were all coughing and spluttering.'

The squad stayed in a normal tourist hotel, the Luxor, right on the main road on Copacabana Beach. Coach Walter Winterbottom later conceded in Dave Bowler's biography of Sir Alf Ramsey that that was a mistake but blamed one of England's leading clubs:

> The accommodation was hopeless – we were stuck on Copacabana Beach. Arsenal had put us up to it, they stayed there the year before, but of course they were on an end-of-season tour, so to be on the beach was uproarious for them! The kitchens were dreadful, the smell used to go up into the bedrooms and the food was swimming in oil . . .

The food seems to have been a real issue. Bert Williams recalls the first meal without any affection: 'It was a bowl of olive oil with a piece of bacon floating about in it. I shared with Alf Ramsey, and I said to him that we couldn't eat this. So Alf went to the desk and asked if we could have some fruit in our room. We were invited out that night, and when we came back the fruit was on the table and there was a black line coming off the table, down the table leg, across the floor, up the wall and then out of the ventilation shaft – ants!'

Some players complained the food was too spicy, others went down with stomach illnesses and a few existed solely on bananas. At one stage, Winterbottom himself went into the kitchens to prepare everything. The players, naturally enough, wanted to go and enjoy themselves on one of the most famous beaches in the world, but they were forbidden to do so after 10 a.m., because they were told the sun would make them lethargic.

The squad had trained for just four days in London before flying out, and the shock on arrival was palpable. The players went from a mild English summer to temperatures in the 80s, and they had to deal with the altitude as well. When they visited the Maracanã Stadium before the first game, they saw oxygen tanks and masks in the dressing room, and then it dawned on them what sort of challenge lay ahead.

England had asked for some lightweight boots in preparation for the heat and humidity, but when the boots arrived the players found they were more like heavy rubber gardening boots. The players' feet sank ankle-deep in the thick grass. With the conditions, the altitude, the food and the hostility of the crowd, the English team had more than just the 11 opponents on the field to overcome.

England might have been one of the favourites, but the stark truth is that in 1950 Walter Winterbottom and his players knew precious little about the threat posed by the South American teams. There was no television, of course, no way that, unless you had seen these teams in the flesh, you would have any idea of how they really played or how good they were. The only information anyone could access about these sides came from reading magazines. Winterbottom himself had never seen Brazil play, and it was only after watching them in their first game, when they thumped Mexico 4–0, that he appreciated the speed and inter-passing of their forwards. He realised then what an enormous threat Brazil posed. The England squad went to that game, but it was the pre-match entertainment that Bert Williams recalls: 'All round the pitch were cages of pigeons, and quite suddenly we thought a bomb had gone off. They had got cannons on the ceiling of the stands, and Bill Eckersley and I had these pieces of concrete falling down on us. We thought we were being bombed!'

With all these obstacles in their way, it seems absurd that England were one of the pre-tournament favourites, and they almost suffered another setback on the eve of the first match, as Rio's desire to beautify itself for the tournament very nearly cost them their centre-forward. The city was tearing down trees to replace them with broad parades, but one worker forgot to fill in a hole and Stan Mortensen walked straight into it. Thankfully, he came to no harm.

In contrast to the enormous excitement and anticipation that surrounds the World Cup today, Bert Williams says it was all very different 60 years ago: 'There was no publicity attached to it at all till the latter games. I'm sure most of the players weren't aware of the importance of it, to be quite honest. We didn't realise it; it's not like today. It was just another match. We weren't aware it was something exceptional like it is today with all the razzamatazz. We didn't realise the euphoria that would be connected with it.'

On Sunday, 25 June 1950 England played in the World Cup finals for the first time. Workmen were still putting the final touches to a revamp of the famous Maracanã Stadium, and fewer than 30,000, in a ground that held 200,000, came to watch England play Chile in the rain.

Laurie Hughes of Liverpool played in the vital centre-half position vacated by the exiled Neil Franklin, and Stan Mortensen of Blackpool played at centre-forward between Roy Bentley and Wilf Mannion of Middlesbrough. Tom Finney was on one wing and Jimmy Mullen of Wolves on the other – in place of Matthews, who had arrived from Canada too close to the game to be considered. A 2–0 win, fought out in bad weather as puddles appeared all over the pitch, was a decent start, even if the team acknowledged they hadn't quite clicked as they struggled with the humidity and the conditions underfoot.

Mortensen scored in the first half, heading in a Jimmy Mullen cross, and Mannion grabbed the second. Bert Williams didn't have much to do in goal. Nicknamed 'The Cat' after the Italian crowd had chanted '*Il Gatto*' at him during a spectacular display in an international at White Hart Lane the year before, Williams was the sort of goalkeeper who liked to be on the move and didn't like to think anything could beat him. One Brazilian radio reporter in the Maracanã surprised him more than the Chilean attack: 'They were taking a corner, and I was at the far post. There was this bloke standing by the post, and he shoved a microphone at me and said, "Say a few words." And I said, "Bugger off." And he said, "Thank you very much!" There were a few more words I would have liked to have added!'

England still had much work to do, but the *Daily Mail* signed off its match report with comforting and, at the time, perfectly reasonable words:

> England came through the first test fairly satisfactorily, considering the strange conditions and the hostility of the crowd. All things considered, England should take the game against the US in their stride as a preparation for the stiff test against Spain.

One can hardly blame the *Daily Mail* for its sentiments, because after all, England, with its team of hardened First Division players, many of whom had great international experience, were now preparing to play a semi-professional American side in the lower altitude at Belo Horizonte. The US had led Spain by a goal to nil until ten minutes from time in the other group game, when the Spanish finally came alive and scored three times. Even the American coach admitted his team had no chance against England. Bill Jeffrey was a Scot who had emigrated 30 years earlier and done wonders with the American national team, but he was so sure they would lose against England he allowed his players to stay up late the night before the game. One London bookmaker offered odds of 500–1 against an American win.

A change of venue meant a change of base for the England squad, and so they gladly moved to be guests of the English-owned Morro Velho gold mine, which employed 2,000 British workers. The squad swapped the hustle and noise of Copacabana Beach for the mountain air and tranquillity of what Roy Bentley remembers as a peaceful place in the middle of a forest: 'It was beautiful up in the hills. When you were in a taxi, you had to drive along with the windows shut, otherwise the red dust kicked up by the car would cover you and get stuck in your ears and nose.' Bert Williams wouldn't want you to think it was some sort of country club, though: 'We stayed in wooden huts, workmen's huts, like army quarters. Lots of the players had been in the army or the navy, and Wilf Mannion used to march up and down, shouting "Halt 1-2-3-4" and "About turn." That was about all the entertainment we got!'

Bentley's room-mate was a Sunderland player who would go on to do great things for England but not with a football at his feet: 'There was a lovely cricket ground there, and every bit of spare time we had I would go and bowl at Willie Watson, who shared with me, and he would knock me all over the place. A lot of people were surprised he didn't get a game in Brazil, and when he got home he was determined to get back into the limelight in the game for which he was known: cricket.' Three summers later, Watson and Trevor Bailey denied the Australians victory in the Lord's Test match with a doughty stand that played its part in the Ashes coming home after a nineteen-year absence.

When he wasn't bowling at Willie Watson, Bentley would go for walks around the forest: 'You could see these monkeys, and they would throw things at us. They had the coldest water in the showers, home-made efforts, and it was like putting blocks of ice on you.'

In Dave Bowler's biography of Alf Ramsey, the full-back recalled the terror of the bus ride from the training camp to the stadium:

Never will the England footballers who made the journey to the camp forget the nightmare experience of being driven round 167 hairpin

bends on a road which seemed to cling to the side of the mountain
... The driver was possibly the only fellow aboard the coach who did
not give an anxious thought to the possibility that the coach might
hurtle hundreds of feet into the valley below.

Stanley Matthews was now available for selection, but, as we have already
seen, whether he played or not was not down to the coach, Walter
Winterbottom, in these arcane times. The team was picked on this occasion
by the one selector on duty, Arthur Drewry, a director of Grimsby Town
and later chairman of the FA and president of FIFA. Winterbottom had
served with the RAF during the war and was now combining the job of
national manager with being director of coaching at the FA. He was initially
met with a degree of suspicion by some internationals who felt they didn't
need coaching at their rarefied level. He had also never managed a club,
which, for some, left an unbridgeable gap in his experience. Bert Williams
outlined it very elegantly: 'I think you respect a person who has seen a lot
of football himself, like Matt Busby, like these top managers. I don't think
anybody had heard of Walter Winterbottom till he came in.'

Winterbottom now had to sit by while Drewry insisted he would not
change a winning team. In today's language, it is like Fabio Capello looking
on helplessly as an FA mandarin refuses to restore a now fit-again Wayne
Rooney to the starting line-up. Winterbottom wanted Matthews to play
to unlock the American defence, and it has even been suggested that
the secretary of the FA, Stanley Rous, went to see Drewry to press for
Matthews's inclusion, but the selector held firm. The journalist Norman
Giller later compared Drewry's decision to 'leaving Wellington on the
beach at Waterloo'.

Tom Finney, for one, certainly thought that Matthews should be drafted
in – he thought it odd Matthews hadn't been with the party since the
beginning of the World Cup – and Roy Bentley was of the same opinion,
even if he knew the Blackpool winger wouldn't have enjoyed all his recent
plane journeys: 'Stan himself was a bit dubious about what was going to
happen. I don't think with his age [he was 35 now] that he was terribly
keen on the travel. He had a routine which he never broke – the same
food – and he had a black holdall he carried round, which had his lotions
and potions in. He was a fanatical trainer and trained like a boxer, which
his father was. He would do the skipping and shadow-boxing all day

long. I was always dancing round doing the necessary, and he would do his routines. He hated travel and smoking.'

So with Matthews sitting idly in the stands in Belo Horizonte, America and England, in unfamiliar blue shirts, took to the field, although Roy Bentley argues it was barely that: 'The ground was an old bullring and not even a first-class bullring. They had it returfed for the game, but it was still sand basically and there were walls all the way round. If you kicked the ball out of play hard enough, it would bounce back off the walls. We thought, "Oh my God, what have we got here?"' The walls were about 12 ft high, and with the stadium still being rebuilt, the dressing rooms were so dirty that England got changed a 5-minute coach ride away at the Minas Athletic Club. Despite the support of the British workers from the mines, the crowd was largely hostile once again, with the locals realising England represented the biggest threat to their own World Cup dreams.

Over the years, many publications have suggested that the US team arrived 'through Ellis Island' or were a sort of 'United Nations' team, but eight of their seventeen-man squad were actually born in the same place: in St Louis, Missouri. On the day of the game, three of the starting line-up – Joe Maca, Joe Gaetjens and captain Eddie McIlvenny, a Scot who eighteen months earlier had been given a free transfer by Third Division Wrexham – were not US citizens, but they had declared their intention to become so and were subsequently allowed to play under US Soccer Federation rules. Of the three, only Maca went on to swear the Oath of Allegiance, but later in 1950 the US were cleared of any violation under World Cup rules.

Their team was made up of semi-professionals: midfielder Walter Bahr was a high-school teacher; Haitian-born forward Gaetjens washed dishes in a New York restaurant; and St Louis provided two postal workers in Frank Wallace and Harry Keough, a dock worker in Gino Pariani, a meat cutter in Charlie Colombo and also the busiest man of the afternoon, the goalkeeper Frank Borghi, who was a funeral director. When the American team turned up for the game, some were wearing cowboy hats and others were smoking cigars.

The game quickly settled down into what both sides anticipated, namely England's attack against America's defence. When, almost 60 years later, I asked Sir Tom Finney about the nightmare of Belo Horizonte, he chuckled softly in his chair in his home in Preston: 'It's best forgotten! We really didn't anticipate any problems. We thought they were just there to make up the numbers. They were classed as just learning the game, and we had twenty-five shots on goal to their one!'

Roy Bentley hit the crossbar three times, two of them headers: 'I got above the bloody keeper for one and really met it and thought, "That's a goal." But I got too much power behind it, so it didn't drop.' The keeper, Frank Borghi, was born to Italian parents and served as a field medic during the war. He was an all-round sportsman, talented enough to play two seasons of baseball in the minor leagues. He started playing football in the winter to keep fit, and with his large hands and excellent hand–eye coordination he had won his first cap a year earlier. Bentley thought he got away with a great deal that day: 'The goalkeeper was diving through the air and grabbing people. He got Tom [Finney] in a rugby tackle.' Even so, it seemed it would be just a matter of time before England's persistence bore fruit, but then, eight minutes before half-time, the unthinkable happened. Walter Bahr shot from 25 yards, and, with goalkeeper Bert Williams seemingly having it covered, Joe Gaetjens ducked and diverted it into the net with his head.

The second half followed a similar pattern, as England kept on pushing for a goal. Alf Ramsey scored from a free kick, but it was disallowed for an infringement, and as the game wore on a feeling of inevitability descended upon the England XI. 'The longer the game went on, the more we didn't look like winning it,' said Sir Tom. 'They were a rubbish side really, but it's hard to explain why it materialised the way it did. It was the most disappointing match of my career.'

Looking on forlornly from the other end as England slipped to an astonishing 1–0 defeat was Bert Williams. 'The reason we lost was simple,' maintains Bert. 'Everybody in the world knew the Americans wouldn't win. They came under the impression that they didn't expect to win, but they didn't want to lose by a hatful of goals. As a result of this, the retreating defence came into operation. Everyone on their side came back onto the goal line, and you couldn't see the goal. We couldn't score if we were still playing now. We couldn't believe it.'

All Stanley Matthews could do was sit and suffer, as he made clear in his autobiography, *The Way It Was*:

The game was purgatory to watch from the stands, and come the final whistle I thanked my lucky stars I hadn't been part of it . . . All I know is that England missed a hatful of chances and never looked capable of scoring, even if we'd played for 9 hours, never mind 90 minutes. Even allowing for the uncomfortable journey to the game, the poor pitch and the fact we dominated the match it was a humiliating defeat.

The crowd chanted 'One more!' as they willed the US towards an astonishing victory, and as full-time neared, the Brazilian fans took out their handkerchiefs to wave England goodbye. Borghi continued to stop everything thrown at him, using his face when necessary to repel England, until, as Brian Glanville wrote in *The Story of the World Cup*, 'at the final whistle, newspapers burned on the terraces, a funeral pyre for England, and spectators rushed onto the pitch to carry the brave American team shoulder-high.' Only one US reporter saw the game. Dent McSkimming from the *St Louis Post-Dispatch* paid for his own airfare to Brazil after his newspaper refused to cover his expenses. 'It was like Oxford University beating the Yankees in baseball,' he wrote.

Gaetjens was 26 and never played for the US again after 1950: he returned to his native Haiti to open a dry-cleaning business. In 1964, during the reign of 'Papa Doc' Duvalier, he was arrested by the Haitian secret police and disappeared. Fifteen years later, the Inter-American Commission on Human Rights published a report that concluded: 'The fact that Mr Gaetjens, a football player of international standing, has not been seen since his detention in 1964 leads to the conclusion that he is dead.' Witnesses later claimed that within days of his arrest he was lined up against a wall and shot.

The disbelief shown by the England players that they had actually lost to this American team was shared by those back home. The website On This Football Day quotes a scene from the *Daily Mirror* offices. Ken Jones, a *Mirror* correspondent, remembers it like this:

When the 'flash' result was passed to a sub-editor he smiled – understandably assuming an error in transmission; he reached for a pen to correct the score – surely, England 10, USA 1. Still smiling, he turned to a colleague and said 'England defeated by the United States. Now that would have been some story.'

It was a busy day on the sports desks, as England's cricketers also lost to the West Indies for the first time in a Test match.

Roy Bentley's father thought there had been a misprint in his paper and assumed England had scored 12 without reply. Bentley can laugh uproariously at the result six decades on, but at the time the FA machine whirred into action as they set about limiting the damage. He calmly recalls how the players received clear instructions on how to deal with this humiliation: 'Whatever you do now, you will be accused of trying to find excuses for a bad display, so just take it on the chin. You can't talk about it. If you start saying "Oh it's a bullring, how do you expect us to play on a bullring?", they will say you're looking for excuses. We will never live that result down, will we?' The American defender Harry Keough had some sympathy for the England players, as Michael Lewis wrote in *Soccer Digest*: 'Boy, I feel sorry for these bastards. How are they ever going to live down the fact that we beat them?'

Walter Bahr acknowledged in an interview with Reuters that his team had ridden their luck:

> We knew it was an upset. Of course we were excited about it. Things went our way and, in the run of play, they should have won the game, but they didn't score. As the game went on, we got a little bit better and they got a little bit more panicky. Nine times out of ten they would have beaten us, but that game was our game.

The British press savagely criticised the team in a manner that has become familiar. The *Daily Worker* called it 'the worst display ever by an England side', and the *Daily Mail* labelled the result 'the biggest soccer upset of all time. England were beaten because of bad shooting, over-anxiety in the second half and the failure to settle down on a small pitch.' England have avoided playing in blue shirts ever since. They had been told not to moan to the press about the conditions or pass on any stories at all, even though the newspapermen were there every step of the way – in planes, in taxis and in the team hotel. Roy Bentley remembers one pressman getting so drunk on the flight out to Rio that he started singing a popular vaudeville song at the top of his voice and trying to open the cabin door 23,000 ft up in the air. 'But they kept that out of the papers,' Bentley noted whimsically.

England retreated to their base in the forests to nurse their battered pride, play cards and watch films, but after setting out as one of the favourites to win the World Cup they had made the headlines for all the wrong reasons. 'Bloody ridiculous,' said Wilf Mannion. 'Can't we play them again tomorrow?'

They returned to Rio for their last group game against Spain knowing they could still qualify for the final stage, but that crushing defeat in Belo Horizonte followed them all the way, even onto the training field. 'We were so deflated after that result,' Tom Finney recalls. 'Spain were rated as an ordinary side, but we couldn't beat them.' Stanley Matthews belatedly made his World Cup bow, and the forward line had a very different look to it, with Wilf Mannion and Roy Bentley making way for Newcastle hero Jackie Milburn and Tottenham's Eddie Baily. 'There was a big gap between Baily and I; he was three yards slower,' says Bentley. 'But in his prime he was a good player and always had that bit of cockney about him, as in, "I'll show you, you buggers!"'

Tom Finney moved to the left wing to accommodate Matthews on the right, and after 14 minutes Milburn headed in a Finney centre, only for the goal, wrongly, to be disallowed for offside. Finney twice had very legitimate penalty appeals turned down, and five minutes after half-time Zarra headed the only goal of the game. Spain won Pool Three and the 'Kings of Football' had to come home with the nation ready for its first World Cup inquest.

Tom Finney returned to Preston, and people would stop him on the street and ask, 'What happened, Tom? What happened?' He and the squad knew that they were far better than their results had shown. The press liked to build up the rivalry between Finney and Stanley Matthews, but as far as the two players themselves were concerned, their relationship was perfectly friendly and built upon mutual respect. They had shown in the defeats of Portugal and Italy that they could play together, and we will never know what might have happened had the dogmatic Arthur Drewry not consigned Matthews to a place in the stands in Belo Horizonte. Neil Franklin was clearly a loss in defence, but England had had more than enough opportunities to win the games against America and Spain.

With England gone, Uruguay stood between Brazil and a home triumph. Having reached the final pool phase of the 1950 World Cup by thrashing their only opponents, Bolivia, 8–0, Uruguay then drew 2–2 with Spain and beat Sweden 3–2 to set up a thrilling denouement with the hosts in Rio de Janeiro. Brazil had been scoring goals for fun in dismantling the Swedes 7–1 and the Spanish 6–1. Ademir had grabbed four against Sweden, and Chico a double in both games. A draw would suffice for this technically brilliant Brazil side to win the World Cup for the first time.

On the morning of 16 July 1950, the streets of Rio bustled with activity as an impromptu carnival readied itself to celebrate a World Cup victory. Hubris was to bring the Brazil side down. Just before going out to face a crowd of somewhere around the 200,000 mark, the Uruguayan captain Obdulio Varela gave an impassioned speech to his team, the rank outsiders, about how they must not be intimidated by the crowd. He finished with the line, '*Muchachos, los de afuera son de palo. Que comience la función*' (Boys, outsiders don't play. Let the show begin).

Brazil went on the attack straight away, but Uruguay's defence, held together by Varela, stood firm and Máspoli was elastic and acrobatic in goal. It was goalless at half-time, enough for Brazil to take the title, and two minutes into the second half Friaça scored. Surely that would do for Brazil, as Uruguay now had to score twice to deny them the title. But far from being demoralised, Uruguay seemed galvanised by the goal. Juan Alberto Schiaffino equalised in the 66th minute, and with Varela now the dominant force, Uruguay went in search of the goal that would claim their second World Cup. Eleven minutes from time, Alcides Edgardo Ghiggia made it 2–1 and the Maracanã was silenced. When the Englishman, George Reader, signalled the end of the match, the World Cup returned to Montevideo after a 20-year absence and the term *Maracanazo* was born: the victory of an underdog in the Maracanã Stadium.

Brazil, and England, would have to try again four years later in Switzerland, and for all the pre-tournament worries surrounding Neil Franklin's defection to Colombia and the inexperience of their defence, England's problems had actually been at the other end of the field. Billy Wright went straight to the heart of the matter in Dave Bowler's book, *Winning Isn't Everything . . .* :

> The England forwards were brilliant in their approach work. Time and again they tore wide gaps in the defence, which tried to halt their progress, but once the penalty area was reached! I can assure you that schoolboys would have been spanked by their masters for

missing the same simple chances . . . the primary lesson being that too many English forwards in their mania for football perfection overlook the fact that it is goals that count most of all.

If England's attack had been guilty of over-elaboration, then the English game as a whole was accused of being an ostrich by its best-known player. Stanley Matthews's frustration is evident in his autobiography:

> If ever there was a time when English football should have sat down and taken a long, hard look at itself, it was in the aftermath of the 1950 World Cup. The standard of British football wasn't bad, in fact it was good, but other countries were catching us up; some had overtaken us. We stood still, our insular attitude reinforced by the notion we had invented the game. We had superbly gifted individual players, but little was done to form them into a unit, a team who could play to a system with players who would help one another so that individual skill and guile also became collective skill and guile.

As soon as England went out of the World Cup, all the newspaper journalists went home and, far more tellingly, so did Walter Winterbottom and Arthur Drewry, as if they would learn nothing from watching the other teams at the latter stage of the tournament – giving further credibility to the supposition that whatever happened in Brazil in 1950, England felt they were superior. They were England, the home of football, the inventors of the game, and everything was in order. That perception was about to be blown apart.

2

SWITZERLAND 1954

Stanley Matthews desperately wanted English football to learn from the 1950 World Cup, but in reality nothing changed. The make-up of the average First Division team remained very much the same: physical, tough players lining up in the 2–3–5 system, hard tacklers, direct wingers and the long ball to the centre-forward. When it came to an England match, there was barely time for Walter Winterbottom to prepare. The team met up on a Monday for a Wednesday game, and the side tended to chop and change, giving further ammunition to those who believed the selectors held all the power and that Winterbottom's influence was minimal. In the season that followed the 1950 World Cup, half of the six internationals were in the British Championship, meaning England had very little exposure to the ins and outs of foreign teams.

If the national side were something of a tactical dinosaur, then there was a team in the First Division that had shown what could be done with a little thinking and tinkering. Arthur Rowe's Tottenham won the Second Division title in 1949–50 and then the First Division Championship itself the following season with their 'push-and-run' style of play, so called because a player would quickly pass the ball to a teammate and then run past his marker into space, to make himself available for the return. In stark contrast to the traditions of strength and power that characterised so many First Division teams, this Tottenham side needed immense fitness, flexibility and nous.

After Spurs thumped Newcastle 7–0, the *Daily Mail* described being there:

[A] privilege . . . on-the-floor soccer, the short passing style one dreams of, constructive ability, speed, attack and first-class finishing. There is none of the first-time nonsense. Backs pass it to halves, the halves to forwards after defenders have been drawn.

They were an English team in a class of their own, attacking from all parts of the field and playing in triangles with a teammate always in support. This Tottenham side represented a part of football's evolutionary tactical journey that would eventually metamorphose into the great 'Total Football' teams with which the Dutch so delighted the world in the 1970s. But Arthur Rowe had had time to mould his players into his system, to cajole, coach and convince them this was the way forward. With so little time before an international, it is hardly surprising that Winterbottom stuck to the methods he and the players knew so well. Interestingly, one man who played in both teams was the full-back Alf Ramsey, whose tactical brain was to come to the fore in the next decade.

Financially, things hadn't changed for the players either. By the mid 1950s, the maximum wage had crept up to £15 a week. In 1952, Palermo of Italy wanted to sign Tom Finney, and they offered Preston £30,000 and Finney a £10,000 signing-on fee. Preston turned it down flat, saying he was irreplaceable, and, with the 'retain and transfer' system still very much in place, that was that. Finney stayed at Preston for the remainder of his career.

The case of Newcastle United illustrates the reality of being a top-class footballer in the mid 1950s. They were a hugely successful team, winning the FA Cup in 1951, '52 and '55. Ronnie Simpson was their goalkeeper, and yet, by the time he was offered a new contract for the 1954–55 season, his weekly wage was actually reduced by £2 to £13 a week, the club using the excuses of both poor recent results and the need to increase incentives. Simpson considered leaving the game altogether: 'I can see that I must sign in accordance with football law, but if I do so on the terms offered, I shall make a request for a transfer.' In the end, he decided to stay.

England forward Jackie Milburn was a Newcastle legend, but he still took every opportunity to make a few extra shillings. Milburn was lucky in that he was high profile enough to augment his maximum wage with some endorsements. In the late '40s, he worked as a coalminer at Hazelrigg colliery, but he stopped because of problems with his ear. He may have been happy at St James' Park, where he was worshipped, but there was still no doubt as to who was running football.

Ivor Broadis played with Milburn at Newcastle and went to the World Cup in 1954, but he told me his memories of St James' Park were very different: 'I couldn't wait to get away. It was an employer–employee relationship. The clubs, and particularly the chairmen, had all the power. They ruled the roost. You couldn't sign a contract for longer than one year. At the end of the year, they either retained you or transferred you, put you on the transfer list. If nobody came in for you, your wages stopped on 30 June and you were out of work, because they still retained your registration. I fought against that all my playing career, and you get a tag as a rebel, because you're fighting for what you think is right.'

With players limited to what they could earn by the maximum wage, there were always stories circulating that some clubs paid money 'under the counter' to attract and retain the best players. That could come in the form of unofficial signing-on fees or a cut from the surplus cash raised by the sale of programmes and merchandise. Other players started businesses to supplement their income and give them some direction once their playing careers were over.

Cinema and television were increasing the exposure of football to the masses, even if attendances did gradually decline from their record high of 1949: down five million from their peak by the time of the 1954 World Cup. Alternative forms of entertainment meant football was now in a more crowded marketplace, in a society coming out of its post-war torpor. Rationing ended in 1954, and the country was enjoying near enough full employment as both the average wage and the standard of living rose.

If Newcastle were the dominant Cup team, then the First Division title was shared around at the start of the decade. As Arthur Rowe's Tottenham team grew old, they were succeeded as champions by Matt Busby's Manchester United, then Arsenal and then Stan Cullis's Wolverhampton Wanderers, captained by the England skipper Billy Wright. The British Championship of 1953–54 once again doubled up as the qualifying group for the World Cup, and England comfortably took one of the two slots on offer. Before that, Wright had led England on a tour of South America in the summer of 1953, a trip devised to prepare for the World Cup the following year. Results were mixed, with an abandoned game against Argentina followed by a win over Chile and a defeat against Uruguay before the Americans were beaten 6–3 in New York: the slimmest of consolations for what had happened in Belo Horizonte, but, of more importance, the team had the chance to train and play together over a sustained period of time.

On their return, in October 1953, they needed a late penalty to earn a 4–4 draw at home against a European XI in a game celebrating the FA's 90th birthday. It was clear by now that England's supposed invincibility at Wembley was slipping. The Republic of Ireland had won 2–0 at Goodison Park in 1949, but with England having drawn four of their last seven internationals at home, it was inevitable that a first-ever defeat at Wembley was coming sooner rather than later.

Hungary visited London on 25 November 1953, a seminal day for English football. Hungary were Olympic Champions, on an unbeaten run of 29 matches, and a game at Wembley was part of their own build-up for Switzerland. Their manager, Gusztáv Sebes, had planned meticulously. He had borrowed the heavier type of balls used by the FA, so that his team could practise with them, and altered his training pitch so that the dimensions matched those at Wembley. He had also arranged practice matches against Hungarian club sides ordered to play in the English style, and a fortnight earlier, when Hungary played Sweden – coached by an Englishman, George Raynor – Sebes decided to play Nándor Hidegkuti instead of Péter Palotás as centre-forward. But Hidegkuti was not used as a traditional type of number nine, and Raynor twigged that it was this floating centre-forward who made the Hungarians tick. As a result, the Swedes did their best to man-mark him in a 2–2 draw. Walter Winterbottom made no such provision, with disastrous consequences.

Winterbottom had seen that game in Budapest, and, as he said in Dave Bowler's biography of Alf Ramsey, he was a worried man:

> The press were laughing, saying our game against them would be a cakewalk! I couldn't believe it; they couldn't read that game. Sweden were a hard-tackling team, the normal European style of play, where Hungary played beautiful football and had a number of near misses. It was obvious that if they clicked they could murder any team. We had time with England to rehearse a few restarts, such as throw-ins, corners and so on, but they were rehearsing movements in play . . . We never had that chance.

England's haphazard selection policy meant the team were always striving for fluency and continuity, whereas the Hungarians played together regularly at international level, in practice matches and many of them at club level, too – with the army side, Honvéd. Hungary had developed a tactically flexible 4–2–4 formation with the shrewd Hidegkuti playing as a deep-lying centre-forward, confusing the centre-half and teasing him as to whether to follow him down the pitch, thereby creating a hole at the back, or leave him alone to pick the ball up unmarked. The smaller Sándor Kocsis was a prolific goalscorer, as good in the air as on the ground. József Bozsik was an attacking right-half of enormous technical and tactical ability, and then there was the totemic Ferenc Puskás, nicknamed the 'Galloping Major' after his rank in the army.

The heartbeat of the side, small, with a low centre of gravity, hair parted neatly down the middle, Puskás had a wonderful first touch and a fearsome left foot; he scored an incredible 84 goals in 85 matches for Hungary. When England captain Billy Wright was called to the centre circle to toss the coin that day, Puskás, his opposite number, was juggling the match ball on his left foot. As Wright approached, Puskás flicked it into the air, caught it on his thigh and let it run down his shin onto the centre spot. The watching British press later reacted in a patronising manner, saying that these seal's tricks before the game were one thing, but pulling them off during the 90 minutes was quite another. The level, and cost, of England's isolation was about to be made all too apparent.

It is impossible to think about England's performances in the 1954 World Cup without appreciating quite what impact this match at Wembley, and the return in Budapest six months later, had on English football and the national psyche. Injury to Bert Williams allowed another Midlander, Birmingham's Gil Merrick, to take over in goal for that infamous day in north London, and I went to see him at his Birmingham home before he passed away. If the years had dulled his memories of the World Cup a little, they had done nothing to cloud the reminiscences of that particular November afternoon. He was eager to remember it and his recollections were sharp: 'We didn't know they were that good. Our strong English game was hard tackling, hard marking, long ball, big centre-forward with wingers crossing it, but they didn't let our defenders tackle. They moved the ball accurately and quickly, and I was wondering what had happened.'

Hidegkuti scored in the very first minute, and although Sewell soon equalised, England were then hit by a three-goal salvo – another from Hidegkuti and two from Puskás, his first the most memorable goal of the whole afternoon. As Gil Merrick sat back in his chair, that moment came flooding back: 'Puskás came down the line, and Billy Wright came over from right-half, and he could see Puskás in the inside-right position inside the box. So Billy comes over at a million miles an hour, and Puskás drags it back and smashes it into the net. I had no chance at all.' It was a move that encapsulated Hungary's play – their intelligence, speed, control and mastery of the ball – and prompted Geoffrey Green, the football correspondent of *The Times*, to write, memorably, 'Billy Wright, defending the edge of the goal area, raced past Puskás as he dragged the ball back before shooting over Merrick. Wright was like a fire engine going to the wrong fire.'

Stan Mortensen pulled one back before half-time, and as the England players walked off the length of the pitch after forty-five minutes, 4–2 down, Merrick remembers centre-half Harry Johnston turning to him and saying, 'Gil, I haven't had a kick. I don't know who to mark!' Hidegkuti was playing just out of range of the centre-half, at the bottom of Hungary's fluid U-shaped attacking system, and Johnston was symbolic of a bamboozled England: he didn't know what to do, and nor did Walter Winterbottom. He had not designated anybody to track Hidegkuti at all. It seems as if a naive England manager simply had no idea how to counteract the Hungarian formation.

Mortensen's goal at the end of the first half proved to be a mirage, as the effortless Bozsik scored with a rising drive and the elusive Hidegkuti completed his hat-trick after an array of dazzling passes. Alf Ramsey scored a late penalty. Stanley Matthews was on the right wing that day and said in his autobiography that the 6–3 defeat served as a watershed in British football:

> How we approached and played the game and how we perceived ourselves would never be the same again. Far from being the masters, on this day we were shown to be the pupils. It was an imaginative combination of exacting ball control, speed of movement and esoteric vision that knitted together to formulate a style of football that was as innovative as it was productive.

The *Daily Mail* suggested the Hungarians set the pattern for the football of the future: 'Now perhaps our soccer will be remodelled, not only at national level but at club level . . . an England team were run off their feet, outlasted for stamina, humbled in every art of the game . . . like an amateur boxer taking on Jack Dempsey.'

Tom Finney was injured and sitting in the stands that day. He told me, 'Hungary were a better side than we had given them credit for. We had dismissed them as just an ordinary team.' The mist that had enveloped Wembley had wrapped itself around the England team as well, and the vast majority of the 100,000 crowd left for home, convinced they had seen the next World Champions. The Hungarians had shown themselves to be far in advance of their hosts with more than just their football. Their kit was lightweight, their boots slimmed down; England wore baggy shirts and shorts and heavy boots. It was the day that led to a gradual change in the way English clubs trained, what they wore and, further down the line, how they lined up tactically.

A 6–3 thrashing at home sent shock waves throughout Europe and the world just nine months before the World Cup, and six players never played for England again, including Alf Ramsey and Stan Mortensen. If any of those present – playing or watching – had not quite appreciated the nature of the lesson handed out by the Hungarians, then it fell to the Austrian journalist Willy Meisl to put it into words. Meisl was a Jew who had emigrated to the UK after the Nazis seized power in Germany, and his footballing credentials were impeccable, his brother Hugo being the coach of the so-called Austrian *Wunderteam* of the early 1930s. Willy Meisl wrote in his book *Soccer Revolution*, published in 1953, 'Isolation, insularism, obstinate resistance to any reforms, refusal to break with outdated methods, from training to tactics, from selecting internationals to educating talent, had put [England] ten light years behind.'

Five years later, that Mighty Magyars team, as they were known, came back to London for a party and invited the England XI to attend, but Gil Merrick was the only one to go: 'I don't know why the others didn't come, but I had a marvellous time and they treated me really well. They had a banquet, and they went to Croydon, because lots of Hungarians were living there. I asked their manager [Sebes] when he had decided on the tactics for the match, the way they were organised, and he said to me, "Do you know, Mr Merrick, it was the night before!"' All the evidence suggests Gusztáv Sebes was probably being very polite and this was far from the case.

If that humbling hadn't been bad enough for England and English football, then worse, certainly in terms of the scoreline, was to come before the World Cup. In May 1954, England played a return match in Budapest, and only four of the team that had been slaughtered at Wembley survived, including Merrick and Wright. Hungary won 7–1, England's biggest defeat in their 90-year history and still the biggest to this day. It was England's last game before the World Cup, but Gil Merrick dismissed the final score as misleading: 'You have to forget about that because with ten minutes to go till half-time Syd Owen got injured. He had been running around so much he got cramp and had to be carried off. So we played with only ten men when we needed fifteen!' The England set-up knew so little about nutrition and taking on liquids in those days that Owen had become dehydrated and seized up.

Billy Wright was not as sanguine as his goalkeeper about the result. Having been embarrassed by Puskás at Wembley, he had now presided over an even bigger thrashing, and he was brutally honest in Norman Giller's book on his career:

> Hungary were even more devastating than they'd been at Wembley. They were unstoppable, and we were just happy to get off the pitch without the score going into double figures. What it confirmed was that we needed to go back to the drawing board.

The *Daily Express* said, 'Billy Wright came off with his face as white as his shirt and looking like a man who has seen a ghost come back to haunt him. As hard as this giant-hearted man tried, he could not get near to suppressing the irrepressible Puskás.'

Inside-forward Ivor Broadis scored England's consolation goal and joked afterwards, as he took off his boots, 'Don't touch my feet, they're red hot!' At the post-match banquet he talked, via an interpreter, to Hungary's right-back: 'He reckoned he had been home twice in two years from the army. Most of the time they spent playing football.' Little wonder they were such a cohesive team. The way they went about the game impressed Broadis, who had already been a player-manager by this time at Carlisle: 'Their positioning off the ball was excellent. Somebody in possession always had two or three alternatives. They had a great understanding and very skilled players.'

There seems little doubt these two matches shaped the short-term future of English football. Two thumpings by the Hungarians had a noticeable effect as the squad prepared for Switzerland, according to Sir Tom Finney: 'There was a crisis of confidence because of the two Hungary results. We had the players to play better than we actually did. We didn't play anywhere near as [well as] we should have done, because we had started to doubt ourselves.' Confidence is a vital factor in all successful teams, and without it sides struggle to achieve success. England went to Switzerland with their ship taking on water before they had even embarked on another World Cup adventure.

As the World Cup approached, Hungary were clearly the outstanding team and the hot favourites; Austria had been arguably the best in Europe at the start of the decade but were now past their best; West Germany had been readmitted to FIFA but weren't fancied by many pundits; both Uruguay and Brazil would pose problems from South America, although the holders weren't an unknown quantity this time; and Italy, if they got their act together, could cause trouble. Scotland deigned to compete this time after coming runners-up to England in the British Championship. If the group sections in the 1950 tournament had been ludicrously lopsided, the ones in 1954 were unnecessarily overcomplicated. There were four groups of four, but two of those teams were seeded and it was decided the seeded teams wouldn't play each other – nor would the unseeded teams. So, with each country playing just two matches, FIFA said extra time would be played and, if necessary, a play-off between countries with equal points would determine the final standings.

England were in a group with fellow seeds the Italians, the hosts Switzerland and, for their first game in Basle, they faced Belgium. Bolton's Nat Lofthouse had been England's centre-forward for most of the time since the last World Cup, and by now he was also known as 'The Lion of Vienna', after his performance against Austria two years earlier. Following a 2–2 draw at Wembley in November 1951, the return in Vienna the following May was looked upon as deciding the best international side in Europe. Lofthouse had endured a difficult game in Florence a week earlier in a 1–1 draw with Italy, at one stage being pelted with coins and bottles by the crowd after a challenge on the goalkeeper, and the calls to send for Newcastle's Jackie Milburn were growing.

The crowd in Vienna that day was swelled by thousands of British soldiers stationed on the Rhine, and Lofthouse had already scored once when, with the game level at 2–2 with eight minutes remaining, Gil Merrick came out to collect a cross: 'As I caught the ball, their centre-forward Dienst slapped it with his hand in an attempt to get me to drop it. But I held on and slung it to Tom Finney in the centre circle. He played it straight through to Nat, and with a pack of defenders snapping at his heels, he knocked it past the keeper into the net, collided with him and was knocked unconscious.'

Lofthouse recalled the incident in the book *The Lion of Vienna*:

> I'd scored the greatest goal of my international career and never seen the ball go into the net. What a day! And what a night! We started off in the privates' mess, moved into the sergeants' mess and finished up in the officers' mess, by which time some of us were decidedly unsteady on our feet.

He returned to the field dazed for the last few minutes, hit the post and on the final whistle the triumphant England players were chaired off the field by the servicemen. The players were so thrilled by the win that they asked Walter Winterbottom if they could keep their shirts. Merrick kept his yellow goalkeeping jersey in the bottom of his kitbag until he lost it.

For the Belgium game, Lofthouse was supported by Ivor Broadis, now of Newcastle, and Manchester United's Tommy Taylor as inside-forwards, with Stanley Matthews on the right wing and Tom Finney on the left. Finney and Broadis were the only survivors from the forwards who had witnessed the mauling in Budapest, and the recalled Matthews was very surprised to see that the defence that had been so easily dismantled by the Hungarians remained completely intact for the World Cup opener.

The match was televised live, and the watching public back home saw goals galore. After only five minutes, England were behind, but with Matthews in excellent form on the right wing Winterbottom's team were ahead by half-time. Broadis converted captain Billy Wright's through pass for the equaliser, and Lofthouse, with a spectacular diving header, gave them a 2–1 half-time lead. When Broadis made it 3–1, it looked like England were going to start with a victory, but, with the defence looking shaky, first Anoul and then Coppens hauled Belgium back level. A score of 3–3 at full-time meant extra time under FIFA's strange regulations, and England went back in front when Lofthouse profited from good work by his two inside-forwards. But, just as an opening win beckoned, Jimmy Dickinson of Portsmouth headed a Belgium free kick into his own net and it finished 4–4.

Of greater long-term significance for England was that Billy Wright moved to centre-half in the closing stages to take over from the injured Syd Owen, who limped out to the wing. Since Neil Franklin's decision to move to Colombia four years earlier, England had tried eleven different players in that position, and now they realised the answer had been on their doorstep all the time. The *Daily Mail* asked, 'Could it be that at long last England have found the pivot they have been seeking ever since the defection of Neil Franklin?' Indeed England had, and Wright stayed there for the rest of his international career, but he was a frustrated man in Basle that night. He knew England had been the better team and that the defence, so ripped to shreds by Hungary and yet untouched by the selectors, had once again been England's Achilles heel.

Gil Merrick remembered the weather in Switzerland more than anything else: 'We played in terrific heat. It was 100 °F in the shade, and I had a bloody woollen jersey on.' Clearly, the lessons of the lightweight Hungarian kit at Wembley the year before had gone unheeded: 'I was sweating buckets, and that's what it was like in every match, as they started at three o'clock in the afternoon. It was absolutely terrible.' Tom Finney recalls the heat and also the lack of spectators: 'The crowds didn't really show any interest. It was disappointing; it changed the atmosphere.'

The squad stayed in Lucerne, and when they went training, Ivor Broadis remembers, Stanley Matthews was a law unto himself: 'We would get off the coach and saunter into the dressing room and take our time getting ready. When we were going out to train, Stan was on his way back in! He knew what he needed. He would take all sorts of things abroad in small bottles, like vitamins and things. Walter Winterbottom left him to it. He trusted the man. Stan got changed, did a few sprints and that was it. I admired him; I thought he was a great fellow.'

The FA tried to keep the mood light within the training camp by inviting the comedian Jimmy Jewell along to entertain the squad. 'It was just something to take our minds off things,' said Gil Merrick. 'The night before a match they brought in Raymond Glendenning to talk to us. What did he know about us?' Glendenning was a BBC commentator, so you would hope he knew a fair bit!

Three days later, England played the hosts in Berne, knowing that victory would see them reach the quarter-finals. Billy Wright started his first game at centre-half and played magnificently, giving the Swiss strikers not a sniff of a chance. Matthews and Lofthouse were unfit, so in came the Wolves pair of Jimmy Mullen and Dennis Wilshaw. Huddersfield's Bill McGarry played in Wright's old position of right-half, and Gil Merrick, after receiving some criticism for his display in the opening match, had a sound game in goal. Again, it was boiling hot, and the players lost several pounds in the heat, but, despite the sunlight, Gil Merrick wouldn't wear a cap in goal: 'I carried one but never wore one. I thought if you put a cap on and it has a peak, when you came out and looked up at the ball, the glare would put you off. I never got caught out, so I must have been as much right as wrong.'

The cap that Merrick carried was a replacement for one that had belonged to his father. He had lost it the summer before the World Cup on the tour of South America, when England were playing Argentina in Buenos Aires. The players were introduced to the Argentinian president, Juan Perón, and then went to warm up. Gil put his father's old flat cap and a second pair of gloves in the net, as usual, when they were all called forward for individual photographs. When he resumed his warm-up, the gloves were there, but the cap was gone: 'It was just a flat cap, and I used to put it in the back of my goal. A little Argentinian lad must have nipped round the goal and nicked it! I never thought I would feel so bad over losing it!'

Back in Berne, a capacity crowd of 60,000 watched expectantly as Switzerland played their first game in their home tournament, but the crowd's cheers were silenced three minutes before half-time. Jimmy Mullen, profiting from Tommy Taylor's flick, rounded the goalkeeper for the first, and there was no way back for the hosts when, midway through the second half, the other new Wolves addition to the team, Dennis Wilshaw, cleverly beat three Swiss defenders before calmly scoring the second. England were into the knockout stages.

Elsewhere, Scotland's first World Cup finals appearance ended with two defeats and no goals scored as they lost narrowly to Austria and heavily to Uruguay. As anticipated, it was the Hungarians who were making all the headlines. They scored an astonishing seventeen goals in their two group games, hammering Korea 9–0 and then dismantling West Germany 8–3. During that game in Basle, Puskás was injured, kicked by a German centre-half called Werner Liebrich. It was a challenge that was to have an enormous impact on the destiny of the 1954 World Cup. The Germans were not at full strength, or even playing at 100 per cent, as Kocsis then helped himself to four goals – even with Puskás off the field for an hour with his injured ankle.

So England prepared to face World Champions Uruguay in the quarter-finals in Basle. On England's tour of South America 12 months earlier, Uruguay had played a floating centre-forward in Míguez, who had given the England defence a torrid time in Montevideo in a 2–1 win for the home side. That wasn't the first time England had seen a forward deployed in such a manner. Ivor Broadis remembers an Argentinian XI playing an FA XI a couple of weeks earlier on the tour, before the full international in Buenos Aires. Broadis was sitting on the grass at the stadium watching the game: 'This stood out for me and the rest of the lads who weren't playing. Here was this fellow, a good ball player and passer of the ball, centre-forward, lying deep in his own half and supplying the two front runners through the middle. We said to each other, "Surely Walter will do something about this in the interval." This player was the first deep-lying centre-forward we saw.'

Matthews and Lofthouse were fit again to take their places in the team, and England were confident of winning, but it turned into a game for Gil Merrick to forget. Uruguay scored early through Borges. 'The fellow picked the ball up inside the 18-yard line and hit it into the far corner. I had no chance,' remembered Merrick, but the goalkeeper was to be heavily criticised for his performance and held responsible for two of Uruguay's goals. Just past the quarter-hour mark, England levelled. Matthews was playing well, and his pass to Wilshaw gave the restored Lofthouse the opportunity to equalise.

England were now on top, but just before half-time Varela's shot from the edge of the area found the back of the net. Immediately after the break, Schiaffino scored a controversial third after Varela was allowed to take a free kick in dubious circumstances, but, with three Uruguayan players limping, England kept pressing, and with twenty-three minutes remaining Finney brought his side back into the game. Man of the match Matthews then came agonisingly close to an equaliser when his shot hit the post and the Uruguayan keeper, Máspoli, pushed another effort round the corner. But it was at the other end that the final significant moment would occur, when Merrick allowed Ambrois's shot into the corner of his net. Uruguay won 4–2, and there was no doubt at all as to who was blamed for England's elimination. It proved to be Merrick's last international for England. He had let in thirty goals in his final ten games, thirteen of them courtesy of the Hungarians, after conceding fifteen in his first thirteen matches.

'We should have beaten Uruguay, whatever anybody says; I think we were good enough to beat them,' maintains Ivor Broadis. 'I don't know how much the two Hungarian games affected Gil, but let's say it's not a great thing for a goalkeeper to be beaten so many times in two matches. If you make a mistake in the outfield, you have about ten players to cover for you. If a goalkeeper makes a mistake, that's it, isn't it? They tend to get hammered if they're beaten from any distance, for example, and I think one of the Uruguay goals was from a considerable way out, but I'm not going to call Gil Merrick anything.'

In his book *The Way It Was*, Stanley Matthews felt that Merrick's discomfort in goal transmitted itself to the whole team:

> When a goalkeeper makes errors he usually does so with catastrophic results. Outfield players can make elementary errors and get away with them; not so a goalkeeper. Uruguay's first goal was a soft one which crept in past Gil at his near post and I am sure it rattled him. When your goalkeeper is not playing with confidence or dominating his penalty area, the whole team senses it. It unnerves you. You are afraid to make a mistake for fear of the opposition going on the attack and scoring another. We had such tension in our play, and, although we were on top for the last 20 minutes, we couldn't take our chances, and England exited from the World Cup.

Merrick, though, does have his defenders. Tom Finney said in his book, *My Autobiography*:

> I felt desperately sorry for him. He was criticised unmercifully in the media: England's public enemy number one according to them. They slaughtered him for days and seemed to have ganged up on him to

ensure that he was banished from the international arena forever. All players make mistakes, and no one individual should ever carry all the responsibility for a result, irrespective of how poorly he might have played. Goalkeepers always suffer for a bad game because their mistakes are vital.

Merrick went on to play for Birmingham in the FA Cup final two years later and managed the club in the 1960s, but his international career was over: 'I was very proud to have played in the World Cup. We did as well as we could. Uruguay were just too good. They must have sussed us out after seeing us play Hungary. You couldn't really enjoy yourself, because you always had the pressure of the game.'

It was also the last World Cup in which Stan Matthews and Tom Finney played together, and for Merrick one of them was the standout player: 'Tom Finney. Great player, great man. I class him in front of Stan, because Finney could be a great outside-left, a great outside-right and a great centre-forward, whereas Stan was a right-winger, a great juggler of the ball. At training, the boys used to ask Stan, "Go on, show us how you beat the full-back," and he used to do it!'

For his part, Tom Finney told me the problems England had that afternoon in Basle went much deeper than any one player having an off-day: 'We could have learnt from the Hungarians in '53 and gone into the World Cup with a more flexible, different approach. We underperformed in Switzerland. We should have been doing better. After the World Cup, Stan [Matthews] and I talked about it on the train on the way to games. Stan didn't have [the] memories of great days playing for England that he did with Blackpool.' In 1953, Matthews had finally won his first FA Cup winner's medal with Blackpool, but 12 months on he played his last game at the World Cup finals.

The problem lay with the prevailing attitude of the FA: We are England and we will let people worry about us. Even after the two Hungarian thrashings, the penny clearly had not dropped. England were not evolving tactically, and now Uruguay, with their own deep-lying centre-forward – and despite carrying three injured players in the second half – had ended rigid England's World Cup aspirations. At some stage, England were going to have to accept that football was changing and that, by being anchored to the past, they were in danger of being left behind.

England bade farewell to a World Cup that turned out to be a goal-fest. One hundred and forty goals in twenty-six games was the upshot of matches like the quarter-final in Lausanne, where Austria beat Switzerland 7–5 in what remains the highest-scoring game in a World Cup match. West Germany saw off Yugoslavia 2–0 in Geneva, and Berne was the stage for the Hungary–Brazil game. This brutal, infamous match was to become known as the 'Battle of Berne'. Puskás was still injured, but Hungary quickly went into a two-goal lead in the pouring rain. Maybe their niggling tackles did irritate the Brazilians, but whoever was to blame, by the second half the game had degenerated into a dirty, hostile encounter. Hungary led 3–2 when, with fewer than 20 minutes to go, Bozsik and Santos were sent off for fighting, the Hungarian having reacted to the Brazilian's stiff tackle. Brazil pushed for an equaliser but were caught on the break, and there still remained time for one more act of on-field violence as the Brazilian inside-left Humberto Tozzi kicked Lóránt and was sent off by the English referee, Arthur Ellis – even though Tozzi, according to Brian Glanville in his book *The Story of the World Cup*, 'fell weeping on his knees to plead with Arthur Ellis'.

There was no question that the English official was man of the match and only his skill enabled the game to be completed at all, but the bad blood spilled over into the dressing rooms. The non-playing Puskás faced accusations that he had hit the Brazilian Pinheiro with a bottle, and the centre-half certainly left the stadium with his head bandaged. Boots, as well as bottles, were used as instruments of attack, and Hungary's manager, Gusztáv Sebes, had his cheek cut. Hungary went through but at the price of football's reputation.

They met Uruguay in the semi-final, and the defending champions promised no violence: a pact they kept to in an enthralling game that lacked a key player from each side. Puskás was still unavailable for Hungary, and Varela, so key in Brazil four years earlier, was absent for Uruguay after being injured against England. Hungary went into an early lead that was doubled by a flying Hidegkuti header in the second half, and the exhilarating Hungarians seemed on course for the final. But, inspired by Schiaffino, the Uruguayans would not bend, and 15 minutes from time he gave Hohberg the chance to halve the deficit. Three minutes from time, the pair repeated the trick, and the Uruguayans celebrated so wildly that Hohberg was either knocked out accidentally by an overexuberant teammate or passed out through sheer excitement. In extra time, the now-recovered Hohberg hit the post, and that was Uruguay's final opportunity. Kocsis scored twice with headers, and a wonderful game was settled in Hungary's favour.

The other semi-final was a local affair in Basle between West Germany and Austria. The Austrians bravely changed goalkeepers for this huge match, and the recalled Walter Zeman had a nightmare as his team, favourites before the game, crashed 6–1. Having just been readmitted to FIFA, West Germany had made the final. Led by the 33-year-old inside-forward Fritz Walter, West Germany were a functional, tough, straightforward team, compared with the multi-layered, skilful, esoteric Hungarians. It was the artists against the artisans in Berne. Gusztáv Sebes knew the final would be as much a test of nerves as of skill and they had one massive decision to make. Puskás hadn't played since the group game against the Germans in Basle – when Liebrich had kicked him – and the rumours surrounding the state of his injured ankle were a blizzard of contradictions.

In the end he did play, but whether the Major was fit was highly doubtful. His return also necessitated a team reshuffle, when they had been playing very well. Sunday, 4 July 1954 was a rainy day in Berne, and half of the 60,000 crowd in the Wankdorf Stadium were behind the Germans, giving the underdogs an atmosphere they could feed off. In awful weather, the Hungarians made a devastating start. Six minutes in, and, fit or not, Puskás's left foot drove the overwhelming favourites into the lead – and Czibor quickly added a second. This terrible opening would have depressed most teams, but not the West Germans. Morlock pulled one back, and, amazingly, barely 16 minutes into the game it was 2–2 as Rahn equalised from Walter's corner. Hungary were faltering; Puskás was clearly slowed down by his ankle, and his cumbersome presence was in danger of unbalancing a team who thrived upon quick and slick inter-passing.

In the second half, the Hungarians stepped up the pressure. Turek in the German goal twice denied Puskás, Kocsis hit the bar and Hidegkuti missed a glorious chance. They were made to pay in the 83rd minute, when West Germany's outside-right, Helmut Rahn, drove in his second goal of the game. Hungary furiously sought an equaliser, and two minutes from time they had the ball in the net when Puskás darted through to score, but their celebrations were cut short by the flag of the Welsh linesman Mervyn Griffiths.

The Jules Rimet Trophy, which had seemed destined for Puskás and Hungary, was handed instead to Fritz Walter. This unexpected win unleashed a wave of euphoria around West Germany, a nation still suffering on so many levels in the aftermath of the Second World War. German historians point to '*Das Wunder von Bern*' (The Miracle of Berne) as a turning point for a beaten nation living in a destroyed country. The German people were once again permitted to enjoy feelings of success and pride in their flag. Hungary's long unbeaten run was over. Gusztáv Sebes blamed bad luck, West Germany pointed to resilience and by the time the best footballers on the planet gathered again in Sweden in 1958, England had built and lost a team capable of challenging for the world title.

3

<hr>

SWEDEN 1958

Just six months after the 1954 World Cup final, England captain Billy Wright had another meeting with his nemesis, Ferenc Puskás, but on this occasion at club level. The start of regular air travel and the introduction of floodlights at grounds meant that European teams began making tours of Britain, with the games proving to be hugely popular. In late 1954, Wolves, the League champions, beat both Moscow Dynamo and Spartak Moscow before playing Puskás's Honvéd team on 13 December. Almost 55,000 packed into Molineux that night, and millions more watched on their black and white televisions at home as Wolves came from 2–0 down at half-time, against a team containing seven Hungarian internationals, to win a spectacular match 3–2 thanks to two late goals from Roy Swinbourne.

Wolves goalkeeper Bert Williams knew this was no friendly match: 'This was an international. We were all keyed up for it. This was something special for Billy Wright. He had got a bit of the run-around against Hungary, and he was looking at this game to re-establish himself as captain of England. The game was live on the radio, and with the last kick of the match, with one of their players through with just me to beat, the line went dead and they said, "Now it's time for the nine o'clock news"! They had to apologise!'

As Billy Wright admitted in Norman Giller's book:

> It was the greatest moment in my club football career. There have been few nights to match it for atmosphere and excitement. To give a team of Honvéd's calibre a two-goal start and then beat them 3–2 was like something out of a fairy story. It helped restore pride and

self-confidence after those nightmare matches against Hungary. The newspapers dubbed us the Kings of Europe, and that triggered the idea for a European club competition.

Watching on with great interest was Gabriel Hanot, a former French international and coach turned sports journalist who, for 20 years, had been proposing some sort of European league. In response to the crowing of the British newspapers over the Wolves win, he wrote in *L'Equipe*, 'We better wait until the Wolves travel to Moscow and Budapest to proclaim their invincibility; but if the English are so sure about their hegemony in football, then this is the time to create a European tournament.' Hanot outlined his latest idea: that one team be entered from each association into a knockout competition over home and away legs, midweek and under floodlights, with a one-off final in Paris.

On 21 June 1955, the fledgling UEFA took over the organisation of the European Champion Clubs' Cup, but despite enormous enthusiasm around Europe for this new puppy, the Football League did not approve. They put huge pressure on the champions, Chelsea, to withdraw, saying the European Cup was incompatible with the League calendar, and, just as they had with the World Cup 25 years earlier, England adopted the same isolationist, suspicious, lofty approach towards a new international tournament. At least this self-imposed exile only lasted for one season. Matt Busby saw the educational benefit to his players and the economic benefit to Manchester United of the European Cup, and the new champions entered for the 1956–57 season.

In 1955, the players' union, the Professional Footballers' Association (PFA), joined the Trades Union Congress (TUC). PFA chairman Jimmy Guthrie made a famous speech at the TUC's annual conference in Blackpool, where he implied footballers were little more than indentured slaves: 'I stand here as a representative of the last bonded men in Britain. We have had enough of human bondage – we seek your assistance to unfetter the chains and set us free!'

Len Shackleton won his fifth and last cap in December 1954, scoring in the win against World Champions West Germany at Wembley, but he was far too much a maverick for both Walter Winterbottom and the football authorities in general. He was handed a third-class rail ticket for the overnight sleeper back to Sunderland, after the FA told him all the first-class tickets had been sold. When he got to King's Cross, he found there was plenty of room on the train and paid for his own upgrade.

We have already seen how Newcastle United treated their goalkeeper, Ronnie Simpson, despite his part in their FA Cup successes, and in 1955 Frank Brennan received an even worse offer. His new contract was worth just £8 a week, a case which Guthrie seized upon as an example of the blatant inequality of the current system. The PFA wanted players to be able to negotiate contracts for an agreed period of time and at a scale of wages acceptable to the player and the club. By now, the PFA had some powerful allies on board. No less than the secretary of the FA, Stanley Rous, put forward the idea of a Super League, made up of 16 to 18 teams, that would help the national team improve its standing – how familiar does that sound? He wanted players to be permitted to earn up to £25 a week, double the maximum wage of the time, arguing that the extra money would act as an incentive for players to work and train harder to get into the First Division.

In 1957, the Fulham midfielder Jimmy Hill took over as PFA chairman, and the force of his personality was to have a huge impact during his four-year tenure. Within months, in April 1957, what was known as the 'Sunderland Affair' blew up. The club were fined £5,000 and four directors and five players suspended for life after accusations of illegal payments. Hill now played a canny game of brinkmanship and demanded a full-scale enquiry. He organised a petition and urged every player who had received an 'illegal' payment to sign it, gambling that so many would own up that the FA would be forced to back down. It worked, and the Sunderland players were allowed to resume their careers, even having their fines quashed at a later date. The scandal made the PFA even more determined to break the maximum wage structure, and if the players felt a sense of frustration at the cap on their earnings, then the country as a whole was suffering from no such glass ceiling, as living standards rose markedly.

The Conservative government claimed that increased production in coal, steel and the motor industry was leading to a rise in wages, export earnings and investment. There was full employment, car ownership had rocketed and more people owned their houses, which they filled with an increasing number of consumer gadgets. In July 1957, the prime minister Harold MacMillan made his famous speech at a Tory rally in Bedford:

Most of our people have never had it so good. Go around the country, go to the industrial towns, go to the farms and you will see a state of prosperity such as we have never had in my lifetime – nor indeed in the history of this country.

The country was becoming more prosperous as a result of hard work; footballers still had a bar on their salaries.

England qualified for the World Cup in May 1957, and later that year they thrashed France 4–0 at Wembley. Manchester United centre-forward Tommy Taylor and Bobby Robson of West Brom each scored twice, and in the book *A Hero for All Seasons*, Billy Wright, now firmly established as the team's centre-half, recalls the excitement at the potential of this team:

I can remember as clearly as anything Walter Winterbottom saying to me at the after-match banquet, 'Bill, I think we have a team that could make a really telling challenge for the World Cup.' Little did we know then that we would never be able to field that side again.

Between November 1955 and the French game two years later, England lost just one game in eighteen internationals, and part of the reason for Winterbottom's optimism was the form of the younger players who had regenerated the team. Fulham's Johnny Haynes had made his debut as a teenager in the autumn of 1954, and his ability to hit 40-yard passes with either foot soon made him a regular, but it was another teenager, from Manchester United, who had made an even bigger impression.

In April 1955, Duncan Edwards played his first game for England in a 7–2 thrashing of Scotland at Wembley, aged just 18 years and 183 days: the youngest England player of the century. He played with such assurance, confidence and skill that Winterbottom knew he had uncovered a gem. Edwards's best game in an England shirt came a year later, in a 3–1 win against World Champions West Germany in Berlin. From his position of left-half, he dominated the match, tackling fearlessly, defending with brio, attacking when he could and scoring a fine goal from 20 yards. At the end, in an echo of Nat Lofthouse in Vienna in 1952, the watching British soldiers carried him off the pitch. Such was Edwards's potential that he was clearly set to become the mainstay of both the United and England teams for the next decade.

But Walter Winterbottom's high hopes at that post-match banquet for the 1958 World Cup ended in the snows of Munich on 6 February 1958. It was Billy Wright's 34th birthday, and on his way back from training on the bus – he had lent his car to his landlady's son as it was his birthday as well – he spotted a billboard outside a Wolverhampton newsagent's that screamed 'Man United Air Crash!' The plane carrying the Manchester United squad back from a European Cup tie in Belgrade had crashed while trying to take off from Munich Airport. Among those who died were three England regulars: the left-back Roger Byrne, the centre-forward Taylor and, succumbing two weeks later to his injuries, the twenty-one-year-old Edwards.

England full-back Don Howe was just 22 at the time of the '58 World Cup and was playing for West Brom, very near to where Edwards grew up: 'He came from Dudley, and I lived down the road in Sedgley, and I knew of Duncan Edwards. Everyone thought he would go to the Wolves, but he went to Man United. His build, his style of play, wherever you put him he could play.' Such was his precocious talent, Edwards played in the United first team aged sixteen, and by the time he died he had already played eighteen times for his country and scored five goals.

Tommy Taylor had already played in the World Cup four years earlier, and his goalscoring record of almost one a game in nineteen international appearances augured well for the remainder of his England career, given that the twenty-six year old was likely to take over from Nat Lofthouse on a permanent basis. Roger Byrne, United's captain and a fine full-back, was another who had been to the '54 World Cup, and he had won 33 caps by the time of that fateful February day.

England's first game after the Munich disaster was away to Scotland in the Home Championship in April. Wolves wing-half Bill Slater had won two England caps in 1954, but the sad death of Duncan Edwards meant he was now recalled: 'In a sense you didn't welcome getting into the team on that sort of basis, but once you were into the game then you're just focused and these things don't strike you. Perhaps after the game you might think a little bit about it.'

Manchester United's Bobby Charlton made his England debut at Hampden as a 22 year old. He had escaped physically unharmed from the Munich crash, but inevitably there were internal demons with which he would have to deal as a result of being in such a catastrophe. He scored a fine volleyed goal in a thumping 4–0 win that seemed to brighten England's spirits just a little. Derek Kevan, replacing the late Tommy Taylor, got two, and Bryan Douglas opened the scoring. The Blackburn Rovers right-winger had just finished a gruelling season by helping his club win promotion from Division Two and reach the FA Cup semi-finals: 'At the time we thought we were doing OK, but time caught up with us in the end to be honest, and it was always in the back of our minds about the Man United players. It was just too soon; after all, three months later we were playing in the World Cup. It was a hell of a blow to lose the three of them. If we hadn't have lost them, we would have got a lot further in Sweden.'

The build-up to Sweden continued with a home win over Portugal, in which Charlton scored both goals, before a chastening and sobering experience in the heat of Belgrade against Yugoslavia. England were hammered 5–0, and if, as they travelled to the World Cup, the Munich disaster played on their minds emotionally, then the thrashing in Belgrade arguably played the same tricks with their confidence on the field. England were disjointed on the day of the Yugoslavia match and couldn't find any rhythm. Don Howe admits, 'It put the team on a downer. It was a very hot day, and they were used to it, while we weren't and we ran out of steam.' Bill Slater said he had never felt so uncomfortable on a football pitch. Aleksandar Petaković scored a hat-trick, and Tom Finney, who was about to play in his third World Cup, admitted to me that 'the 5–0 thumping in Belgrade damaged the team's confidence'. The dressing room was a very subdued place afterwards, as Billy Wright accepted the team had, perhaps inevitably, gone backwards since Munich.

There was one more game before setting off for Sweden, and that was in Moscow. Bobby Charlton paid the price for a poor display in Belgrade and was dropped. Controversially, he wouldn't appear again till after the World Cup. Bryan Douglas remembers the Russian trip, and the 1–1 draw, more for what happened off the field to an outspoken, uncapped centre-forward: 'We had a practice match the day before – and you could usually tell a Walter Winterbottom team by the practice match line-up – and Brian Clough was at centre-forward. But when the team was announced for the Soviet Union game, it was the same 11, except Derek Kevan was in for Brian. I've always wondered whether Brian had a go at Walter on the way home and was left out of the '58 squad as a result.'

At that time the big debate in football circles focused on who was going to play centre-forward in Sweden: the prolific but as yet uncapped Clough of Middlesbrough, who had scored 42 goals that season – albeit in the Second Division; the hugely talented but inexperienced Charlton, who had just come through the horrors of Munich; or the strong, straightforward, bruising Derek Kevan of West Brom. The latter two went on the trip, and Clough's two England caps had to wait till the following year.

The 1958 World Cup in Sweden was, and still is, unique in that all four Home Nations qualified. Wales beat Israel in a play-off, winning 2–0 both home and away. John Charles was their outstanding player, and after an excellent first season in Italy for Juventus, he and the squad travelled to Sweden in good heart. Scotland had qualified admirably by beating Spain in their group, and Northern Ireland got the better of another traditional European powerhouse when they saw off Italy. Peter Doherty was a savvy manager of the Northern Irish side and Danny Blanchflower its heartbeat on the field.

The 1958 World Cup was the first that journalist Brian Glanville covered, and he has been attending them ever since. A former correspondent of *The Sunday Times* and columnist for *The People*, he is still a prolific writer today. The tragedy of Munich meant that England were significantly weakened in all three areas of the field – in defence, midfield and attack – but Glanville says the selectors added unnecessarily to the handicap: 'The three key players being killed was compounded by the lunacy of England not taking their full complement of players. They could have taken two more. One could have been Stanley Matthews and one Nat Lofthouse. He [Lofthouse] came back in the autumn and created absolute chaos against Russia: a Russian team we twice tried to beat in Gothenburg, but couldn't, but absolutely overwhelmed at Wembley.'

Lofthouse had just scored both Bolton's goals in the FA Cup final but had been suffering from a shoulder injury. He played twice more for England after the World Cup but was ignored for Sweden. Stanley Matthews's international career had ended 12 months earlier. The last of his 54 caps had come in a qualifier against Denmark in May '57, when, at the age of 43, an England career that had spanned the war, and started when he was a teenager, finally came to an end. He felt he should have been in the '58 squad, and so did Tom Finney, but the year before, the selectors decided they wanted the Preston man to play on the right wing so that David Pegg of Manchester United could come in on the left. That meant the end of the road for Matthews. Pegg was to perish in Munich, and in the end Finney continued playing mainly on the left. Brian Clough was another who could have gone to Sweden, given his scoring record that season, and so was Chelsea goalscorer Jimmy Greaves, an England under-23 international who certainly felt he was ready.

England arrived in Sweden just two days before the start of the tournament and found they didn't even have a proper training ground. Their hotel was in the centre of Gothenburg, and Glanville remembers having reasonable access to the players: 'Sir Stanley Rous [secretary of the FA at this point and later president of FIFA] was anti-press. He had a Swedish interpreter who was very good at shutting the door in your face in the Park Avenue Hotel. You could drop in of an afternoon and talk to Bobby Charlton, but generally speaking relationships between the press and the players were not very good.'

Bryan Douglas recalls a very relaxed atmosphere around the hotel, with trips to a nearby beach and various functions put on to keep the players from being bored. Occupying the squad when they weren't training or playing wasn't the issue in Sweden that it was going to be in Chile four years later.

Bobby Charlton's omission from every game in this World Cup was to be a major talking point. Being of a similar age, he and Don Howe would go around together a lot in Gothenburg: 'They had these parks, and the two of us would go on the rides. One day the squad went to the Brazilian camp in another part of Gothenburg. They weren't there! They were out and about, relaxing, sitting in the sun with one or two ladies about. They used to come and train by the hotel. We could live as normal. We were in the middle of town, and if we wanted to go out for a couple of hours we did. We didn't get flooded with newspapers; we made our own entertainment. We were a happy and determined group full of winners and fighters. We had ten to twenty newspaper reporters with us, and we socialised with them, plenty of laughter and joking.'

Walter Winterbottom was about to embark on his third World Cup as the England coach, and he still had to deal with the vested interests of the FA councillors, who wanted to make their mark on the England scene. Don Howe feels that, inevitably, politics did play its part: 'Walter had to deal with all the various committees at the FA as well as coach the team. They would sit round a big table and say, "Who do you want, Walter?" And he would go through them. There would be one or two club chairmen who would lean towards players at their own clubs. The chairman at West Brom was a Major [H. Wilson] Keys, and he was a big man at the FA. I don't know whether he pushed for me or not, because I wasn't there, but I think he thought I was good enough for the England team.'

Brian Glanville maintains that, although technically not involved in picking the team, Winterbottom probably did select the starting 11: 'He had the selectors in the hollow of his hand but made a mess of it. I liked him very much, but he was a bloody awful team manager! He stayed 16 years as the England manager, because he was a Rous puppet!'

Winterbottom was a fascinating mix of former player, schoolmaster and RAF wing commander – as he had previously been – and now national director of coaching, as well as England manager. Don Howe would go on to coach England at three World Cups himself and thought his manager in 1958 to be 'a bit schoolmasterly but very intelligent and thoughtful'. Howe also says, 'He was very modern tactically. As director of coaching at the FA he went round the world watching other countries – to Brazil, to Italy and Spain – to watch the way they played. Then he would come back with some ideas. One time we had a training session of forwards against defence with one or two in midfield. The defence would do their work and he would make various points and the same with the attack, telling them where they could be dangerous and where they could shoot. That's not schoolmasterly; that's really studying the game.' The paradox of Winterbottom was that he was both a schoolmaster and a student of football.

At last FIFA had settled upon a more straightforward system for the World Cup, and the top two teams from each group of four would qualify for the quarter-finals. If teams were level on points, they would face a play-off, the fate that befell three of the Home Nations. Northern Ireland were drawn with defending champions West Germany, Czechoslovakia and Argentina. The Scots faced up to France, Yugoslavia and Paraguay. Wales had hosts Sweden, Mexico and the fast-fading Hungarians, denuded of many of their stars like Kocsis and Puskás, who fled the country after the 1956 revolution; and England were in Pool Four along with the Soviets, Brazil and Austria.

Gothenburg's new Ullevi Stadium was the setting for England's first game against the Soviet Union, and Winterbottom's team received a blow from which they couldn't recover. Tom Finney, England's one world-class forward in the baffling absence of Matthews, Lofthouse and Charlton, was kicked on the ankle, and, though he made it through to full-time, his World Cup was over. England did well to get a point after being 2–0 down ten minutes into the second half. Simonian and Ivanov had given a smart Soviet team a comfortable lead when, with 25 minutes remaining, Derek Kevan's blond head dragged England back into the game.

Six minutes from time, Bryan Douglas was tripped in the area and England had a penalty. Douglas had taken over on the right wing from the incomparable Matthews the previous October: 'Stan was a hero of mine, an icon of the game. To replace him and make sure he never came back, well I was very proud but well aware I was taking over from the great Stan Matthews.' Lev Yashin, the outstanding Soviet goalkeeper, clad all in black, was so disgusted at the awarding of this penalty that he span the referee around and then threw his cap at him! Incredibly, he wasn't sent off.

Despite his injury, Tom Finney decided to take the penalty. When I asked him all those years later whether he was nervous, he laughed gently. Quite the contrary, his reply shows how relaxed he was: 'I used to take them against normal sorts of keepers with my right foot, but I decided to take this one with my left. I thought it would be something new!' Finney scored, and England escaped with a draw.

Northern Ireland began their World Cup adventure with a 1–0 win over Czechoslovakia, thanks to Wilbur Cush's header; Scotland came away from their opener with Yugoslavia with a highly creditable 1–1 draw; and Wales got a similar result against Hungary – John Charles scoring. England next played Brazil, who had cruised to an opening 3–0 win over the Austrians.

Seventeen-year-old Pelé had been injured at the start of the tournament and still wasn't available, while the brilliant but inconsistent Garrincha wasn't trusted. The right-winger had contracted polio as a child, leaving him with misshapen legs – hence his nickname, which translated as 'Little Bird'. There was no doubting his speed or prodigious skills, but he didn't yet have the faith of the Brazilian manager, Vicente Feola. Didi was the star of the midfield, whose 'falling-leaf' free kick – so called because he could get the ball over the wall and then back down under the bar by putting spin on it – had earned a vital 1–0 win over Peru in their last qualifying match. The teenage José Altafini was at centre-forward, now going by the name of Mazzola owing to his resemblance to the legendary Torino captain Valentino Mazzola, who was killed in the Superga air disaster of 1949.

England's management team now got to work on creating a system to combat Brazil. Winterbottom's assistant was the Tottenham manager, Bill Nicholson, and the pair of them ran through the opposition in great detail. They had Don Howe's rapt attention: 'Walter talked tactically about how they would play. He started with the goalkeeper all the way through to Zagallo at outside-left. I can remember it like it was last week. Gilmar, the keeper, did he kick it or did he throw the ball to his defenders? Those two full-backs were gods to me: Djalma Santos [who didn't play in this game] at right-back and Nílton Santos at left-back. Both great and the type of full-back I wanted to become. Nílton overlapped, and there was no publicity about it. Everyone gives Brazil credit for their technical ability, but they were very knowledgeable tactically.'

Despite everything the Hungarians and Uruguayans, in particular, had shown them in the previous five years, England were still lining up in the same way, but on this occasion they were tactically adept. Their management team deserve great credit for the way they tackled the game. Don Howe was at right-back with Tommy Banks of Bolton at left-back, but Winterbottom and Nicholson had both noticed that although Zagallo played outside-left he didn't play up the field in the traditional sense of a winger. He played deeper than that, and they didn't want Howe dragged out of his position following him, so the instructions were that when Zagallo dropped into those deep positions Howe would tuck in alongside centre-half Billy Wright, with left-half Bill Slater tightly marking Didi.

That Slater was in Sweden at all was down to his ability to juggle being a fine wing-half for the champions Wolves with his teaching physical education at Birmingham University. Remarkably, he wasn't even a full-time professional footballer and initially thought he would have to turn down the opportunity to represent his country at the World Cup: 'I played with the Wolves first of all as an amateur, and then the university agreed I could become a part-time professional. But there was a special clause in my contract that made it clear that teaching and commitments at the university would have priority if there was a clash. In order to go to the World Cup, I had to take leave of absence. The competition was during the summer vacation, but there were the matches in Yugoslavia and in Russia as well, and all the training, so I took a six-month leave of absence from the university. The payments for playing in the England team at that time just about matched the loss of salary, so I was OK financially.' Compared with today, it is extraordinary to think that someone who wasn't even a full-time pro could play in the World Cup and that the honour might have cost him financially.

Although Brazil were just a couple of weeks away from their first world title, they already had an aura about them, as Bryan Douglas remembers: 'They weren't just another team, even though they had never won the World Cup at this stage. We had beaten them 4–2 at Wembley two years earlier and knew they were very, very skilful. They were the best side in the world at this time.'

Vava was brought into the Brazilian line-up to play alongside Mazzola for the game in Gothenburg, as Brazil followed Hungary in adopting a fluid 4–2–4. Although Brazil had territorial possession, England's tactics worked well. Burnley's Colin McDonald had a fine game in goal, saving well twice from Mazzola, and Vava hit the bar, but England should have had a penalty in the second half when Bellini brought down Derek Kevan. Bill Slater did what was asked of him and stuck to Didi like the proverbial glue: 'I rather enjoyed playing as an attacking wing-half normally, but I had to discipline myself not to let him make their game, as it were. He was their playmaker, so I just marked him as tightly as I could. It wasn't the most enjoyable game I have ever played, because to some extent it was restricted by this requirement not to let him dominate the game. But sometimes you get your instructions on occasions like this and you have to accept them.'

A goalless draw with Brazil was an excellent result and meant that a win over Austria would almost certainly see England into the quarter-finals. They returned to their city-centre hotel in good spirits, knowing they had carried out Bill Nicholson's finely prepared tactics with just the precision needed, but there were worries going into the final group game. Tom Finney's ankle wasn't responding to treatment, and the energy levels of several players who had just finished an exhausting domestic season were a concern.

The supremely talented Johnny Haynes had given his all in the vain attempt to win Fulham promotion to the First Division, and although Ronnie Clayton's and Bryan Douglas's efforts with Blackburn were more successful, the season had left its mark, as Douglas concedes: 'I was a tired boy, to be honest. I didn't do myself justice, and a lot of the players didn't perform. It was difficult with the South American players just starting their season, and we were coming off the back of a hard season.'

England had players in key attacking positions struggling to find a spark, and their best forward of all was injured. Tom Finney's ankle wasn't up to it, and his replacement, Liverpool's Alan A'Court, was 'a straight up and down winger, a second-class player', according to Brian Glanville, who was watching in the stands. There was still no call for Bobby Charlton, and if that might have been understandable, given that England were widely expected to beat Austria in their final group game, it became ever harder to fathom after the match.

England were unchanged for the game in Borås against a team who had lost both their opening matches. Winterbottom's side had anticipated tight games against both the Soviets and Brazil, but this was a match they knew they could win. In the end, they simply didn't play well enough. Austria led at half-time through Koller's long strike, and although Johnny Haynes conjured up an equaliser just after the break, England were behind again when, with 20 minutes remaining, Austria scored once more from a distance, this time through Körner. Derek Kevan, who had always had a bad press for looking clumsy and inelegant and for keeping Bobby Charlton out, scored the second after Haynes set him up, and England thought they had won it when Bobby Robson scored – only for the goal to be harshly chalked off for a foul by Kevan on the goalkeeper. A 2–2 draw was an enormously disappointing result.

Goal average counted for nothing in the group stages, and so three of the British teams now entered the play-offs for the quarter-finals. Northern Ireland had followed up their win over Czechoslovakia with a 3–1 loss to Argentina and a thrilling 2–2 draw with West Germany. That meant, tied on three points apiece, the injury-hit Northern Irish faced the Czechs for a place in the last eight. Manchester United goalkeeper Harry Gregg was injured, replaced by Norman Uprichard of Portsmouth, but manager Peter Doherty promised an Irish win in Malmö, and, astonishingly, they delivered after going behind in the 19th minute. As half-time beckoned,

Peter McParland equalised after Cush had twice been denied, and McParland volleyed the winner in the first period of extra time.

Wales drew all three of their group games. They repeated their opening 1–1 scoreline against Hungary in their second game against Mexico. Ivor Allchurch's goal seemed to have won it, but Jaime Belmonte equalised right at the death, and Wales followed that up with a goalless encounter against hosts Sweden, in Solna – meaning another encounter with Hungary. One-nil down at half-time, the Welsh turned it around in the second half. Allchurch scored again, and Terry Medwin put Wales into the knockout stages with the winner 14 minutes from the end. That October, Allchurch finally left Swansea for Newcastle United, and Santiago Bernabéu, president of the dominant club side in the world, Real Madrid, called him 'the greatest inside-forward in the world'.

For both Northern Ireland and Wales to reach the quarter-finals was a magnificent achievement, but Scotland couldn't follow them. After the opening day draw with Yugoslavia, they lost by the odd goal in five against Paraguay – then 2–1 to France, for whom Just Fontaine scored one of his record thirteen goals in the tournament. Scotland lived to rue John Hewie's missed penalty.

The day that England were labouring to their 2–2 draw with Austria was the day that Brazil unleashed both Pelé and Garrincha against the Soviets in Gothenburg. Brazil won 2–0, at a canter. Pelé had been an international for almost a year by now, and Garrincha owed his place in the starting line-up to peer pressure. The players asked manager Feola to include him, and Garrincha immediately justified his presence, hitting a post early on. Pelé followed up by striking the other post, but Brazil didn't have to wait long, Didi setting up Vava for the first. The Soviets somehow held out till 13 minutes from time, when Pelé played Vava through for his, and Brazil's, second.

The margin of Brazil's win meant England and the Soviets had the same number of points and had scored and conceded the same number of goals, even if they had had very different results. Two days later, they met for the second time in Gothenburg. The stakes were extremely high but Don Howe was confident: 'You couldn't get anybody better than Bill Nicholson as your coach, and he watched the team you were going to play and did the team meeting. He was spot on with everything he said. That team was an outstanding team.'

The big question was a simple one: would Bobby Charlton play? The absence of Finney convinced some in the media that this would be the time to bring Charlton back. Billy Wright was convinced that Winterbottom wanted to but was outvoted by the selectors, who thought Charlton was too young. Even if they didn't necessarily discuss it among themselves, this was clearly the one topic the squad were thinking about.

'I was surprised and I think most of the players were surprised Bobby didn't play,' said Don Howe. 'They opted for the old-fashioned centre-forward, like Derek Kevan. A few of us would say, "Yes, play Kevan up front and let Bobby play a bit deeper, like he does at Man United." Kevan was good in the air, good at the back post, and I think that's why Walter plumped for him. In those days, opponents couldn't cope with high crosses to the back post, goalkeepers couldn't come out and catch the ball, they didn't know what it was – apart from Yashin!' This was the same Yashin who England were now about to face.

The author Bob Ferrier collaborated with both Walter Winterbottom and Billy Wright for a book called *Soccer Partnership*, published in 1960. The following passage explains, just maybe, why Charlton was ignored in Sweden, even at this crucial stage.

> Even against Portugal [in May '58] when he scored both England's goals – the first a 'twister', the second quite remarkably brilliant – little was seen of him as a footballer helping his team and being part of the team effort. He did not feature well in progressive, linked movements and his defensive play was non-existent. So it seemed England would have to 'carry' Bobby Charlton solely for his scoring potential, or discard him in favour of a better all-round and more workmanlike performer . . . His method of loitering with intent, or drifting around hoping for a scoring strike to turn up, made one wonder if that alone would be enough in a team, which, because of its lack of general class, now demanded solid and continuous work from everyone. There was the additional consideration that now he might be feeling delayed effects from the air crash.

It seems clear from this passage that Charlton was never going to be considered for a starting place in Sweden – as much because of the shortcomings of the other forwards as anything else – and that he was being brought along solely for the experience.

England did make changes, though, for the game, and in light of what we have just learnt about Bobby Charlton, it seems extraordinary they brought in two uncapped forwards. The Chelsea right-winger Peter Brabrook replaced Bryan Douglas, and inside-right Peter Broadbent of Wolves came in for Alan A'Court. To pick two debutants in a game of this magnitude was a massive gamble. Brabrook struck the post twice, and the Soviets hit the upright as well, in a game that was always likely to be decided by the finest of margins. With 23 minutes left, Anatoli Ilyin, the outside-left, scored the only goal. The otherwise faultless Colin McDonald had carelessly thrown the ball out, and right-back Don Howe remembers it only too well: 'He had the 11 on his back, but he moved about and I didn't always know what to do. Shall I go with him, or shall I let him go and not move out of position and let them exploit the gap? It was a very close game, and we just needed a bit of luck.'

For Tom Finney, his illustrious career was coming to a close. He played just one more international, that autumn in the 5–0 demolition of the Soviets when Nat Lofthouse scored – what might have happened in the play-off game against the same opponents in Gothenburg if they had both been available and picked? – and the 1959–60 season was his last as a professional footballer altogether.

Forced to watch from the sidelines in Gothenburg, he thought England were missing a trick: 'It was strange Bobby Charlton didn't play. He was an up-and-coming player who could have given us something different, particularly against the Soviets second time around, when we needed something special.' That was a road Brazil were happy to go down in this same competition with a raw, hugely talented 17 year old – and he had a massive bearing on its outcome. It is hard to escape the conclusion that whereas Brazil were happy to throw Pelé into an admittedly fine team and see what he could do, England – rigid, predictable, same old England – were not prepared to do the same with a player who might just have been the catalyst for their World Cup adventure.

Tom Finney had played all three World Cups that England had deigned to enter, and the Preston man had played for pride and honour. Talking to him, it is clear that the English game barely progressed in the last five years of his international career, since that momentous match against Hungary at Wembley: 'I didn't think we would ever win the World Cup, because I didn't think we were good enough. It's sad to say that. The players were good enough, but English football wasn't advanced enough. I don't think they realised the opposition had done something special in the way they lined up. We were a bit too predictable: wingers, big man in the middle, two wing-halves, two full-backs and a centre-half. It was clear to the opposition what we were going to do.'

As the decade drew to a close, English football was still highly cherished and respected, but it certainly wasn't feared on the biggest international stage of all. Nothing had changed in terms of England's formation and how they played, while, abroad, the Hungarians, the Brazilians and the Swedes had shown what could be possible with some thoughtful tactics and fluid movement.

As a disappointed England flew home, Northern Ireland and Wales had the honour of representing the Home Nations in the last eight. Wales were cruelly denied the services of the injured John Charles, but with Jack Kelsey in inspired form in goal they pushed Brazil all the way in Gothenburg. With a quarter of the game left, Pelé's shot was deflected in by Stuart Williams's foot, and Brazil squeezed through into the semi-finals. A weary and injury-hit Northern Ireland made the 210-mile journey to Norrköping only the day before their quarter-final with France – and were no match for the French as Fontaine added two more goals to his World Cup tally in a comfortable 4–0 win.

With Sweden and West Germany winning the other two quarter-finals, the semi-finals were now an engaging mix of the thrilling Brazilians, the World Cup holders West Germany, the hosts Sweden – under an English coach, George Raynor – and a free-scoring French side. Sweden had finally allowed professional footballers to play for the national team, and thus, bolstered by stars such as the AC Milan pair of Nils Liedholm and Gunnar Gren and urged on by a passionate and enthusiastic home support, they approached their semi-final against the holders in buoyant mood. Sweden pushed at the boundaries of good sportsmanship by allowing their cheerleaders onto the pitch itself prior to kick-off in Gothenburg, but during the match the Swedes had to come from a goal behind to win their place in the final. The hosts eventually won a fractious affair 3–1, after Juskowiak had become the first German ever to be sent off and Fritz Walter, the winning captain of four years earlier, had been fouled so badly he spent the next day in bed.

Brazil's semi-final with France promised to be a thriller but was ultimately ruined by an injury – in the days when substitutes were not permitted.

Raymond Kopa of Real Madrid was France's conductor and gem from the middle of the pitch, and he was a constant menace for a Brazilian side that took a second-minute lead through Vava. The prolific Fontaine equalised just seven minutes later, but when the French defender Bob Jonquet was hurt, Didi scored almost straight away, and, with the French team shorn of defensive stability, Pelé went to town, helping himself to a hat-trick.

World Cup final day in Stockholm was a rainy one, and the World Cup committee forbade any repeat of Sweden's gamesmanship before the final, banning the cheerleaders from taking to the field. Djalma Santos, one of the full-backs so revered by Don Howe, made a surprising reappearance in the Brazilian team, but it was Sweden who struck first, thanks to their AC Milan axis. Gren supplied Liedholm, and, after beating two players, his precise shot past Gilmar meant Brazil were behind for the first time in the tournament. Their response was led by Garrincha, whose speed and swerve set up two goals for Vava, and when, ten minutes after half-time, Pelé got a third, the game was up. For many people around the world, it was the first goal they would ever see him score. He controlled a high ball in the area on his chest, flicked it over a defender's head and thundered the volley in. Zagallo joyously added a fourth, and although Simonsson reduced the deficit, the final word went to the 17 year old from the heart of the state of Minas Gerais. Pelé acrobatically headed the fifth, and the World Cup triumph Brazil had assumed to be theirs by destiny eight years earlier in Rio had finally come to pass. No one would ever dispute that the best team on the planet had won the World Cup.

England had much to reflect upon. They had suffered from the Munich disaster but also from some self-inflicted wounds. Sir Bobby Charlton quotes one newspaper report in his autobiography, *My England Years*:

> There were too many simple, straightforward players earning their prosaic bread and butter in our attack and that is why we failed. Without the injured Finney, no curtain call for Charlton, and with Stanley Matthews twiddling his thumbs elsewhere, we lacked the vital sparks that count.

When Walter Winterbottom was met at the airport by his young son, Alan, the boy summed up the thoughts of millions of football fans in England: 'Daddy, why didn't you play Bobby Charlton?'

4

–––

CHILE 1962

In the summer of 1959, England went on a four-game tour of North and South America. Billy Wright admitted that his team just weren't in the mood for such a trip on the back of another exhausting domestic schedule, and after being beaten 2–0 in Rio by the World Champions Brazil, in front of a crowd of 185,000, the squad became demoralised. England were hammered 4–1 in Lima by Peru, beaten 2–1 by Mexico and the 8–1 win over the US in Los Angeles was only notable because it turned out to be Wright's 105th and final cap.

England had now played in three World Cups with very little success and had endured a horrible summer away. The press waded in. Former England international David Jack concluded in his column in the *Empire News*: 'Make no mistake this is crisis time for England. The game we gave to the world is no longer played with the required skill in these islands.'

Sweden had just reached the World Cup final under an Englishman, George Raynor, and yet the following year, 1959, he was in Skegness, working as an assistant storeman at Butlins and coaching the part-timers of Skegness Town for £10 a week. He had also guided Sweden to the 1948 Olympic gold medal, third place in the 1950 World Cup and bronze medal in the 1952 Olympics. Sweden's national football museum is in Degerfors, and its curator, Goran Berger, said, 'It really seems amazing that England didn't want him when he came home. For us, he's simply the most successful national coach of all time. He taught us how to win.'

In October 1959, Raynor was back with Sweden, masterminding their 3–2 win at Wembley, which was only England's second-ever home defeat in London by foreign opposition. He told the press that night:

I feel like a football fifth columnist. I got some sort of satisfaction out of the result, but not enough. I would much rather have been doing the same sort of thing for the country of my birth. All I consider is that the people in England have had their chance. I want to work in England – for England. They want me in Ghana, in Israel, in Mexico and in Sweden. I am a knight in Sweden and have a huge gold medal of thanks from King Gustaf. I have a letter of thanks and commendation from the Prime Minister of Iraq. My record as a coach is the best in the world. I don't smoke. I don't drink. I live for football.

Walter Winterbottom, though, remained in charge, still combining his job as national team manager with that of director of coaching for the FA – and still having to deal with self-interested parties who wanted to stick their oar in to team selection.

Real Madrid's brilliance in the European Cup final of 1960, when they beat Eintracht Frankfurt 7–3 in a scintillating match at Hampden Park, showed up the stark contrast between some of the continent's top sides and England's leading teams. Manchester United's thrilling young side had threatened to pick up the baton for flowing football in the late '50s, but when that dream was snuffed out at Munich, Wolves dominated the end of the decade, winning the title in '58 and '59. They were a direct, physical, pragmatic side whose manager, Stan Cullis, had studied the analyses of Wing Commander Charles Reep. His statistics showed Cullis that 50 per cent of goals came from no more than one pass and 80 per cent from no more than three. As a result, Wolves wing-halves were instructed to 'hit the corners', giving the wingers something to chase, and there were certain types of player, however good, that simply did not fit into the blueprint.

Jimmy McIlroy, who helped Burnley win the League title in 1960, is quoted in *Never Had It So Good* as writing that year:

> Artistry with the ball is not all-important with Wolverhampton Wanderers: therefore, it is now being treated as something of an expendable luxury by managers all over the country. These managers to their eternal shame are breeding a race of footballers who would be more at home in a wrestling stadium than on a football field.

McIlroy was the schemer in a fine Burnley team, and their successors as League Champions fell into the same bracket – a team who would today be saddled with the rather quaint tag that 'they like to play football'. Bill Nicholson's Tottenham not only won the League but were also the first side in the twentieth century to do the League and FA Cup Double.

As the '60s began, there was just a feeling that skill might be getting the upper hand over power, that fluency was winning over directness and that changes were seeping into the national side. Winterbottom had lived through the chastening experience of the Hungarian defeat, had seen how a fluid Brazil won the World Cup in Sweden and now realised it was time for England to evolve. The 2–3–5 system that England had been chained to throughout the 1950s was about specialist players in specialist positions; it was effectively about 11 individuals and not the team. The approach now had to be about all-purpose footballers, in a unit, who could move the game forwards and backwards together cohesively – not the percentage play of the previous decade. So at the start of the 1960–61 season, Winterbottom gathered his squad together at Lilleshall and told them they were going to play in a fluid 4–4–2 formation.

As Winterbottom was changing the dynamic of the England team, so the PFA chairman, Jimmy Hill, was intent on altering the lives of the leading players. Hill and Tottenham captain Danny Blanchflower had appeared on television in 1959, claiming their contracts and conditions of employment rendered them virtual slaves to the Football League clubs. The following year, Newcastle refused to grant George Eastham a transfer at the end of his contract. Hill, together with union secretary Cliff Lloyd, decided to challenge the 'retain and transfer' system and the maximum wage, which, at the time, was £20 a week during the season and £17 in the summer.

The momentum towards changing the status quo was gathering pace. Lloyd asked Blackpool's Jimmy Armfield to make sure his teammate Stanley Matthews attended a meeting in Manchester, which he did, and in 1961, backed by a 100 per cent strike ballot, Hill threatened to bring the game to a complete halt. The bearded Hill, known by such nicknames as 'the bold buccaneer', was undoubtedly a chairman with personality who understood the influence of the media, especially television. He successfully managed to highlight the anomaly of a maximum wage in an increasingly affluent society, claiming that players' earnings had actually fallen behind average working-class pay. Hill also maintained that footballers were not working-class men themselves but professionals in the entertainment business who should be rewarded accordingly. European clubs could now sign up the best British talent as well – as in the case of Leeds's and Wales's John Charles – and the threat of that, alongside the spectre of illegal, under-the-counter payments, added to the bullishness Hill showed in presenting the players' case.

The pressure on the Football League was immense, and finally they folded, conceding that, for the first time since the nineteenth century, players were free to earn whatever their clubs would pay them. Within weeks, England captain Johnny Haynes was the first player to be paid £100 a week, as Fulham sought to hold on to him. It took another two years and a court case before George Eastham successfully challenged the League's 'retain and transfer' system, so making it possible for players to move at the end of their contracts.

Haynes led a markedly different England side from the one that had competed in the 1958 World Cup. With a new direction, England went on a goalscoring spree in the run-up to Chile. They beat Wales 5–1; famously thrashed Scotland 9–3 at Wembley in April 1961; and the following month hammered eight without reply past Mexico, before winning 3–2 in Italy. That they were an attacking team is self-evident.

Jimmy Armfield was the original overlapping full-back at right-back, Ray Wilson was at left-back, with Charlton and Bryan Douglas, two survivors from the '58 squad, providing the width. Johnny Haynes was the fulcrum of the side in midfield, while Jimmy Greaves was transferring his prolific club form onto the international stage. But just two months before the World Cup started, Greaves's fellow striker Bobby Smith hurt his ankle in a 2–0 defeat at Hampden. Smith had been Tottenham's leading scorer in their Double season of 1960–61, and with Greaves moving to White Hart Lane after an ill-fated stay at AC Milan, the pair had formed a deadly partnership for both club and country as Tottenham retained the FA Cup in May 1962. Smith's injury, though, meant England would not get the benefit of that understanding in Chile, as he had to withdraw from the squad.

That wasn't the end of England's bad luck. In the Switzerland game at Wembley in May, West Brom's Bobby Robson was injured, and though he went to Chile, he then chipped a bone in his ankle in a practice match.

An even bigger misfortune befell centre-half Peter Swan. The first choice centre-back went to South America with flu and then came down with dysentery, which ruled him out of every game. Swan was excellent in the air, a great ball winner on the ground and had established a good understanding with the other defenders, especially his Sheffield Wednesday teammate in goal, Ron Springett. Maurice Norman of Tottenham now had to come in: a very good centre-half but one very inexperienced at international level. He won only his second cap in England's World Cup opener against Hungary. Much worse was to follow for Swan when, in 1964, he was accused of fixing a game to stage a betting coup, was banned for life by the FA and sent to jail. Swan would definitely have been in the squad in 1966 but, instead, had to watch England's triumph painfully from the sidelines.

The hosts had problems as well – of a different nature. In May 1960, with preparations well under way, Chile suffered an enormous earthquake. Measuring 9.5 on the Richter scale, it was the biggest of the twentieth century, and in the face of this colossal setback, the president of the Organising Committee, Carlos Dittborn, appealed to the hearts and minds of football lovers everywhere. 'We must have the World Cup,' he said, 'because we have nothing.' Chile's team responded to the challenge of rebuilding the country and hosting the tournament by making a memorable charge to the semi-finals, while Brazil, on their home continent, were always going to be the team to beat.

Losing three key players forced Jimmy Greaves, for one, to re-evaluate his high hopes that England could mount a significant challenge for the Jules Rimet Trophy. England had to reshuffle their side, but the question of who was going to replace Robson in midfield was answered by the debut of a cool 21 year old from West Ham United in the final warm-up game in Peru. The 4–0 victory in Lima was the day Bobby Moore arrived on the international stage.

England were drawn in a group with Hungary, Argentina and Bulgaria. The Hungarians were a better team than the one that had lost to Wales in '58; Argentina boasted an inside-left, José Sanfilippo, of whom much was expected; while Bulgaria were durable but unexceptional. Chile being the long, thin strip of a country that it is, the group games were dotted around, with one group in the capital, Santiago, another in Viña del Mar, on the coast, a third up by the Peruvian border in a remote spot called

Arica and a fourth – where England's group was to play – in Rancagua, an hour south of Santiago.

The players stayed in Coya, up in the hills, as guests of the American Braden Copper Company in what was essentially a mining camp. By today's standards, what they had there was positively primitive, but some of the squad had done National Service and it was perfectly passable. The players shared rooms that contained simply two single beds, two chairs, a chest of drawers and a basin. The squad were divided into two huts separated by a ravine that one group had to cross, by bridge, at mealtime. Once a day, the players would swallow sulphur tablets to try to keep their stomachs in order.

Access to the base was via a single-gauge railway that wound its gentle and unassuming way up the mountains. The scene was picturesque: to the west there was a view down to the Pacific and behind were the Andes themselves. There was a nine-hole golf course nearby and a little cinema with wooden seats for the miners, who were mostly working away in the hills. A skittle alley and a table-tennis table were also provided, but, unsurprisingly, boredom became a big factor for some.

Centre-half Ron Flowers of Wolves had been an England regular since the autumn of 1958, and being a massive golf lover, he felt lucky. He always had something to do: 'I played a lot of golf out there. The boss of the copper company was an American and a fanatic like me. He used to ask Walter if I could go and play golf with him. Walter used to look at me and say, "Well, what about your training?" This chap entertained me most of the time. The course was in beautiful condition, and I'll always remember that it was like having my own golf course.'

Not everyone was as fortunate as Ron Flowers. 'We were based at what seemed like the end of the world,' remembers Bryan Douglas, who had scored a vital goal against Portugal in the qualifiers. 'The last couple of World Cups there have been WAGs and fantastic hotels and whatnot. In '62 you had to book a phone call home 24 hours before you wanted to call. We were stuck up a mountain, and you expected Wyatt Earp to come past at any time. We were invited one night to a church, where they showed us a little dance on stage; the selectors came with us. They tried to occupy us. We trained during the day, and there was little else. I was very homesick. You couldn't just pick up the phone and ring home.'

Peter Swan had been reluctant to take his sulphur pills and ended up battling dysentery, but the night of the church concert he felt a little better and went along with his teammates. 'Peter looked dreadful, really dehydrated,' said Ron Flowers. 'He just happened to recover one night when we were going to a concert. He had been writing to his wife about how ill he felt, but this night he was having a little dance at the end. Well, of course, a photograph appeared in the Sheffield paper, and his wife saw it – after all the complaining to her about how ill he felt!'

As always, the squad came into the World Cup off the back of a hard domestic season. Centre-forward Gerry Hitchens was the only one playing outside of England, and, unlike Jimmy Greaves, he was enjoying his Italian adventure – his at Inter Milan. When Hitchens arrived in Chile, dressed to kill, Douglas remembers him hanging up six Italian suits in his room.

England had one more formality to fulfil before their opening game against Hungary. The squad dressed up in their flannels and blazers and hopped onto the train down the mountain to stand in Rancagua's main square while the mayor welcomed them. The band played, England had done their duty and been the attentive guests and they then went back up to their base to prepare for the first match.

Hungary had beaten England two years earlier in Budapest. Flórián Albert was now the focal point of their attack – a latter-day Nándor Hidegkuti in some ways – and Lajos Tichy was a goalscorer of note, while Kálmán Mészöly was one half of a formidable defensive pair. Bobby Moore's assured debut in Lima and Bobby Robson's injury meant the team pretty well picked itself. Moore kept his place, Norman replaced the stricken Swan to line up alongside Flowers at centre-back and up front Hitchens partnered Greaves.

The crowd in Rancagua was a measly 7,938. 'It felt like Accrington Stanley got more than we did,' Bryan Douglas recalls disappointedly. 'There were no crowds, no atmosphere. It was like playing on an open park; teams in non-league today have better grounds. We were supported by the British Embassy people and a few soldiers, but you feed off the crowd; they are your 12th man.'

Douglas and Jimmy Armfield had developed a very fruitful partnership down England's right-hand side. The full-back was encouraged to get forward, and whenever he did, Douglas would drop back and fill in. Armfield says, 'The ground was never full for any game, and by modern standards it's almost laughable, but in those days they tried to move the World Cup around. It wasn't about television. It was Chile's turn, they got it and after the earthquake they needed it to revitalise the country. The climate was good as well: it wasn't too hot.'

Johnny Haynes was the key to this England team: a hugely skilful player, described by Bryan Douglas as 'a fantastic lad. A bastard on the field, where he would holler and shout, but off it a fantastic guy.' England's man of the tournament eight years later in Mexico in 1970, Alan Mullery was on the ground staff at Fulham when Haynes was in his pomp: 'In those days, the ball weighed sixteen ounces when it was dry, and when it was wet it was like ten bags of sugar. When he started, it had a lace in it as well, and he could kick that ball 60 yards farther than a goalkeeper. A keeper would take a goal kick and just about reach the halfway line in those days, but I used to watch him doing it every day in training when I was a ground-staff boy at Fulham. I thought the second-best passer of a ball I ever saw was Glenn Hoddle; the best was Johnny Haynes.'

Haynes had been troubled by blisters on his feet in Sweden four years earlier, but now he was twenty-seven, in his prime, and this should have been his stage. Yet if England had a problem, it was that they relied on Haynes too much. Yugoslavia man-marked him in a friendly at Wembley in 1960, and now Hungary put a man, Rákosi, on him, realising much of England's attacking play went through their captain and number ten.

On a day of pregnant cloud and intermittent drizzle, England's 1962 World Cup got off to the worst possible start. After 16 minutes, Lajos Tichy sent a fierce shot from outside the area past the dive of Ron Springett. Flórián Albert then missed a great opportunity to make it 2–0 as a frustrated Haynes exhorted for more effort from his teammates. One Bobby Charlton cross led to a near thing as Gerry Hitchens collided with the Hungarian goalkeeper, Gyula Grosics, a veteran of the great Puskás team, but this was the day Kálmán Mészöly would come of international age.

The sturdy defender repelled nearly everything England threw in the air at the Hungarian defence, and it was only after a mistake from the goalkeeper that England drew level. Under pressure from Hitchens, Grosics allowed a Douglas cross to escape from his grasp, and when Jimmy Greaves's goalbound shot was handled on the line, Ron Flowers equalised from the penalty spot. Flowers, though, was soon to go from elation to despair when he slipped on the sodden surface and Albert rounded Springett and shot past Ray Wilson, who was trying to protect the goal. England had to reflect upon a disappointing 2–1 defeat as they dragged themselves back up the mountain in the rain.

Chile won their opening game 3–1 against Switzerland on a beautiful day in Santiago, with the snow-capped mountains a lovely setting. The defending champions, Brazil, opened up with a 2–0 win over Mexico, Pelé scoring one and providing the other for Zagallo. But after beginning the tournament in such good form, Pelé was to last no longer than 25 minutes of the second group game, against Czechoslovakia. Receiving a pass from Garrincha, he shot powerfully against the post, tore a thigh muscle and hobbled out of the World Cup. Both teams settled for a goalless draw.

The second round of group matches was most notable for the infamous 'Battle of Santiago' between Chile and Italy. The background to the violence on the pitch that day in June 1962 was multi-layered. The Chileans were already antagonised by the practice of *oriundi*: the Italian habit of poaching Latin American players with Italian ancestors. José Altafini, Italy's chief goalscorer, had played for Brazil in the 1958 World Cup. Humberto Maschio and Omar Sívori, a talented inside-left, were set to turn out for Argentina in 1958, before Italian clubs came knocking on the door. Italian scouts hanging around the training camps of the South American teams merely ratcheted up the tension, and then two Italian journalists sent home derogatory reports about the conditions in Chile, provoking more local anger.

It all added up to a combustible mix, with the hostility of the crowd in Santiago transmitting itself too easily to the players on the field. Chile's Leonel Sánchez broke Maschio's nose with a left hook, an act that was televised around the world but ignored by the linesmen, who did nothing to help the unsighted referee, England's Ken Aston. He called the match 'uncontrollable' and was forced to send off two Italians who had risen quickly to the Chilean bait. Giorgio Ferrini was sent off for hacking down Landa, although it took minutes for the Italian to leave the field, and Mario David followed him – taking out his own retribution on the pugilistic Sánchez by kicking him in the head. Reduced to nine men, Italy held out till the last quarter of an hour, when Ramírez headed in Sánchez's free kick and Toro got a second in the last minute. It had been a black day for football.

England's next opponents were an Argentinian side who had started with a narrow 1–0 win over Bulgaria, so victory was imperative if England were to stay in the tournament. Argentina boasted a new star: the toast of Buenos Aires, José Sanfilippo was a languid inside-left whose reputation had reached English ears. Juan Carlos Lorenzo was a hardline coach determined to put some backbone into a team all too often found wanting, as had been shown when the Czechs turfed them out of the 1958 World Cup with a 6–1 thrashing.

Argentina had intimidated the Bulgarians and would try to do the same against England, for whom Alan Peacock of Middlesbrough was brought in at centre-forward – to make his international debut no less – in place of Gerry Hitchens. England played by far the better football. In front of another paltry crowd, of 9,794, Moore, Flowers and Norman tackled hard, the Douglas–Armfield partnership worked smoothly down the right-hand side and the tall debutant Peacock, in the words of the watching *Sunday Times* correspondent Brian Glanville, 'had a very good game, although he was badly maltreated by Ruben Navarro, the centre-half, who was bashing the back of his neck all the time. Peacock played a real Grenadier's game.'

Bobby Charlton had an excellent match at outside-left, constantly beating his marker, Vladislao Cap, and his cross led to the first goal when Peacock's header was handled by Navarro and Flowers scored his second penalty of the World Cup. Flowers scored a record six penalties for England, the same number as Alan Shearer, and the centre-half thinks the lack of supporters in Chile was a boon when it came to spot kicks: 'I didn't get nervous. If the atmosphere had been there and the crowds had been there, that makes a difference really. I just picked a corner out and hit it! You've got to make your mind up as to what you're going to do.'

Charlton scored the second himself before half-time with a low shot, after fooling the defence that he was about to go round the full-back again, and Jimmy Greaves got the third with a quarter of the match remaining. Greaves was 22 at the time and had made his international debut aged just 19 in May 1959. In both the 1958–59 season and in 1960–61 he was the leading First Division goalscorer, before his brief sojourn in Italy with AC Milan. Billy Wright wondered whether England shouldn't have taken a chance with him for the 1958 World Cup, when they didn't even take the full complement of players to which they were entitled.

By the time they came to Chile, Greaves was a regular in the England side, and the year before, at the British Home Championship, he had achieved the remarkable feat of scoring seven goals in three games as England won the title. Greaves scored 44 goals in 57 appearances for England, third on the all-time goalscoring list behind Bobby Charlton and Gary Lineker, but that goal in Rancagua against Argentina was the only one he scored in the finals of a World Cup. Jimmy Armfield was unequivocal when I asked him about Greaves the goalscorer: 'He didn't have the best of World Cups by his standards, but he's the best finisher I have ever seen. I've never seen anyone better than Jim. Left foot, right foot, header, inside of the foot, outside of the foot, dribble, speed, control – he had the lot and all, too, with a smile on his face.'

The ineffective José Sanfilippo scored a late consolation, which only went to underline how much he had been overhyped, and he quickly faded from the Argentinian scene. As Jimmy Armfield says, 'Sometimes these players take very well to World Cup football, and sometimes they die a death.' Sanfilippo was clearly in the latter category. England were back in the World Cup, and skipper Johnny Haynes was quick to tell the travelling press that they had written off England's chances all too readily.

Armfield came off the pitch knowing he had been in a match: 'The left-back let me cross the ball, and then he came in late on me and it didn't half hurt. It really hurt me, but in those days you didn't lie down, you didn't let them see they had hurt you, so I got up and limped away. I remember the blood coming through my white sock.'

Elsewhere in the group, Hungary thrashed Bulgaria 6–1, with Flórián Albert grabbing a hat–trick, and then eased back on the throttle against Argentina, knowing that a point would suffice for qualification. A goalless draw ensured Hungary won the group as Mészöly gave another outstanding performance. England duly qualified as runners-up after a goalless draw of their own against Bulgaria the following day, in a game that Sir Bobby Charlton describes in his book, *My England Years* as:

> [A] match so bad, so depressing, so opposed to all that I believed in and had been taught at Manchester United, that when the final whistle confirmed our place in the quarter-finals after a goalless draw with one of the least talented, least ambitious teams to have played in

the World Cup, I found myself involved in a loud and angry dispute with my captain.

Frank McGhee of the *Daily Mirror* agreed. He said afterwards, 'I had six cups of coffee during the match, but that still didn't keep me awake.'

Johnny Haynes felt the achievement in reaching the last eight was a cause to celebrate, no matter the quality of the game that had got them there, but Charlton heatedly made his point to the contrary. Bobby Moore later described it as one of the worst internationals of all time, and part of the problem was that Bulgaria knew they couldn't qualify but wanted to go home with some honour in the shape of a single point won. Bulgaria's approach was totally foreign to England's way of thinking. 'Every game you played to win in those days,' says Jimmy Armfield. 'I don't think they had a shot for an hour. We had all the play but couldn't score. We would get to the halfway line, and no one would come near us. We were playing 4–2–4, virtually.'

As is often the case in these sorts of games, Bulgaria had one chance that could have caused massive embarrassment to England when the winger Ivan Kolev whipped in a cross that no one converted – with the goal gaping. But however much the nature of the match disappointed the Bobbies Charlton and Moore, England were through to the quarter-finals of the World Cup. That was the good news; the downside was that the holders, Brazil, were waiting for them.

England's progress in the World Cup was also bad news for those in the squad who knew they had no chance of playing and who, thousands of miles away from home, were bored. This is always a potential problem at any major tournament, but in Chile in 1962, with telephone calls difficult to make and local entertainment thin on the ground, it was a more acute issue. Writing in his autobiography, Sir Bobby Charlton accepts this was a major issue:

> This may sound a little harsh, an offloading of responsibility perhaps, but one thing was evident enough to me during the course of the tournament. It was that the squad lacked any real sense of unity and purpose, a problem increased by the effects of homesickness, particularly in some of the fringe players.

Bryan Douglas says that for those having to watch from the sidelines the tournament was dragging on: 'One or two of the players knew they weren't going to get a game and wanted the thing over with and [to] get home. They were fed up, and I don't think they wanted us to win. I can think of one or two fringe players who knew they would only play if someone got injured, and they weren't too worried when, eventually, Brazil beat us and they knew we would be coming home.'

Jimmy Armfield had his own experience of looking in from the outside, as it were, when he was a non-playing member of the triumphant 1966 squad. Of course, that was easier to deal with, because the tournament was at home, but he appreciates what those not in the 11 were going through in South America: 'For those not in the team, in Chile, it was hard. Then it's up to the individual; it's part of your job to help the *esprit de corps* of the team. Even though I didn't play in '66, it does reflect on you that you were part of the squad. In '62, you really were thousands of miles from home, and if you weren't playing it would have been tedious at times, because you weren't even getting the big-match atmosphere as the grounds and crowds were so small.'

At least for those who were not going to be involved in the quarter-final against Brazil there was a change of scene. England came down from their mountain-top eyrie and moved to the coast, to Viña del Mar, where they could eat lobster at night and spy pelicans wading in the shallow water. Brazil had edged past Spain 2–1 to top Group Three and set up a meeting with England for the second successive World Cup – after their goalless draw in the group stages in 1958. In place of the stricken Pelé, Brazil's coach, Aymoré Moreira, had gone for Botafogo's inside-left, the 24-year-old Amarildo, who didn't appear to be weighed down by the shadow of the man he was replacing.

England were confident: they had outplayed South American opposition already, in the shape of Argentina; there was no Pelé to worry about; and they had shown themselves to be ready, physically and mentally, for what lay ahead. Jimmy Armfield was symbolic of that quiet determination: 'I thought this was our opportunity to win the World Cup. I thought we were good enough. I had seen the other teams, and I thought, "We'll beat them", even when we lined up against Brazil. They didn't have Pelé; they had Amarildo instead – cute little bugger – and Vava, Didi, Garrincha, Zagallo and two animals behind them who kicked everything in bloody sight, and because it was in South America they got away with it. I thought we were the best team in the tournament, and we didn't win it.'

That England lost on 10 June 1962 in the Sausalito Stadium was down to a combination of individual errors, indifferent finishing and a virtuoso individual performance from Garrincha. Freed, perhaps subconsciously, by the absence of Pelé, Garrincha was magnificent, flowing down the right wing and making Ray Wilson work overtime in an attempt to subdue him. Everyone knew about his tremendous speed, his dexterity and his crossing, but now he showed his ability in the air, out-jumping Maurice Norman to head in a corner after 36 minutes. Garrincha gave away six inches in height to the England defender but still sent a header past Ron Springett in goal. The keeper then pulled off a fine save to deny Amarildo before England equalised. Gerry Hitchens was back in the side because of an injury to Alan Peacock, and when Jimmy Greaves headed against the crossbar, Hitchens popped in the rebound.

It was 1–1 at half-time, and England, despite Garrincha's display, were still in the game. They had their moments, and Jimmy Armfield remembers the opportunities that got away with great frustration: 'At 1–1 Jimmy Greaves missed a chance and Gerry Hitchens missed another, and we were all over them. I don't know how we didn't score. Bobby Charlton was running past their right-back, Djalma Santos, and Bryan Douglas was too clever for Nílton Santos on the other side, and Zagallo was running back to try to prop him up. We just wanted the second goal. I spent most of the game attacking!'

The second goal, though, wouldn't come for England, and Garrincha turned the game. After 53 minutes, England, fatally, gave away a free kick within shooting range. Garrincha took it. Bryan Douglas remembers what happened next all too well: 'Springett went to catch it, and it bounced off his chest and Vava headed it in. Then, half an hour from the end, Garrincha bent one in from twenty yards, and after that we couldn't get the ball off them. Once they were in front, it was increasingly difficult.'

Ron Flowers thinks the type of ball they used in Chile contributed to England's downfall: 'We should have won that match. We were on top, and they scored against the run of play. The ball was swinging a little bit – a bit what they're like today, a very light ball – and the idea was to hit it straight at the keeper and get the movement going before it got to him, and then he couldn't get hold of it. Ron Springett stopped the ball and would have caught it easily, but, of course, it was moving about and it came back off him for Vava to head in. Ron was right behind it, but the ball was going all over the place.'

Garrincha was the master on the pitch that day, and the only thing he couldn't tame and control was a woolly black dog that had run onto the field as if to celebrate his performance. The dog evaded the 'Little Bird' but not Jimmy Greaves, who got down on hands and knees to trap it and take it off the field.

It wasn't a World Cup to remember fondly. There was too much defensive, safety-first play, with too many fractious matches resulting in dozens of players being taken to hospital. Greaves later told Brian Glanville: 'There are a lot of very good players there [in Chile], and they're not doing anything because they're afraid they're going to get killed, as the boot was coming in all the time.'

Jimmy Armfield was named as the tournament's best full-back, but he has never received whatever memento FIFA had in mind. Back in the hotel after the Brazilian defeat, he went to the bar: 'When we lost, I was really miffed. I had a beer with some of the press lads. I really thought we were going to win it or get to the final at least. The team was so good with so few weaknesses. We had young Bob [Charlton], who was settling in; we had everything.' Football has forever divided opinions, and not everyone saw the game that way. Brian Glanville viewed it through the prism of Brazil's outstanding right-winger: 'I don't think England were ever in the same class as Brazil that day. Garrincha was doing exactly what he liked.'

It was arguably the game of Garrincha's life, but it was definitely the last day of Johnny Haynes's international career. After 56 caps, many of them while playing in the Second Division with Fulham, he never played for England again – although the new manager, Alf Ramsey, did toy with the idea. Later in 1962, Haynes was involved in a car crash in Blackpool one Saturday night. The Fulham team had played at Bloomfield Road that afternoon and were staying over before a game at Burnley on the Tuesday. Haynes had gone to meet a friend of his, while Alan Mullery went out for a few drinks with his teammates: 'We were all walking back to our hotel, and in one of the little hotels on the way home, there was this little sports car which had literally gone through a brick wall and was hanging halfway down into the basement. We didn't realise Johnny Haynes was in it.'

Mullery said he didn't notice any discernible dip in Haynes's performance once he had returned to full fitness, and whenever Alf Ramsey asked another of Fulham's England internationals, the full-back George Cohen, for an update on Haynes, the England manager always received glowing reports. Ramsey would not budge, though, and Haynes admitted later in life that the England manager was quite right not to recall him to England colours.

The career of Johnny Haynes is curious when considered from afar: the first £100-a-week player, one of the first to have an agent, whom he shared with Denis Compton, and one of the first to use his name to advertise various products – his nickname was the 'Brylcreem Boy'. He had a sponsored car, captained England on twenty-two occasions and was renowned for being a marvellous passer of the ball, and yet, by deciding to stay with Fulham for his entire career, he didn't win a single honour in the game and his two World Cups were a disappointment. In Sweden, he was exhausted after a tiring domestic season and dogged by blisters. In Chile, he was man-marked in the opening game by Hungary and undone by Garrincha's brilliance in the quarter-final, his head hitting his chest in frustration at the realisation that his World Cup dreams were going up in smoke. The year he died, I ran into him by chance in a bar at Lord's during the Ashes Test match. He chatted amiably about football and showed no envy for what contemporary players were earning. He was of his time and they are of theirs.

As Johnny Haynes and his team flew home, Chile were continuing their remarkable surge through their own World Cup. Against the Soviet Union in the quarter-finals, Leonel Sánchez, he of fighting fame from the 'Battle of Santiago', scored the first from 25 yards, and, after Chislenko had equalised, Eladio Rojas beat the great Lev Yashin from 35 yards for the winner: a strange aberration for a goalkeeper of his class. Yugoslavia edged out West Germany 1–0 in Santiago, and Czechoslovakia beat Hungary by the same scoreline in Rancagua. Here a goalkeeper was the hero, not the villain, as Schroiff, in the Czech goal, kept out everything the Hungarians could hurl at him and Scherer scored an improbable winner for the outplayed Czechs.

Chile's semi-final was due to be played in Viña del Mar, but their surprise appearance at this stage prompted the organisers to ask FIFA to switch the game to Santiago. A capacity crowd of 76,000 watched the home country's improbable tilt at the world title come to an end as Brazil asserted the natural order of things with a 4–2 win. Garrincha continued his excellent form, and he scored twice before Chile could get on the board: a left-foot shot and another header from a corner. It seemed that even the constant baiting from the partisan crowd couldn't put him off his game, but the crowd had something more positive to shout about when Toro brought Chile back into the game just before half-time.

Vava restored Brazil's two-goal advantage right at the start of the second half when he headed in Garrincha's corner, but the indefatigable Chileans wouldn't buckle and Sánchez narrowed the gap once more from the penalty spot. Finally, Brazil put the match to bed when Vava headed in a fourth from Zagallo's cross. But in the closing minutes, Garrincha's patience eventually snapped, and, tired of being kicked, he retaliated against Rojas and was sent off. As he left the field to a chorus of boos, he was hit on the head by a bottle and his head was cut open. For the moment, Garrincha would be suspended for the final. Landa was later sent off for Chile.

Garrincha had been the star of the tournament, and the press, naturally enough, wanted to know if he was going to be available to play in the final. Brian Glanville was with the BBC commentator Kenneth Wolstenholme when he rang Sir Stanley Rous, the president of FIFA, for an update. Sir Stanley told them that the disciplinary committee had met that morning.

'And what did they decide?' asked Wolstenholme.

'Just a minute,' said Sir Stanley. 'I've got my papers here. Seven and nine. Seven was cautioned and nine suspended.' And that is how they found out Garrincha had been allowed to play in the final, for he was wearing the number seven shirt in the semi-final and Landa the number nine. The Chilean would be banned for the third place play-off match.

The all-Eastern European semi-final was an altogether different affair, watched by fewer than 6,000 in Viña del Mar. The Czechs survived till half-time, and after going into a fortunate lead, they were once more indebted to their goalkeeper, Schroiff, after Yugoslavia seemed to have wrestled the momentum back with a 69th-minute equaliser. Scherer followed up his winner in the quarter-final with a breakaway goal ten minutes from the end and then scored a penalty to give the Czechs a 3–1 win. After their goalless draw in the group stages, the game in which Pelé was injured, Brazil and Czechoslovakia would meet again – this time in the final.

Brazil were clear favourites to retain their world title, but then Czechoslovakia had been underdogs in both their quarter- and semi-finals and had passed the test. That was in large part due to the outstanding form of Schroiff in goal, but on the biggest stage of his career he fluffed his lines. The Czechs guarded Garrincha closely early on and even took an 18th-minute lead when Masopust converted Scherer's clever diagonal pass. For the second successive World Cup final, Brazil were behind.

It took them just four minutes to equalise – four minutes for the Czechs to realise that Schroiff was not going to repeat his heroics of the last two rounds. Amarildo dribbled down the left wing, and, as the keeper guarded his near post, the centre-forward espied enough room on the far side to slam the ball into the side of the goal.

With a quarter of the match left, it was still 1–1 and the Czechs were sticking gamely to their task, twice testing Gilmar in the Brazilian goal. The game could still have gone either way, and then Amarildo, the Pelé replacement – but the man who had stepped up to the plate so effectively for Brazil – worked himself some space down the left-hand side and crossed for Zito to head in. Thirteen minutes away from their coronation they got a third: an atypical Brazilian goal. Djalma Santos booted a high up-and-under into the Czechs' box, and Schroiff dropped it at the feet of Vava, who calmly knocked it in. For the first time since the 1930s, the reigning World Champions had retained their title.

As England flew home, it was clear Winterbottom's reign was coming to an end. He had held the post since the end of the Second World War, and he left to become the head of the Council of Physical Recreation, having lost out, unexpectedly, in the voting to pick a successor to Sir Stanley Rous as secretary of the FA. It was time for the England team to head in a new professional direction where the manager, and the manager alone, picked the team, unfettered and unencumbered by FA councillors, selectors and the like, with their differing parochial interests. Alf Ramsey was officially named manager on 1 May 1963 – although he took charge of a couple of games before that – and England, chosen as hosts to celebrate the centenary of the codification of football, had a World Cup at home to look forward to.

The 1962 World Cup has tended to become lost in the mists of time a little, because of its distance from Europe. Jimmy Armfield sums it up neatly: 'Because of where it was, in such a remote place, no one ever talks about the Chilean World Cup. It's the furthest point in the globe. It's incredible they didn't have a match in Tierra del Fuego at the bottom. For me, it was my World Cup, and I'll never forget it. When we set off in '62, I thought we were going to win.' England would have to wait another four years for that privilege.

5

ENGLAND 1966

England's defeat in Viña del Mar wasn't Walter Winterbottom's last game in charge, but it was clear he was coming to the end of his shelf life as manager. His constant battle with the system was tiring him out, and after a draw against France in a European Nations Cup qualifier and a couple of perfunctory wins in the Home Championship, he was replaced by a man who had surprised the football world by bringing the League title to Ipswich in 1962.

Former England full-back Alf Ramsey, whose international career had ended the day the Hungarians stormed Wembley ten years earlier, had taken the unfashionable Portman Road club from the Third Division South to the top of football's pyramid in just eight years. He wasn't the FA's first choice – that was the Burnley player Jimmy Adamson, who had helped coach the England team in Chile – but when Adamson turned them down, the job fell to Ramsey.

The new manager was no fool. He had seen how Winterbottom was undermined by the selection committee, and Ramsey took the job on the proviso that he, and he alone, picked the starting 11. As the leadership of the England national team was undergoing a sea change, so was society both here and abroad. The Cuban Missile Crisis, the assassination of President Kennedy, the Profumo Affair and the revelations of home-grown spies in the British Civil Service all changed the shape of domestic and international politics. There was no longer the reflex deference to the Establishment that there had once been, and satirical programmes like *That Was The Week That Was* reflected the growing confidence people had in questioning the status quo. The emergence of the Beatles, Mary Quant and the birth-control pill heralded the real start of the so-called 'Swinging Sixties'.

The new England manager was a quiet, introverted character, but from the outset he made a bold statement that flew in the face of all logic. While still at Ipswich, Ramsey oversaw two England defeats in the spring of 1963 in his capacity as caretaker manager. The first was a 5–2 thrashing in Paris in a European Nations Cup qualifier. 'We do not lose to the French – well, certainly not like that,' he told the players. He was then forced to watch Scotland win at Wembley. His antipathy towards England's great rivals north of the border was to become legendary.

So by the time Ramsey officially took over, morale was low. Back-to-back losses hard on the heels of a World Cup quarter-final defeat had done nothing for the mood of English football, but Ramsey surprised everybody. 'We will win the World Cup,' he announced publicly. 'We have the players, the ability, the strength of character and temperament to win the title in 1966.' Few people in football believed him, and plenty thought him deluded. There was nothing to suggest he might be right, but Ramsey's strength was making the players believe in themselves and in him, the way he wanted them to play and the formation he would eventually fall upon. His seemingly outlandish prediction was more a rallying call, and in the forty-two games that followed, England lost only four matches in a run that culminated in winning the World Cup.

The FA had appointed a shrewd, tactically savvy, firm but fair man – a players' man who wanted flexibility and total commitment from them. The team and its structure was everything; that mattered first and last, and if it meant that better players were omitted, then so be it. He never had the easiest relationship with the press, he never wanted the players to take their places in his squad or the starting 11 for granted and he was acutely aware of his east London background – to the extent that he took elocution lessons to modulate his Estuary English. The resulting hybrid accent sometimes caused unintentional amusement.

His World Cup-winning team became known as the 'Wingless Wonders', but it didn't start out that way. He played with wingers on his first European tour, in the summer of 1963, in a 4–2–4 system, and fielded one different winger in each of the three group games in '66. When at Ipswich, he had tried replacing the wide men with midfielders who would drop back and help out in defence. This would baffle opposing full-backs, who were used to seeing wingers running at them with the ball – instead the play would go mainly through the middle.

Using this system in the run-up to the World Cup, the seminal moment came in Madrid in December 1965. Spain were the reigning European Champions and yet were comfortably beaten 2–0. The full-backs, Reija and Sanchís, didn't know what to do, because they had no one to mark; they were completely nonplussed. Spain had become the first real victims of the 'Wingless Wonders', and Bobby Charlton, so central to England's World Cup challenge, knew they had alighted upon a system that could threaten the very best. Even Fleet Street swooned. The flamboyant writer Desmond Hackett, of the *Daily Express*, wrote:

> England can win the World Cup next year. They have only to match the splendour of this unforgettable night and there is not a team on earth who can master them . . . England's football was as smooth as the brush of a master – precise, balanced and as lovely to watch as the ballet.

The win in Spain marked a watershed for both the manager and the players. They knew they had a manager with his eye fixed firmly on the ultimate prize: a man who was not going to be swayed by anything. Ramsey knew he had the players to make his prediction come true. Nine of those who started in Madrid played in the World Cup final the following July. From then till the start of the tournament, it was all about fine-tuning for Ramsey. The results that followed, though excellent, were secondary to the way the team was coming together.

As the countdown to the World Cup continued in the summer of 1966, the England captain found himself in a real quandary. Bobby Moore was hankering after a move away from West Ham to Tottenham, but his manager at Upton Park, Ron Greenwood, later England's manager in the 1982 World Cup, wouldn't let him go. Moore's contract ran out on 30 June, and for the first seven days of July he was training for the World Cup without being contracted to any club. England's first game was on 11 July. Legally, Moore didn't exist as a player in the eyes of the FA, who were about to stage the world's biggest tournament. Ramsey knew this was an intolerable situation, and Greenwood was summoned to the team hotel, Hendon Hall, in north London. He and Moore disappeared into a side room, and the England captain quickly signed a month-long deal to tide him and everyone over.

The image of Bobby Moore holding aloft the Jules Rimet Trophy is one familiar to every football fan in England, no matter when they were born. Moore was the golden boy, England's unflappable captain at the back, but, had the Fates conspired differently, it might have been another Englishman altogether who politely wiped his dirty hands on the velvet of the Royal Box before receiving the trophy from the Queen on 30 July. Right-back Jimmy Armfield was Ramsey's first England captain, but when he ruptured his groin on the final day of the 1963–64 season at Portman Road, George Cohen took his place in the 'Little World Cup' in South America that summer. Bobby Moore assumed the captaincy.

Armfield's injury took about five months to heal, but he received a boost at the end of 1965 when Ramsey phoned, telling him he would definitely be in the World Cup squad. He was the first player to know officially that he would be in the 22, and by May '66, with Norman Hunter given a run-out in place of Moore, he was back in the side as captain for the game against Yugoslavia at Wembley. England won 2–0 and then flew to Finland. They were 3–0 up in Helsinki, and Armfield remembers he was playing well: 'It was the last minute, and I'm running down the wing when this bloke comes across and cracks me on my little toe on my left foot.' An X-ray showed he had broken his toe: a hairline fracture that would take two to three weeks to mend. There were now 15 days till England played Uruguay in the opening match. Cohen came in for the next warm-up match against Norway, and Alf Ramsey never tinkered with the defence again. If Armfield's ruptured groin two years earlier had realistically ended his hopes of being England's captain at the World Cup, now a broken toe – a metatarsal, long before David Beckham had made it famous – had done the same to his being in the starting 11.

I have had the pleasure of working with Jimmy Armfield for 15 years, and I have always wondered whether that horribly unlucky break has troubled him – whether he has lain awake at night cursing his bad fortune. As Jimmy's wife, Anne, plied us both with fondant fancies one spring afternoon in Blackpool, I got my answer: 'Not changing the defence in the World Cup was right, as they did very well. It wasn't hard for me to watch. We all want to play, but I think some things you have to take. A lot of good things have happened, so you've got to take the downers as well.'

Injury cost both Jimmies a chance of playing in the final. Jimmy Greaves had been injured against France in the final group game and never regained his place. Jimmy Armfield remains very philosophical about it: 'That's football, and you've got to put up with it. I know people think I've got a soft centre, but deep down I'm quite a strong person.' He feels that growing up in the war and having to do National Service made him better equipped to deal with the vicissitudes of football, even when a World Cup final spot was at stake: 'We expected less, and it does make a big difference. When I was a boy, we lived in pretty humble surroundings. I lived in a boarding house, with just a bed, a radio and books to read at night. What did Wordsworth say? "The Child is father of the Man."' Jimmy became the unofficial leader of the 'second 11' during the World Cup, and Alf Ramsey used him as a go-between – asking him how those players were getting on and using Jimmy to relay messages to them. One day the 'second 11' played Arsenal in a training match and beat them. The England players carried Jimmy off shoulder-high.

Even though Bobby Moore took over as captain after Armfield's injury, the West Ham defender's place in the team was subject to some conjecture in 1966. Don Revie was among those campaigning for Moore to be dropped in favour of his own Leeds United player: the aggressive Norman Hunter, who played in his place in two warm-up games in May and June. Moore held off his rival's challenge, but the major players in Ramsey's World Cup squad and starting 11s were a mix of the regulars who had put in the hard yards and those who came with a late surge. Banks, Cohen, Wilson, Moore, Stiles, Greaves, Bobby Charlton and Hunt had miles on the clock to prove their worth, and they were supplemented by well-judged additions in Jack Charlton, Ball, Hurst and Peters.

That West Ham's Martin Peters should arrive with a perfectly timed run-in to the team was entirely appropriate, for that was completely in keeping with the way he played. His manager at Upton Park, Ron Greenwood, described him as 'ten years ahead of his time' for his style of play and his ability to ghost into spaces, but at Christmas-time 1965 a World Cup spot seemed a mile away. Peters hadn't even played for the Under-23 side for some time, but Greenwood kept badgering away at Ramsey about his ability, and, after a game for the Under-23s in February, Ramsey decided to give him his chance. Peters made his debut against Yugoslavia in May – the game in which Jimmy Armfield returned as captain – but found out about his selection in rather strange circumstances: 'Someone phoned up saying they had seen the matchday programme for the Yugoslavia match and my name was in it. That was about four to five weeks before the game!' Peters didn't waste his opportunity.

The World Cup had to endure one final hitch before the best players on the planet gathered to see whether Brazil could win for a third time in a row. The trophy had been on show at the National Stamp Exhibition in London and was promptly stolen, causing huge embarrassment to the FA. After a week's fruitless searching from the Metropolitan Police, a Londoner called Dave Corbett was walking his dog, Pickles, one day in south London when the dog disappeared into a hedge. Pickles started wrestling with a brown parcel, and when Mr Corbett bent down to examine it he was astonished to find the missing World Cup. The discovery of the trophy made headlines in all the papers, which were gearing up for the three weeks of football. The 1966 World Cup was the first to enjoy comprehensive coverage on television, still something of a rarity for the viewers who had been introduced to *Match of the Day* only a year previously. The viewing figures that July played a large part in convincing the BBC that there was a massive audience for football on television in highlights form.

England were scheduled to play all their group matches at Wembley, and they went into the first match against Uruguay well prepared, in good form – they had won their last seven games – and with a tangible will to win: a sense of determination sharpened by every fresh criticism of Alf Ramsey that the manager wasn't getting the right team together. The press were still far from convinced, and the manager had a conundrum: who was he going to play out wide? He knew he wanted to play 4–3–3, which probably meant one traditional winger.

Spain had been beaten in Madrid by a side containing no traditional wide men, and in the last warm-up game, against Poland, Ball and Peters wore the number seven and eleven shirts, but Ramsey took more notice of the critics than he dared admit. He brought in winger John Connelly of Manchester United for Peters for the opening game. The West Ham man was philosophical about the decision: 'I didn't expect to play. I was the new kid on the block, so happy to be part and parcel of the squad. To be around those great players is what I really wanted. Geoff Hurst and I sat together watching in the stand.' Just 19 days later, the West Ham teammates would be out on the pitch scoring the goals that lit up England's greatest ever day.

The Uruguay match was an awful game: a goalless draw that did little to reassure the watching public that England were about to make a genuine challenge for Brazil's title. The Uruguayans came to deny their hosts, and despite 16 corners and 15 shots on goal England rarely threatened. The players were under enormous pressure, and, realising they needed a break, the following day Ramsey took them to Pinewood Studios, where a James Bond movie was being shot. The manager caused total hilarity when he thanked Sean Connery for his hospitality by referring to him as 'Seen'. Bobby Moore apparently said to Jimmy Greaves, 'That's the funniest thing I've ever sean.' Sean Connery told Jimmy Armfield that if England reached the final he would lay on a party at his house. Anne Armfield was very keen to go, surely not the only player's wife who wanted to . . .

Alan Ball had a slight injury and was replaced by Martin Peters for the Mexico game, while Southampton's Terry Paine came in for Connelly. Again the visitors were dogged and resolute in defence, but seven minutes before half-time Bobby Charlton scored a wonderful goal from distance outside the area. It lifted the tension. Charlton had gone from a left-winger, in Chile in 1962, to a midfielder with a creative licence, the link between the attack and Stiles sitting in front of the back four, whose job it was to win the ball and then look for him. Jimmy Armfield is unequivocal about Charlton's role in England's triumph: 'We wouldn't have won the World Cup without him. The turning point was that goal against Mexico. He hit this 30-yarder, which sparked everything off. He was the one player every other team feared. He was the ace in our pack.'

In the second half, Jimmy Greaves's shot was saved by Calderón in the Mexico goal and Roger Hunt gobbled up the rebound. England were on their way, without hitting any great rhythm, and Ramsey again persisted with just one winger for the French game, this time bringing in Ian Callaghan of Liverpool for Paine. A draw would be enough to win the group, while a 2–0 win for France would see them through at England's expense. As it was, England reached the last eight with a brace of goals from Roger Hunt in a 2–0 win. Hunt had won thirteen caps over four years, and so his good start to the tournament was enormously encouraging for him. 'You were never certain of your place, so if I was scoring goals I would keep my place,' the Liverpool and England striker told me. 'My career with England had been up and down; I didn't have many regular games altogether. It was a couple of games here and there, so I was delighted to score three goals in the first three games.'

England's progress to the quarter-finals, though, was overshadowed by a furore over Nobby Stiles's tackle on Jacky Simon. Stiles was the gap-toothed, diminutive, infectious, limited yet important cog in Ramsey's team: 'The destroyer and policeman around the area who would give the ball to Bobby Charlton,' according to George Cohen. Stiles caught Simon with a late tackle, and FIFA warned the Manchester United player about his conduct. This message filtered through to the FA, who asked Ramsey whether Stiles was really necessary to the England cause. Ramsey was outraged. 'If Nobby Stiles doesn't play, then England don't play,' he said.

The team loved it; it underlined their 'all for one and one for all' approach. Even 43 years later, sitting talking to me in the pavilion at Lord's, where he had just launched *Our Sporting Life*, a nationwide show of sporting memorabilia, George Cohen is still angered by the reaction to Stiles's tackle: 'What is the most unbelievable cheek is that worse fouls were perpetrated, especially on Pelé, and the Portuguese doled out some nasty treatment to the Brazilians, and yet Stiles was reported to FIFA and his worth queried. I find that unbelievable cheek and absolutely terrible that our FA even listened to the question and posed one afterwards.'

While Alf Ramsey was dealing with the fallout from the Simon affair, Jimmy Greaves was coming to terms with the fact his World Cup was almost certainly over. England's most natural goalscorer had fourteen stitches inserted in a leg wound after a tackle from Joseph Bonnel, and, with just ten days till the final, he realised Ramsey was unlikely to change a winning team should England make it. It was a cruel blow for someone so popular, a certain starter who had fought so hard to get back to his best after being laid low with hepatitis. Geoff Hurst had only made his debut in February, and now he came in for his sixth cap to play alongside Roger Hunt, a partnership that had functioned smoothly in a 4–3 win over Scotland in April.

With Alan Ball restored to the team, Ramsey abandoned any pretence to play with an orthodox winger. Now this side really were the 'Wingless Wonders', and more balanced for it: less 4–3–3 in the eyes of Nobby Stiles and more 4–1–3–2, with Stiles patrolling in front of the back four, Charlton, Ball and Peters in midfield and Hunt and Hurst up front. Martin Peters believes Greaves's unfortunate injury was a blessing in disguise for the manager: 'I do believe Alf got pushed into changing things because of Jimmy's injury. He had a six-inch gash in his shin, a bad gash, and he never wore shin pads, because he said it gave him two extra yards of pace not to wear them. So Geoff came in, and Alf changed the system, whereas before he had kept trying wingers. Alan and I were young enough to get forward and back. It was ideal for us, because we were the two youngsters in the squad. Charlton went wherever he liked, and Nobby stayed in the middle. The system worked really, really well. We could pull off wide to receive the ball from the full-backs.'

The press reaction to England's displays so far was lukewarm, and that reflected the public's attitude towards Alf Ramsey's team. He seized upon the media's indifference, turning it to the team's advantage as he built up a siege mentality. To escape from the football he would organise trips – mandatory visits – to the cinema in Hendon. He loved cowboy films, and Jimmy Armfield remembers that they would be sitting around the team hotel when Ramsey would tell trainer Harold Shepherdson it was time for an outing: 'Alf would take us all down the hill to the Hendon Odeon like some sort of glorified school trip to the cinema, the players struggling to keep up and put their coats on.'

England now faced Argentina in the quarter-finals, the country that Ramsey had identified as a major threat after seeing them beat Brazil 3–0 in the 'Little World Cup' in 1964: a result which meant he wrote the Brazilians off. Their World Cup campaign came crashing down after the Portuguese kicked an unfit Pelé out of the tournament, and the deposed holders went home muttering of conspiracy theories and bad refereeing. Such mutterings in South America grew even louder after the game with England. West Germany and Argentina had played out a bad-tempered goalless draw in the group stages, and in the dressing room before the quarter-final, according to the book *Bobby Moore: The Life and Times of a Sporting Hero*, Ramsey accurately forecast what was in store at Wembley that day: 'Well gentlemen, you know what sort of game you have on your hands this afternoon.'

The Argentinians were provocative from the start, niggling away, and although England were riled by their behaviour, and actually committed more fouls in the game, George Cohen said to resort to the visitors' level would have been detrimental: 'I was very angry at their snide tactics. They were pulling ears, raking your Achilles, tweaking chests and putting in late tackles. We were very fortunate to come in at half-time without serious injury, and Alf was absolutely incensed at what was going on. They had this destruct button that when things didn't go their way they resorted to stupidity, and they did commit some of the worst excesses I have ever seen on a football pitch, and that's why Alf called them animals afterwards. He was even more incensed when he had to apologise for saying that.'

Argentina's approach was a waste of a very good side, full of players with excellent technique: good one- and two-touch footballers who had won Brazil's 'Little World Cup' two years earlier. They were marginal favourites at Wembley, and their volatility would have been accepted in South America as part of the game, but in Europe it was greeted with disdain. The irony is that if they had just concentrated on their football, they would have been a very serious threat to Ramsey's ambition. As it was, their captain, Antonio Rattín, a wonderful player who was trying to run midfield and referee the match as well, played the pantomime villain, constantly chirping away at the official from West Germany, Rudolf Kreitlein. Nine minutes from half-time Kreitlein's patience snapped. Rattín objected to the booking of a colleague, and, though he spoke no Spanish, Kreitlein had had enough and sent him off. Chaos ensued as Rattín refused to go, and at one stage it looked as if the whole Argentinian team would leave the field. One of them, Ermindo Onega, spat in the face of a FIFA commissaire, and the head of the World Cup referees, Ken Aston – who had endured that horrendous match in Santiago in 1962 – appeared on the touchline.

The delay went on for seven or eight minutes, and Roger Hunt remembers how unreal it all was on a beautiful July Saturday in the London sunshine: 'It was incredible. Rattín wouldn't go off. Some players sat down, and then it flashed up on the scoreboard that North Korea were beating Portugal 3–0. The crowd noticed it and cheered, because the winners were due to be our next opponents. Portugal were very much fancied to win the Cup, and they were three down. All this was happening when Rattín was being sent off, and people were trying to get him off. It was so strange.' Finally, reluctantly, Rattín made his laborious way round the pitch, stopping to exchange insults with the crowd and wiping his hands on a corner flag.

The ten men kept England at bay until twelve minutes from time, when a move straight off West Ham's training field eased England into the last four. Martin Peters went down the left-hand side and knew instinctively what he should do: 'Ron Greenwood had introduced this move that Geoff

Hurst or Johnny Byrne would make a run to the near post. I was OK with my left foot, and I knew I needed to hit it as best I could to the near post, knowing Geoff would get on the end of it. It was a great run from Geoff and a great leap. It was a typical West Ham goal.' England were through, but Alf Ramsey was so angry with the Argentinians that he refused to allow his players to change shirts with their opponents, running 20 yards to stop George Cohen from swapping with González. The referee needed help to get away from the visitors, some of whom made a beeline for the England dressing room, looking for a fight. One stopped to urinate in the tunnel. Alf Ramsey's 'animals' accusation so inflamed Argentinian sensibilities that the British Ambassador in Buenos Aires, Sir Michael Cresswell, needed a special police guard afterwards.

The quarter-final win at Wembley represented a turning point in the relationship between the England team and the press and public. Now they started believing that Alf Ramsey's prediction of three years earlier might just come true. The players felt that, whatever happened now, they hadn't let anybody down by reaching the last four. In many ways, the hardest hurdle had been overcome, and although their semi-final opponents, Portugal, had the great Eusébio in their line-up, they had conceded three goals to North Korea in their quarter-final before storming back to win. Bobby Moore was supremely confident, as he outlined in Jeff Powell's book:

> I had no doubts by then. I never felt that Portugal could beat any England team. This was probably their best side ever. Yet they had needed Eusébio to pull them out of trouble against North Korea. And Eusébio didn't have the stomach for Nobby Stiles.

There was a row over the semi-final venue, with the early indications being that if England got that far they would play at Goodison, but, in reality, nothing had been decided upon in advance. The World Cup Committee took the pragmatic approach; Wembley would be sold out for an England semi-final, and there was much more money to be made by leaving the hosts to play in the capital. With Greaves still not fit, the team picked itself, and Nobby Stiles was charged with the biggest responsibility of his professional career: to keep Eusébio quiet. Portugal's star striker had burst onto the scene for Benfica at the beginning of the decade, scoring twice in their 1962 European Cup final win over Real

Madrid, and he had been the European Footballer of the Year in 1965. As the crowd filed into Wembley that night, with renewed heart ready to roar England on, Stiles knew what he had to do, and he responded to Ramsey's instructions – and the manager's faith in him after the Jacky Simon tackle – by playing the game of his life.

George Cohen watched his performance with awe: 'When Nobby tackled you he gave you all the ten and a half stone he had. If anyone wants to know how good he was, watch him in that semi-final against Eusébio. Watch how he marked a man who was four yards faster and four inches taller – and one of the world's great goalscorers – completely out of the game, without fouling him more than a couple of times. He made sure he played Eusébio in every negative situation on the pitch. It was a classic. It should be shown to every young midfield player.'

With West Germany already waiting in the final, England and Portugal produced a fabulous match, quite unlike most semi-finals. For the first time in the World Cup, the crowd were animated and involved, realising England were on the verge of something special. Bobby Charlton had his best game of the tournament, and one of his best ever for England, scoring both goals before his brother gave away a penalty, converted by Eusébio, which led to a tense last eight minutes.

Martin Peters is in no doubt as to where the credit for the win lies: 'Portugal had the leading goalscorer, Eusébio. He was strong and physical, and they had a great squad. Nobby won it for us. He didn't foul Eusébio; he just marked him for 90 minutes. Then Jack, like a big fairy, stuck out his hand and handled it late on. I was right behind him, and I couldn't believe it.'

Back at the team hotel, Ramsey loosened the leash on his players just a little. They were allowed a beer and sandwiches, and some of the wives came to visit, but they weren't allowed near the bedrooms. 'There was,' said Bobby Moore in *The Life and Times of a Sporting Hero*, 'no fun and games. We'd been with the squad for the best part of eight weeks and not a soul had stepped out of line. Now there were only three days to wait . . . and one game to play.'

Alf Ramsey awoke on the Wednesday morning with the big debate already raging: would Jimmy Greaves play in the final? Would he come in for Geoff Hurst, or possibly even Roger Hunt, or would Alf Ramsey stick to the side that had won the two knockout matches? Bobby Moore actually went down with tonsillitis on that Wednesday, but the team doctor caught it early, and Jack Charlton had a cold on the Friday night, meaning Ron Flowers was on standby if the Leeds centre-half woke up poorly on the Saturday morning. As it was, the defenders were fit to take their places, and, as he accurately forecast while lying on his bed examining his gashed leg after the France game, Jimmy Greaves was left out.

The team had improved with every game and were functioning superbly. Hurst and Hunt had struck up a strong running partnership that was allowing Bobby Charlton to score goals – and the West Ham triumvirate had added to the team understanding. It had all come together for Alf Ramsey, and he wasn't going to change it now – not that Roger Hunt was taking anything for granted, because of what had happened on the Scandinavian tour prior to the World Cup: 'When we were given our squad numbers, Jimmy Greaves was number eight, Bobby Charlton nine and Geoff Hurst ten. I felt Alf's first eleven numbers would be his team to start with, and I still think that. I was number twenty-one. Only Martin Peters and I weren't numbered one to eleven. There was a lot of support for Jimmy: he was then England's leading goalscorer. Geoff had added something else. He was very good in the air. He had scored against Argentina and played well against Portugal, so I didn't know what to expect. I hadn't had long runs in the team, so I wasn't certain I was going to play, even though I had played all five games.'

It was on another of Alf Ramsey's cinema trips, the night before the final, that Roger Hunt received the good news that he would be in the 11. Both Martin Peters and his roommate Geoff Hurst found out at the same time. 'Geoff didn't know if he was going to play, as Jimmy might have been fit. I found out the night before the final when Alf told me in the reception of the cinema. It was *Those Magnificent Men in their Flying Machines*. We went back to the hotel, and Geoff told me he was playing and we were like two big kids.'

When Bobby Moore stirred on the morning of Saturday, 30 July 1966, he found his roommate and friend Jimmy Greaves packing. Greaves knew he wasn't going to be recalled and wanted to make a quick getaway after the game. George Cohen had known him since he was 16 but didn't know what to say to him that morning: 'I never found the courage,' he admitted. 'I never felt comfortable in asking him the question. Nobody could think about anything else except their own thoughts on the most important game of their lives. I recall seeing Nobby going out of the hotel. He had to come to about two feet away from me because he was so blind! I asked him where he was going and he said, "To find a Catholic church, to pray and confess." He told me he was off to Golders Green! I didn't have the heart to tell him. He came back two hours later complaining the church didn't give change!'

England were confident. They had beaten West Germany twice in the last 14 months, home and away, and they felt as a team that they were coming to the boil at just the right time. They were not alone. Hans Keller was an Austrian musicologist and football fan brought up on the great pre-war Austrian '*Wunderteam*', and he wrote in the *New Statesman*, 'Next week I will describe how England won the World Cup and what we can do about it.'

At eleven o'clock, the twenty-two-man squad was run through West Germany's line-up by Ramsey in the lounge at Hendon Hall. Franz Beckenbauer was the heartbeat of their side, the one player capable of producing the unexpected, and although Ramsey felt the Germans were more afraid of Bobby Charlton than England were of Beckenbauer, he still wanted Charlton to be his shadow – to track him every step of the way in the manner Nobby Stiles had done with Eusébio. Beckenbauer was given exactly the same instructions. The players then boarded a coach to Wembley, and the enormity of the occasion sank in during the journey. There seemed to be a flag hanging from every house. Supporters along the way were dressed in red, white and blue, and one banner proclaimed simply: 'Nobby For Prime Minister'.

England's changing room was a hive of media activity; TV cameras, arc lights and photographers swarmed around, and at half past two, half an hour before kick-off, there were still a hundred people in there, according to Bobby Moore.

The players were held up in the tunnel as the Queen and Duke of Edinburgh took their seats, and George Cohen wasn't quite sure what to expect as he made that famous walk: 'You could hear a hum, but as you hit the open air, the noise was amazing and it drove all thoughts out of your mind. All you could see was a mass of colour moving around, and I thought, "Oh my God," and it got to me a bit.'

West Germany scored early after a mistake from Ray Wilson, but six minutes later, the West Ham axis worked again, as a quickly taken Bobby

Moore free kick was headed in by Geoff Hurst. With 12 minutes left, England won a corner. Martin Peters took up his usual position on the near post: 'Bally took it, and it went deep. It went to Geoff Hurst, and he hit a crap shot. Their right-back did a terrible clearance, and it shot across the six-yard line. I had one thing on my mind: hit the target. I got my knee over it, and the goalkeeper went one way and the defender the other.'

It seemed certain that Martin Peters had scored the winning goal in the World Cup final, until the final minute, when the referee controversially gave the Germans a free kick within shooting range. It was Peters's job to line the wall up: 'Nobby was pushing and shoving and trying to get as close as possible to the ball. We were too deep; the players behind us should have been level with the wall.' The free kick hit George Cohen on the shin, and he maintains that Schnellinger then handled the ball as it ricocheted around the area before Weber slid in to score at the far post. Amid the German delirium and the English disappointment, up in the stands Alan Ball's wife, Lesley, fainted.

This was the last World Cup before substitutes were allowed, so the non-playing 11 members of the England squad were sitting up in the stands as well. Ramsey had told Jimmy Armfield to bring them down to the bench five minutes from the end, whatever the score: 'I sat with Norman Hunter, and I wore this red pullover right through the bloody competition. I'm not superstitious, but Norman carried his mac right through as well – can you believe that? – and we sat with Bobby Charlton's dad. He was more worried about his pigeons that he had left behind in the North East. Ten minutes from time, we came down the lift under the Royal Box, and as we came out, I saw the German goal go in. Most of the lads didn't see their equaliser. Alf had left a seat for me. I was half sat behind him.'

Alf Ramsey was soon off his seat delivering the greatest team talk of his life. As Bobby Moore admitted, if he had berated the team for the sloppy manner of the German equaliser, he would have deflated them there and then, probably with the direst of consequences. Instead, he made sure the players remained standing, while several Germans were lying down having massages, and his words are easy for George Cohen to recall: 'He said, "They're finished – you've won this game once. Now go and win it again. You must get on top of them straight away. You must show them that you're not finished in any way. They're flat out." And it was true. We were a very physically strong outfit. The pitch at Wembley was spongy and made you go two yards slower and the ball two yards faster. You could see they were running on fumes, while some of our guys had plenty of running.'

Chief among those still with plenty of energy was the baby of the team, Alan Ball. Another one of Ramsey's shrewd picks, Ball was just twenty-one and playing his fourteenth international. His father had built up his fitness through cross-country running and boxing, and this was the day the nation would be grateful for that upbringing. Ball was perpetual motion, and his cross from the right in the first half of extra time led to arguably the most controversial goal in the history of the World Cup. Geoff Hurst turned sharply and smashed a shot onto the underside of the bar. Roger Hunt rushed in for the rebound: 'I was a goalscorer and desperate to score, especially in a World Cup final. I was four yards away, right in the middle of the goal, when the ball hit the bar. I was so convinced it was over the line and then going to bounce into the roof of the net that I turned round, instinctively, because normally I would score if I could. I turned away with my hand raised, and when I looked back, the defender, Weber, was heading the ball away. People say why didn't I head it in? I don't think I would have been able to. It came back at an angle to my left. Denis Law said to me afterwards I wouldn't have got it.'

Bobby Moore felt that Hunt's reaction convinced the linesman, Tofik Bakhramov, to give the goal – and England were ahead again. There was no controversy over the fourth, though, as Geoff Hurst decorated Kenneth Wolstenholme's famous commentary with a stinging shot into the top left-hand corner. England had won the World Cup, and a bouncing Nobby Stiles – minus his teeth as ever – couldn't resist kissing George Cohen: 'Now I know what it's like to be kissed by Mick Jagger! It was right in front of the Royal Box and quite embarrassing, but he was obviously overjoyed, deliriously happy. I can't say I was euphoric, because I was too bloody tired. My first thoughts were, "Thank Christ for that." We had been away from home for a long, long time.'

That night, the players celebrated at the Royal Garden Hotel in Kensington in London, but they celebrated amongst themselves – their wives weren't allowed in; they were downstairs in a brasserie. The FA gave them three little pairs of scissors in a leather case: not exactly WAG material. Anne Armfield still has hers somewhere at home. Bobby Moore led the players onto the hotel balcony to wave to the crowds, and at midnight, after the official banquet, there were thousands still there to cheer them as they came out of the hotel. Jack Charlton led one gang to the clubs of east London, while Geoff Hurst, Nobby Stiles and Alan Ball headed for Danny La Rue's club and asked Martin Peters to go with them. He declined: 'I hadn't seen my wife for six weeks, so I said no, took a bottle of champagne to my hotel room and stayed in with my wife! Geoff booked it without asking me!'

And England captains past and present, Bobby Moore and Jimmy Armfield, went with a group to the Playboy Club in the West End, driving up Park Lane through the tooting cars and celebrating hordes. Bobby Moore's life would never be the same again. No one has yet matched his achievement of leading England to World Cup glory. Jimmy sang on stage that night, but Anne Armfield never did get to go to a party at Sean Connery's house. To this day, her husband is not sympathetic: 'Why did she want to go and see James Bond when she had James Armfield, the great lover . . . ?'

6

MEXICO 1970

England were the World Cup winners, and suddenly footballers were household names and in fashion. The world of commerce wanted them to sell products, and football was enjoying a golden age before the traumas of the '70s. The press descended on Geoff Hurst's house on the day after the final, looking for an interview, and found the only man ever to score a hat-trick in a World Cup final going about his mundane everyday business: he was mowing the lawn.

England might have been World Champions, but the players hadn't got rich from their previous three weeks' work. The pot for the whole squad was £22,000, which they agreed to split equally, even though George Cohen knew what he was doing was madness: 'I was entitled to £1,500 for playing all six games, but we all agreed to an even split among the squad. As a professional footballer, you don't give away your bonus – ever. It's probably the most unprofessional thing I've ever done, but also one of the nicest. I understand the Germans were paid £10,000 for losing. To give our players just £1,000 before tax was mean and parsimonious.'

The first big challenge the new World Champions faced was in April 1967, when Scotland came to town. It was England's first game since Alf Ramsey's knighthood in the New Year's Honours List, and Scotland won 3–2, leading to some, north of the border, claiming they were now morally the new World Champions. The game was part of the qualification for the 1968 European Championship – a much smaller-scale tournament than that of today – in which England came third, the final stages being held in Italy. Yugoslavia beat them 1–0 in the semi-final in Florence in a bad-tempered match, blighted by 49 free kicks, during which Alan Mullery became the first Englishman to be sent off in a full international.

He had made his England debut in 1964 but didn't make the final 22 in '66 and watched the World Cup final on television while having lunch with his wife. After winning the FA Cup with Tottenham in May 1967, he replaced Nobby Stiles in the England team, fulfilling the exact same role: 'I sat in front of the back four, and I knew if I got the ball and gave it to Bobby Charlton there was a good chance I would be in the next team! It's as simple as can be. If there was someone special in the other side, it was my job to latch on to them.' Mullery was to get very up close and personal to Pelé in the next three years.

On this day in Florence, 5 June 1968, Yugoslavia's hardman Dobrivoje Trivíc had kicked both Alan Ball and Bobby Charlton, and in the last minute Mullery lashed out in retaliation and was sent off. Nobby Stiles was still in the squad and knew Mullery was in trouble. Stiles rushed over to his dismissed teammate, saying, 'Quick, get into the dressing room; Alf will go potty,' Mullery told me when we met at a hotel at Gatwick. 'I heard the final whistle blow as we walked down the tunnel, and we got into the dressing room and Nobby said, "Get in the bath." And as the door opened, I put my head under the water. It was Alf, and he grabbed me by the hair and picked me up and said, "I'm glad some bastard decided to get their own back." And he dropped me back in the water!'

Alf Ramsey stood by Nobby Stiles over the Jacky Simon furore in '66, and now he did the same for Mullery. The Tottenham player was fined £50 by the FA, and Ramsey paid it. The England manager was confident enough to stand up to the FA when he felt it mattered. News of the sending off reverberated around the world: England players were not supposed to get sent off. They were not supposed to retaliate. They were expected to take all the kicks and blows in the face and treading on feet, but Mullery's sending off meant that perception changed. England had crossed the Rubicon, and now they were acknowledged to be like every other football team in the world – with their own strengths and weaknesses, their own level of tolerance and restraint.

For Alf Ramsey, the 1968 European Championship was part of the build-up to the defence of the World Cup and by no means an end in itself. In 1969, they went on a tour of South America as preparation for the following year. The team had changed a fair bit: Mullery in for Stiles; Everton's Brian Labone for Jack Charlton in central defence; Franny Lee of Manchester City was partnering Geoff Hurst up front; Colin Bell, also of City, was pushing for a place; and there were new full-backs, too: Keith Newton of Blackburn and Terry Cooper of Leeds.

The goalless draw in Mexico was Cooper's fourth cap. He was a fit, quick, mobile, overlapping full-back with good crossing ability. He hailed from the mining village of Knottingley, near Pontefract, in west Yorkshire, and talking to me from his home in Spain, he admitted he never quite got over his inferiority complex: 'I was just in awe of Bobby Moore and Banksy [Gordon Banks] – great people, ordinary human beings, no edge, great lads – but I just used to think, "Bloody hell, what am I doing here playing with these?"

'I can remember once, after a Leeds game, Jack Charlton and I being delayed meeting up with England. And when we got to the hotel all the other lads were already having dinner, and I thought, "Christ, we've got to walk in there, and the players will give us stick for being late!" As I came out of my room, I met Jack at the lift. And he was wearing a big cravat, and I thought, "Jesus, he's going to take all the pressure off me!" because footballers don't wear cravats. And, sure enough, we walked into the dining room and Bally and Bobby Moore jumped on him. Jack had a couple of gentleman's fitters in those days, and thought he was James Bond, but you could put him in a £3,000 suit and he would still look as if it was worth a tenner.'

Cooper was a fine player in a Leeds team that was one of the dominant forces at the turn of the decade. He had won the League Cup and the League Championship by this time, so I was fascinated as to why he seemed to be doing himself down: 'I always felt intimidated, because I came from this little mining village, and you never think you're going to play for your country. It's your make-up. It's your background. I started working down the pit at 15, and then it all happened so quickly, Leeds and England. I loved it.'

Cooper didn't play again on the 1969 tour, because he contracted tonsillitis and so missed the 2–1 win over Uruguay in Montevideo and a defeat by the same scoreline in Rio against Brazil. The draw for the group stages in 1970 had already been made by then, so when the two teams met in the Maracanã on 12 June, they knew it was a dress rehearsal for twelve months later in Guadalajara.

Pelé was the obvious threat, and Ramsey decided it was time for another man-marking job. There was only one candidate, Alan Mullery: 'I was a bit nervous in '69, because I had seen him, when I was a kid, playing in Sweden in '58, and I thought, "Blimey, I am going to play against a fellow who was a star 12 years ago!" Alf said [to] follow him wherever he goes, so, as I say in my after-dinner speaking, I'm the only fellow to play for England to go into the Brazilian dressing room and have a pee – because Alf told me to follow him wherever he went!'

Officially, the crowd was 135,000 in the Maracanã that day, but unofficially many more crowded into the ramshackle stadium. Just as Bert Williams had experienced in 1950, in Brazil reporters with microphones were everywhere. They were on the pitch as the players warmed up and then ran on when Brazil scored through Tostao and Jairzinho, demanding an instant reaction. And people think the British media are too intrusive! England lost to a late penalty, and years later, when Santos came to Craven Cottage to play Fulham, Pelé admitted to Alan Mullery that the closeness of that match meant England were the one team Brazil were apprehensive of in 1970.

That South American tour had shown the England players what was in store for them a year later, both on and off the field. Mexico had lobbied hard to win the right to stage the finals at Argentina's expense, and the conditions were going to pose serious obstacles to the Northern European teams in particular. The heat was likely to be intense, rising to well over 90°F, and the altitude would make breathing difficult. Added to those handicaps was the decision of the World Cup Committee to play certain games, including the final, at midday – for the purposes of international television. This was the first World Cup to be shown in colour and the first to be seen live in virtually every country of the developed world, thanks to satellite technology. There were now two substitutes allowed, red and yellow cards and even a new ball: an Adidas black-and-white-checked Telstar. The game was exploding in glorious Technicolor for the world to enjoy.

If Ramsey couldn't control the weather or the conditions, he could do something about his team's PR, and this is where he fell down badly. After the goalless draw in Mexico City in 1969, he was asked if he had anything to say to the Mexican press:

Yes. There was a band playing outside our hotel till five o'clock this morning. We were promised a motorcycle escort to the stadium. It never arrived. When our players went out to inspect the pitch, they were jeered by the crowd. I would have thought the Mexican public would have been delighted to welcome England.

As a quick afterthought, he added, 'But we are delighted to be in Mexico, and the Mexican people are wonderful people.'

A few days later, after making a presentation to a local state governor, he chased the local press out of the dressing rooms in Guadalajara – he would have done the same to the British press – and the die was cast. With feelings already inflamed in Latin America after his 'animals' reference to Argentina four years earlier, England needed to build bridges with the Mexicans – but Ramsey's attitude merely alienated them. He should have employed a local liaison officer in 1970, but he wouldn't have trusted one, and it was easy for the press to build up the picture of a grumpy 'Little Englander' who was suspicious of foreigners and got angry with photographers and journalists. England had a bus brought out, rather than using those supplied, and Ramsey insisted on flying meat out, but the steaks never made it past customs and were promptly burnt. A sponsorship deal meant that fish fingers and chips – with bottles of HP Sauce supplied – partially compensated for that, and England even brought fruit with them, to a region well known for producing it.

The Brazilian approach was quite the opposite, charming the Mexican birds out of the trees. The hosts were never likely to go beyond the quarter-finals, so the locals were always predestined to fall in love with Brazil's attitude and artistry. Although they are rightly remembered for their intoxicating, fluent game in 1970, they approached the finals in a very pragmatic manner as well. The then World Champions had had a shock in 1966, surprised by the physical and powerful approach of the European teams, and they were determined not to be found wanting again. They trained for three months in Brazil and then spent a month in Mexico getting used to the altitude.

For all the flair and finesse of Pelé, Gerson, Rivelino and Tostao, the captain, Carlos Alberto, realised they had to match the European teams in the battle as well. 'We knew we had to prepare our team physically, 1,000 per cent, if we wanted to start to think about beating the Europeans,' he told me on my BBC 5 Live Sport programme. 'We knew that if we were in the same condition physically, then technically we were better.' That is not to say that everything was sweetness and light for the Brazilians in the build-up. Just three months before the tournament started they changed coaches. João Saldanha had left Pelé out of a warm-up game – relegating the great man to the bench with the number 13 shirt on his back – and in the ensuing power struggle the increasingly erratic Saldanha came second. He was replaced by Zagallo, a teammate of Pelé's in the winning teams of 1958 and 1962.

The England squad departed in early May on a high, capturing the upbeat mood of the nation by releasing a record before they flew off. 'Back Home' was number one for three weeks with its catchy melody and cheery lyrics. The press photos of the time show a group of happy men in dinner jackets and bow ties, with plenty of hair and some sideburns, all mucking in and having fun. Terry Cooper says, 'There were a few ringers in it. I've got a Silver Disc, and I keep telling my granddaughters, "Be careful, I've got a Silver Disc!" Pan's People were on that night, and I was watching them!'

Alf Ramsey would later say that he had a better squad at his disposal than four years previously, and, like the Brazilians, they were leaving nothing to chance in terms of their preparation. England left a month before the tournament started just to make sure they were properly acclimatised. They had two warm-up matches scheduled, first in Colombia and then Ecuador, and on 18 May they arrived in Bogotá and checked into the Tequendama Hotel.

After changing for dinner, Bobby Charlton and Bobby Moore went into the Green Fire jewellery shop inside the hotel to kill some time. They browsed for a few minutes and then went and sat in the foyer, but moments later the shop owner approached them, quizzing them about the alleged disappearance of a bracelet. Alan Mullery remembers, 'The police arrived within five minutes, and the girl from the shop pointed at Bobby Moore. They moved all the cushions on the chairs and the settees, and she accused Bobby of stealing a bracelet.'

Terry Cooper insists, 'Everything in the shop was behind glass anyway; it wasn't on show. We couldn't believe what was happening; we thought it was a joke. If you knew Bobby Moore, he would have been the last one to do such a thing. He took the responsibility of being England captain very seriously.' What no one in the England party knew, until the former Brazilian coach João Saldanha told them he had undergone a similar experience, was that this was a Colombian speciality: accusing visiting celebrities of theft in an attempt to extort money from them.

Both players made statements to the police, and two days later England beat Colombia 4–0 before the whole squad flew to Quito, where Ecuador were beaten 2–0 on 24 May. The journey to Mexico the next day for the start of the tournament necessitated a stop-off back in Bogotá, at the same hotel. Alan Mullery picks up the story: 'We were watching *Shenandoah*, the James Stewart film, and every time I see that film it reminds me of that day. We were sitting there watching it in the basement of the hotel, and the doors burst open. The police came in, and they wanted to take both the Bobbies. It was frightening; they had guns, and they were speaking Spanish.'

Now England really did have a problem. Bobby Moore was taken to a courthouse, and the team flew on to Mexico without him. Jeff Astle was a nervous flyer, and when he arrived in Mexico City in a state of some disarray, one newspaper latched onto it, describing England as a 'team of thieves and drunks'. The chairman and secretary of the FA stayed in Bogotá, as the shop girl, one Clara Padilla, claimed to have seen the England captain pocket a gold bracelet studded with emeralds worth £625. Diplomatic efforts to have him released went into overdrive, but five days away from England starting their defence of the World Cup on 2 June, the England captain was still under house arrest in Bogotá.

On the morning of 28 May, he was allowed to train on an open pitch, and after he had finished his sprints and exercises, he found himself surrounded by his smiling guards and a gaggle of excited boys with a ball. In a magnificent PR coup, the England captain had a kickabout with this motley crew, which meant, in his words in Jeff Powell's book, 'Overnight, I was transformed from a jailbird into a national hero.' The Colombian people were already highly suspicious of the shop's motives, and newspapers denounced the plot as a national scandal. Moore was offered a conditional release on the basis that he would make himself available for future questioning if necessary, and on 29 May he was on a plane for Mexico City and then to Guadalajara: the venue of England's opening match.

Alan Mullery was in a room of four at the Hilton Hotel in Guadalajara with goalkeeper Alex Stepney of Manchester United and Liverpool winger Peter Thompson. The bed reserved for the England captain hadn't been slept in since they arrived five days earlier. Mullery was on his way downstairs to sit in the shade by the pool: 'As I got to the lift, it opened and there he was. Bobby hadn't shaved – and he always looked immaculate – and he still had the England tracksuit on, which we had to wear everywhere. I gave him a big hug, took him to our room, phoned Alf and said, "He's back!" Alf said, "Order a bottle of champagne and five glasses!" So I rang room service, which we were never allowed to do, and Mooro took off his top, which he had been wearing for about a week, and threw it out of the window. Down below, all these Mexican kids in the road were fighting for his top, and he said, "I'm never going to wear that bloody tracksuit again!"'

If losing Moore had been destabilising, then his return so close to the World Cup starting was a massive fillip. Martin Peters admitted, 'When we got him back, it was fantastic. He was our captain, our leader. Everyone loved him and rightly so. He was such a great player. He had been to the previous two World Cups, he had all the experience and he knew these sorts of things could happen. He took it really well, and he was the same old Mooro he had always been.'

Now England could prepare for Romania without any niggling little doubts at the back of their minds. Moore had lost 7 lb while under arrest but soon showed in training that he was fit and ready to lead his country once more, and he felt England had the best squad in its history: one very capable of winning the World Cup again. Guadalajara was at 5,200 ft, and the heat in the Jalisco Stadium was likely to be ferocious, but England were in supreme condition.

'I don't think I've ever felt so fit in my life,' agreed Alan Mullery. 'Alf flogged our balls off in training. Five thousand people used to watch us training, and Alf would say, "We're going to impress everybody." The Mexican bodyguards would read to us what the papers were saying, and it was "Super-fit Englishmen". Some of us would come back spewing in the dressing room, but he wanted to create the impression that we really were super fit – and we were.'

Super fit or not, playing at that altitude and in that heat meant sometimes a player had to make a judgement about what was possible. Terry Cooper was a fabulous overlapping full-back, but he just couldn't play in Mexico as if it were Elland Road on a Saturday afternoon in November: 'It was draining at altitude, so you had to be selective when you got forward, because I knew I had to get back! Inevitably, the conditions curtailed my game. Playing in Colombia and Ecuador was like running with an army pack on your back, but it was lower in Mexico, so it eased off a bit. But you couldn't run about like you did in England.'

Even if he was selective about his forays, Cooper had a fine match against Romania as England began with a 1–0 win against a team quite happy to indulge in some of the darker arts of the game: fouling and then grabbing the England player by the back of the neck as he was helped up, in the hope of provoking a reaction. The game kicked off at 4 p.m., and there were 30 portable oxygen canisters and a resuscitation unit to hand, just in case. All lost weight during the 90 minutes, some about 7 to 8 lb, but Martin Peters shed 13 lb. Wearing all white, Geoff Hurst scored the only goal with a left-foot shot in the second half.

Romania's striker, Florea Dumitrache, had been chirping away, saying how he was going to score twice against the World Champions, and Alan Ball hadn't forgotten his pre-match boast. He recalled in *Playing Extra Time*:

> The days were sweltering. I kept meaning to fry an egg on the pavement but never got round to it. That first match wasn't as uncomfortable as it might have been. The rain was coming down when we scored. At the final whistle I couldn't resist sticking up two fingers at Dumitrache and saying to him, 'Where's your two then, pally?' He just shrugged. I could be irritating at times!

The following day, the England players took their places in the stands to watch Brazil beat Czechoslovakia 4–1 in the other opening Group Three game, the highlight of which was a swerving, banana free kick from Rivelino that brought Brazil level. Now the eyes of the world were on Guadalajara and the meeting of England and Brazil on 7 June. England had stayed at the Hilton in the middle of town the year before on their tour of South America, but they had misjudged just how much of a magnet the location would become 12 months later. The hotel was built in a quasi-Colonial style, with a swimming pool that the players could swim in but not lie by – as Alf Ramsey was convinced the sun would exhaust them. Eventually, the two parties came up with a compromise straight out of the *Carry On* movies. The players were allowed 15 minutes on their front and 15 on their back, and the trainer Harold Shepherdson would time them on a stopwatch, running out to say 'Turn over!' or 'Come in!' – much to the hilarity of the relaxing Mexicans.

As the players gathered to eat together on the evening of the 6th, so did a large crowd outside the hotel, banging old wrecks of cars with sticks, honking horns and chanting '*Bra-sil! Bra-sil!*' The England players had a difficult night's sleep amid the noise, but the Brazilian team – even if they had the overwhelming backing of the neutrals – were apprehensive too. Back home, the Brazilian people were doubtful they could beat the World Champions, and captain Carlos Alberto knew this match held the key to the whole tournament: 'This was *the* game. We knew before we started the competition that England was our main opponent, and we knew we had to win the group, because the winners would stay in Guadalajara and the runners-up would go to the altitude of Leon and have to play West Germany. We knew this match would be the key to getting to the final.'

It was a classic football match played in a temperature of 98°F. Tommy Wright came in for the injured Keith Newton at right-back in the only change to an England side who played their part in one of the best football matches in history. The brilliant Gerson was injured and replaced by Paulo César in the Brazilian line-up. The teams were preparing to come out and Terry Cooper was fixing his mind on the busy 90 minutes ahead when he received a bit of a shock: 'Both teams were standing at the top of the stairs before we went down onto the pitch, and I've looked across and who should I be standing next to but Pelé! And when I looked at him, I thought, "Jesus Christ, he's got massive thighs; he looks like a middleweight boxer!" He was so physically toned, and I thought, "We've got our work cut out today!" And then Pelé looked across at me and said, "Hello Cooper!"'

England created enough openings to get at least a draw. Alan Ball hit the bar, Franny Lee headed straight at the hitherto shaky Felix in goal, Geoff Hurst missed a good chance with a shot and the sub Jeff Astle of West Brom missed the best opportunity of the lot, dragging his shot wide from an excellent position 12 yards out. Terry Cooper had been the source of the move, and in the absence of traditional wingers – just as in 1966 – it was the full-backs who were providing the width: 'My cross fell to Jeff, and he had just come on and fluffed it. They either go in or they don't, and that one didn't.'

In the book *Winning Isn't Everything . . .*, Peter Thompson, who was still with the party even though he wasn't in the official 22, wonders whether Astle was really ready:

> Emlyn Hughes was on the bench and he was sitting next to Jeff. It was so hot, just watching in the midday sun was tiring. Emlyn told me that Jeff was just nodding off when Alf told him to come on, so he was still half asleep when he got on the pitch.

By then England were behind, the goal coming 14 minutes into the second half. Tostao was its creative force, although he seemed to foul Bobby Moore in the build-up, and when he played it across the penalty area to Pelé his lay-off was crashed home by Jairzinho. The Brazilians celebrated wildly, gambolling up the touchline like young Thomson's gazelles. The significance of winning the game had been drummed into them.

Thirty-nine years later, Alan Mullery's enthusiasm for this epic remains undimmed. As in the Maracanã the year before, he was on Pelé duty: 'The quality of Jairzinho, Pelé, Tostao, Rivelino – they wanted a ball each. There was probably only one mistake in the match, and that was made by me literally losing Pelé for the only time that day. It was the best game I ever played in. The technical ability was so high. I haven't seen technical quality like that since. I loved it. I was privileged to play in a game like that.'

Bobby Moore was almost faultless that day, the precise timing of his tackling and composure of his game acknowledged by Pelé afterwards as they embraced and exchanged shirts in the most sporting manner possible. The photograph of them doing so is one of the most famous ever taken in football. They agreed they would meet again in the final. Later, Pelé would concede that Moore was the best defender he ever played against and a gentleman as well.

That Pelé hadn't scored was down to a stupendous save from Gordon Banks. Carlos Alberto crossed from the right, and Pelé's header was destined for the bottom-left corner when Banks dived to his right to scoop the ball up and over the bar. 'He leapt like a salmon leaping up a waterfall,' said an admiring Pelé later. Carlos Alberto admitted to me that Brazil had ridden their luck in this game, but they had the precious victory they craved. Now, to make the last four, England would have to deal with the twin threat of altitude and a West Germany side wanting revenge.

The squad were disappointed but certainly not downcast. 'We thought if we were good enough to play like that against Brazil in that sort of heat, we were confident of going on,' says Alan Mullery. 'I was extremely confident in my own form, and I had made up my mind when I was sent off in 1968 that I wasn't going to let Nobby Stiles get back in the side. He only did when I was suspended.'

By the time England faced Czechoslovakia, they knew a point would suffice. The 4–4–2 system employed by Alf Ramsey was very demanding on the forwards in the Mexican heat, so both Franny Lee and Geoff Hurst sat out, with Jeff Astle and Alan Clarke of Leeds starting. Jack Charlton played what turned out to be his last international in place of Brian Labone, Keith Newton returned at full-back and Colin Bell replaced Alan Ball. England turned in a very ordinary performance and scraped home thanks to an Alan Clarke penalty, somewhat dubiously awarded. England had played well in losing to Brazil: a game sandwiched by two narrow wins that wouldn't linger long in the mind. They needed to improve for the much tougher test that lay ahead.

The quarter-finals saw the end of the Mexican dream in Toluca. They actually led Italy 1–0 early on, but then Riva scored twice on the way to an ultimately comfortable 4–1 win. Uruguay beat the Soviet Union 1–0 in the Azteca in Mexico City, the winning goal a controversial one from Espárrago in the embers of extra time, and Brazil, staying in Guadalajara as they had wanted, saw off Peru 4–2 in a game full of dazzling attacking play.

England travelled up to Leon, 722 ft higher than Guadalajara, where the Germans held the advantage, having played all their games there so far, but for one so professional, Alf Ramsey's preparations were somewhat shambolic. No hotel had been booked in advance, and the squad found themselves in a motel used by the West German wives and girlfriends. However, a much bigger storm was brewing.

On the eve of making the journey, Gordon Banks was unwell, spending much of the night being sick. His room-mates, Bobby Charlton and Keith Newton, suffered milder symptoms. Ever since, what exactly happened to Gordon Banks has been the subject of barroom chat and outlandish theories. The then *Sunday Times* correspondent Brian Glanville is in no doubt: 'Gordon Banks was almost certainly poisoned. I believe that now and I've spoken to him since. There was no explanation for it. He pointed out he ate and drank exactly what everyone else in the squad did, and he was the only one to get ill. I think something very strange was going on.' Peter Osgood had come on as a sub in two of the group games, and he agrees with Glanville, as he outlines in Dave Bowler's book:

> Somebody got at him. We all did everything together as far as food and drink was concerned. We all ate the same things, we were all on salt tablets and various other pills to protect your stomach which is why it was so hard to understand.

But who? Why? Why would someone want to nobble England's keeper? There are as many conspiracy theories as you want to take off the shelf. One is that with a new military junta in place in Brazil, the CIA didn't want England to win the World Cup again – as a third World Cup triumph would bring peace to Brazil. So the CIA poisoned Banks. It's a conspiracy theory. Make up your own mind.

Banks made the five-hour coach journey to Leon but had to miss training the next day. On the morning of the game, he was named in the side, and the players put on their tracksuits and flip-flops ready to board the coach. 'I was a terrible traveller,' says Alan Mullery. 'I got terrible car-sickness, so I sat at the front next to Alf. He was chatting away, sitting on the inside seat. He said to [the trainer] Harold [Shepherdson], "Everybody on board?" Harold counted everybody and called back, "Twenty-one Alf, we're one short. Somebody's missing." Alf responded, "Who the bloody hell's that? Come on, we want to get down there and do a bit on the pitch. Who is it?" And Harold replied that it was Banksy, so Alf said impatiently, "Get him out of his room." Harold went to Banksy's room and came back and leant across me to Alf and said, "He can't get off the loo. He's got Montezuma's revenge; it's running away from him. He looks awful. He can't do it." So Alf got off the bus and went to see Banksy, came back, got on the coach, stood up and calls to the back, "Catty, you're playing," and sits down.'

So it was that Peter Bonetti of Chelsea found out that he was playing in the biggest game of his life. This was only his seventh cap and his second competitive game. Gordon Banks was acknowledged to be the best goalkeeper in the world; England would be forced to go into a World Cup quarter-final without him.

The West Germans had scored ten goals in winning their group – as opposed to England's two – and the press hadn't been impressed by what they saw from the reigning World Champions. The media felt England, with their cagey approach, were doing just enough to get by and no more. On the other hand, that expedient approach was eminently sensible in the eyes of some; it was hot, there were three more games to go and getting through was all that counted as the team sought to come to a peak at the right moment.

England began excellently in Leon and played so well for an hour that a semi-final place seemed inevitable, Banks or no Banks. Apart from his enforced absence, England went in with the team who had started the tournament, and after half an hour Keith Newton and Alan Mullery combined to give them the lead. 'I still think about it now,' says Mullery, his eyes lighting up at the memory of scoring such a goal in such a game. 'I picked it up outside our box, and I looked out of the corner of my eye and saw Keith bombing down the wing from right-back. I smacked this 40- to 50-yard pass with my left foot and then sprinted 60 to 70 yards. Keith smashed it across the six-yard box, and I swung a boot at it. Berti Vogts tried to tackle me, but it flew in.'

Four minutes into the second half, England went further ahead, and again Newton was key, crossing to the far post where Martin Peters ghosted in, as he did so often, to score. England were 2–0 up and surely home and hosed. It was thirteen games since someone had scored twice against them, but now substitutes were permitted in international football and how the two managers used them made all the difference. The German, Helmut Schön, made the first decisive move, changing his right-wingers after 55 minutes – with Grabowski coming on for Libuda. It is worth reiterating that in Ramsey's 1970 team the full-backs got through an enormous amount of work, getting up and down the line and being the outlets out wide, witness Newton's role in both goals in Leon. Now left-back Terry Cooper had a fresh pair of legs to encounter: 'Libuda was a flying machine, but I liked flying machines. Quicker players like him would push it; you just gave yourself a yard, and you could take the ball off them. I didn't like playing against people who stopped then went again then stopped. They were difficult. Grabowski was a stopper and a starter and a jinker. I had expended a lot of energy, it was midday, it was hot and I knew it was going to be a problem.'

Grabowski was full of pace and intent, asking questions straight away of the England defence, but with just over twenty minutes remaining England still held their two-goal advantage. Then Ramsey decided upon a change. Bobby Charlton was thirty-two, he had done a lot of running and, with the semi-final three days later in Mexico City, a further 1,500 ft higher up, Ramsey felt he needed to protect him. As in the World Cup final at Wembley, Beckenbauer had shrivelled under the shadow cast over him by England's experienced statesman, but just as Charlton noticed that Colin Bell was preparing to replace him, Beckenbauer scored. Franny Lee blocked his first shot, but the follow-up, from the right-hand side just outside the area, went under a diving Bonetti for a soft goal.

Charlton immediately came off for Bell, and the shackles fell away from Beckenbauer; he was freed. 'He had been looking after Bobby and suddenly he started to cause problems for us and the game went away from us,' said Terry Cooper. 'That was crazy as we were absolutely cruising it. Alf was looking after Bobby for the next game, and I still think he was correct, because you're trying to win a tournament, not just one game.'

Without rancour, both Alan Mullery and Martin Peters sadly agree on the significance of Gordon Banks's absence. 'I think Banksy would have saved Germany's first goal quite easily, the one that went under Peter's body,' said Mullery. 'I think Peter will admit he should have saved it.' Nine minutes from time Norman Hunter replaced Martin Peters as Ramsey tried to see the game out, but the Germans immediately grabbed a fortunate equaliser as Uwe Seeler's back-header looped over Bonetti to make it 2–2. 'Seeler's header was a complete fluke. All he was doing was trying to flick it on, and he flicked it on so hard Peter was three yards off his line as it went in,' said Mullery frustratedly.

There was still time for Hurst and Lee to very nearly combine for the winner before the full-time whistle meant Alf Ramsey had to conjure up another World Cup pep talk. Ramsey took them into the shade. It was now just after 1.45 p.m. local time, and Alan Mullery remembers how he began: 'His opening gambit was, "Well, we beat them in 1966, we'll do it again." And I opened my mouth and said, "Yeah, but it wasn't 100 degrees in the shade, Alf!" A bit of a defeatist attitude, but we were knackered and they were in the ascendancy.'

In the second period of extra time, Grabowski stopped and started in the way Terry Cooper hated, and, having got the better of his full-back, the winger delivered a cross that was headed back over Brian Labone by Löhr towards the pocket poacher Gerd Müller, who volleyed in the winner. Even now, talking to Terry Cooper, it is easy to see the hurt and disbelief of that defeat: 'We were absolutely distraught afterwards, because it was there for us. We thought we would play Brazil in the final. Distraught because we knew it was there for us, but with Alf trying to do the right thing he ended up doing the wrong thing.' For Martin Peters, Wembley and Leon are the yin and yang of football, the ecstasy of 1966 and the sorrow of 1970: 'We were distressed and destroyed. We blamed ourselves as you would in any game when you were 2–0 up and lose.'

England dragged themselves back to their motel, and the players flopped down on the grass, scarcely able to take in what had happened. Alex Stepney went to see Gordon Banks in his room, where he was watching a delayed transmission of the game. Banks was ecstatic as England were leading 2–0.

Alf Ramsey was full of contrition, as Alan Mullery, voted England's player of the tournament, acknowledges: 'He was so apologetic, because it had gone wrong at the end. He was very humble. I can't think of anyone talking till we got back to the hotel, and he called everybody together and opened up the champagne. I still don't believe it now that we lost that game. Losing has stayed with me for years, but it doesn't detract from what I did. I played over seven-hundred-and-fifty games in my career, and people ask me two questions: you were the first man sent off for England, and I try to describe the situation, and the Bobby Charlton substitution. Even people not born know the story.'

It seems axiomatic that Ramsey made errors with his substitutions, and he never really got to grips with using them. For a man who liked consistency so much, bringing on replacements was too much of a gamble. At the tail-end of the Poland game at Wembley that would signal the end of his career three years later, he brought striker Kevin Hector on with just two minutes remaining. In Leon he left on the overlapping, hard-working full-backs and took off the calming and influential Bobby Charlton, who had the mockers on Franz Beckenbauer. Brian Glanville sadly maintains, 'Ramsey went mad. He took Charlton off, which gave Beckenbauer complete leeway. It was clear after a certain time that both full-backs, Newton and Cooper, who had been doing superb overlapping, were completely knackered. And what needed to be done was they both needed to be relieved. Schön put on Grabowski, and he ran Cooper ragged, who was dead on his feet.'

England were probably guilty of trying to play out time too early as well, and Alan Ball admitted that subconsciously they probably took their collective foot off the pedal. Safe to say there are many reasons for England's shocking defeat in Leon: Banks's illness, Ramsey's strange substitutions, a touch of complacency at 2–0, the extra altitude, the stress the 4–4–2 system imposed on the full-backs and the Germans' will to win – but Banks's sickness remains the most significant.

Schön's team couldn't advance any further, however, as they lost a thrilling semi-final 4–3 to Italy after extra time. Brazil exorcised the ghosts of their predecessors 20 years earlier when they came from behind to beat Uruguay 3–1 in a game that said everything about the favourites' tactical flexibility. Brazil were a goal behind nearing half-time when Gerson approached his captain, Carlos Alberto: 'Gerson said as he was being man-marked he would drop into midfield and that would give Clodoaldo, normally a defensive midfielder, the freedom to go over the halfway line. Five minutes later, Clodoaldo equalised. Zagallo gave us the freedom to change the game, not to wait till half-time and be told what to do.'

Clodoaldo was not so popular in the final when his awful back pass allowed Italy to equalise just before half-time. The team shouted at him, telling him any repeat of that nonsense would cost them the World Cup, but just after the hour mark the Brazilians took over. First Gerson made it 2–1, then Jairzinho 3–1 and then the captain, Carlos Alberto, roared forward into the vacant left-back spot to rifle home the fourth. As FIFA. com said, 'Nothing captured the beauty of their football better than their fourth goal . . . Pelé teeing up his captain Carlos Alberto to conclude a seven-man move by arrowing a first-time shot past Enrico Albertosi and into the far corner.'

The captain told me he wasn't surprised he got a chance to score: 'We knew before the game that that situation might happen. Zagallo told us the Italians play man-to-man marking, so he told Jairzinho, "If possible go to the left, and Facchetti, the left-back, will follow you." He told Tostao to go the left side, and that would leave only Pelé in the middle, so when the ball came to me from Pelé there was nobody on my side!' – and he thumped it in.

The world of football joyously celebrated a win for a team recently voted the best of all time. As Brazil got to keep the Jules Rimet Trophy, the lights were about to go out on English football.

7

SPAIN 1982

Little did anyone realise as the England players hauled themselves from the field in Leon that it would be another long, dark, depressing 12 years before they played in the World Cup finals again. Despite the huge disappointment of losing in the quarter-finals in Mexico – and being outplayed by Günter Netzer of West Germany in the quarter-finals of the 1972 European Championship – there didn't seem anything terrifying about the qualifying group that England were landed in, as they battled with Wales and Poland for the right to go to West Germany in 1974. Poland lost in Cardiff, and a circumspect England were beaten in Chorzów, where Bobby Moore made a rare mistake and Alan Ball was sent off, but victory in the return match at Wembley in October 1973 would mean Alf Ramsey leading his country into the World Cup for the third time.

The game at Wembley is seared into the consciousness of every England football fan, even if, like my generation, they do not remember it or were not even born; they have heard or read about it that often. Brian Clough's description of the Polish goalkeeper Tomaszewski as 'a clown' is one of the most infamous and errant in the history of English football, as he proved himself anything but. Alan Clarke's penalty salvaged a draw but no more, and for the first time since 1938, when their absence was self-imposed, the world's best footballers would gather without England.

It was the end of an era. World Cup winner Martin Peters admitted, 'It was a disaster and basically the end of my England career. We played so well that night, but the goalkeeper played out of his skin. You can't be on top all the time in this game.' Alf Ramsey limped on for two more matches before the most successful manager in England's history was unceremoniously sacked in 1974. Leeds United's Don Revie took over, but he failed to steer the team into the last eight of the European Championships, and the draw for qualifying for the 1978 World Cup in Argentina pitched them in with Italy – with only the group winners going through. Italy won in Rome 2–0 in November 1976, which effectively condemned England to a second successive World Cup on the sidelines – and hastened Revie's end.

That season ended with the Scottish fans swinging deliriously on the Wembley crossbars and taking home pieces of turf for posterity after their 2–1 win in the Home Championship. When England flew to South America for their summer tour, the manager turned up late. Ipswich Town's Paul Mariner was a young, strong striker with two caps to his name: 'I remember sitting in Rio – and I was naive and raw – and one of the players telling me that Don had gone to the Middle East. I hadn't a clue. I thought he had gone scouting or something. That was a major, major turning point in English football. People remember all that.' Revie had been plotting his exit strategy for some time, probably since the loss in Italy, and he resigned as manager on 11 July to soak himself in Emirates petrodollars as the manager of the UAE. The manner of his going grated, as he told the *Daily Mail* before he informed the FA. Football League secretary Alan Hardaker said, 'Don Revie's decision doesn't surprise me in the slightest. Now I can only hope he can quickly learn to call out bingo numbers in Arabic.'

The travails of the England team on the pitch were mirrored by a rising threat of hooliganism off it. Segregation of fans came in after Manchester United's relegation to Division Two in 1974. The same year, a teenage Blackpool supporter was stabbed to death at Bloomfield Road – the first hooligan-related victim at a football match – and Tottenham were banned from playing two European games at White Hart Lane after fans rioted at the UEFA Cup final in Feyenoord. English fans were at the centre of more disturbances abroad the following year in the European Cup final, as Leeds supporters rioted in Paris. Manchester United's expulsion from the European Cup Winners' Cup in 1977, after violence marred their game with St Etienne, was later rescinded, but the malevolent threat of trouble was increasingly, and depressingly, a scar on the national game.

The Chelsea 'Headhunters' and West Ham's 'Inter City Firm', names of hooligan groups, were entering the lexicon of everyday language. Inevitably, perhaps, attendances suffered. In the 1970s, the overall figure for crowds in the top four divisions in England fell from 29.5 million to 24.6 million, and those watching the First Division dipped from 14.8 million to 12.2 million. England, now under Ron Greenwood, did qualify for a major tournament in 1980 – the European Championship in Italy – but that experience was marred by rioting fans in Turin during the game with Belgium, for which England were fined £8,000. The police had to resort to tear gas to regain control.

So, by the time qualification began for the 1982 World Cup, the game here was in desperate need of a boost. The club sides might well have been dominating the European Cup, but the reputation of English football was being trampled underfoot by a hooligan element that had welded itself to the national team. Then, the World Cup Committee came to the rescue of the national team by expanding the 1982 tournament from 16 to 24 teams. Now the top two in the European qualifying zones would reach Spain, and, as Greenwood admitted, a five-team group containing Norway, Romania, Switzerland and Hungary looked reasonably easy.

An admired coach at Arsenal, Greenwood took over at West Ham in 1962, leading them to the FA Cup and Cup Winners' Cup, and he helped shape the Upton Park triumvirate that was central to England's 1966 success. He became the club's general manager in 1974, before answering England's call three years later after Don Revie's defection. Now he was charged with taking the team to the World Cup, and he embarked on the most schizophrenic of campaigns.

England began with a comfortable 4–0 win at Wembley on Wednesday, 10 September 1980 against Norway, still a team of part-timers. It was the first game I ever went to at the old Wembley, with my father, and I still have the programme at home, priced 50 pence. The cost of standing on the terraces was £3.50. In the programme, Ron Greenwood wrote, 'We have a good draw and a good chance of qualifying. But, remember, there are no easy internationals these days.'

I was twelve, and the two things I remember most are the traffic on the North Circular Road and, particularly, the scoreboard. Terry McDermott scored the first goal, and in those days the scoreboard spelt out all the names of the countries and goalscorers via individual bulbs that would light up accordingly. On this night, a few of them were a bit temperamental and had trouble illuminating the last 't' in the Liverpool player's name. 'McDermot' appeared without any problem, but then followed a few moments of frantic effort by the last few bulbs to complete the task, as the crowd watched with increasing amusement; sometimes his name would be completed, but then several bulbs seemingly died of exhaustion, to the groans of the crowd, until finally all were permanently lit. Terry McDermott's full moniker was then correctly spelt, the crowd cheered in that typically British over-the-top way and we all got back to watching the football.

Despite the encouraging start, by the end of the 1980–81 season the results had been mixed and qualification was by no means certain. Romania had beaten England 2–1 in Bucharest and taken a goalless draw away from the return match; Switzerland had lost 2–1 at Wembley. Now came two away games in a week, in May and June, that would go some way to determining what the players would be up to come the summer of 1982. The pressure on Ron Greenwood and the players was intense: to fail to qualify for three World Cups in a row would have an enormously detrimental effect on the game in England.

Sir Trevor Brooking had made his debut in Alf Ramsey's last game in charge, back in 1974. Now one of the most senior and experienced players, he thought four points from the two games would be par for the course. That was an impossible target after the game in Basle, where the England fans reacted to a defeat by causing £6,000 worth of damage. 'The 2–1 loss in Switzerland was what we didn't anticipate,' said Sir Trevor. 'To lose was a shocker, and then there was more crowd trouble because the game was going badly – and there was tear gas. It made for a pretty grim few days building up to the game in Budapest that people assumed we were going to lose because they [Hungary] were top of the group. It was apparent if we lost in Hungary we weren't going to the World Cup.'

Liverpool's win in the European Cup final in Paris meant an English team had won that trophy five times on the bounce, and yet the national team was, as *The Times* put it, 'stumbling its troubled way along a seemingly endless and dark corridor'. Greenwood responded to the biggest crisis of his reign by bringing Brooking back into the team along with Mick Mills of Ipswich Town – it was Ron's 'Dad's Army' according to the press – and it was, frankly, win or bust. Hungary had two wins and a draw from their opening three games, and they cranked up the atmosphere at the Nep Stadium before kick-off by parading the great Ferenc Puskás on the pitch.

If Trevor Brooking is always remembered for his unlikely winning header in the FA Cup final when it comes to his West Ham career, then it is this game in Budapest that is instantly recalled when people talk about his England days. On a lovely playing surface and in a fine setting, the game was poised at 1–1 in the second half when Brooking scored a goal, his second of the game, that I can still remember seeing on a little black and white television: 'It was weird,' said Sir Trevor. 'I hit it with my left foot sweetly, and it stuck in the stanchion of the goal, and I just continued running and celebrating. Ron Greenwood and a lot of the players said that, initially, they thought I had scored, by looking at me. But they couldn't see the ball dropping into the net or bouncing, so they started looking behind the goal. They saw me still running, being chased by some of the lads, and they were still bemused – until they saw the goalkeeper trying to punch it out of the stanchion. It was really freakish. I was one of the few who knew for sure that I had scored.'

Phil Thompson was in the England team that night, fresh from leading Liverpool to that win in the European Cup final against Real Madrid, but for all his success at domestic level, he knew at 28 that a World Cup finals appearance was slipping by. While Southampton's Dave Watson headed everything away in Budapest, Thompson organised, covered, swept and watched as England came away with a priceless 3–1 win: 'Viv Anderson came up to me and put his arms around me and said, "You know what, Thommo, I've always thought you were a good player, but tonight you've proved to me that you're a great player, a top-class player. You've given one of the best defensive performances I've ever seen." Coming from another player, that was a great honour for me. I wanted to go to Spain, to the challenge of playing at the very pinnacle of football.'

The experience of the 'Dad's Army' had paid off, as England boarded the plane home on the Sunday morning with their World Cup destiny back in their own hands – but if they were expecting a quiet, relaxed journey then nothing could have been further from the truth. On the plane with the England squad were many of the journalists who, because of the time demands of the first editions of their papers, had had to write their pieces before the game – and they had filed them assuming England were not going to Spain. Trevor Brooking sat back in his seat and picked up a paper: '[It] had seven of us with a cross on our face, saying we were no longer needed – that we were over thirty, too old – but of course they had written all that without knowing we had actually won 3–1.'

For Ron Greenwood, sitting further up the plane, the premature reports of the demise of his England team were one torrent of criticism too much to bear. After all the flak he had received during the qualifiers and the doom and gloom after the loss in Basle, he was now seeing his team being pilloried in the Sunday papers, even though they had won. England captain Kevin Keegan confided in his Liverpool teammate Phil Thompson: 'Kevin said to me, "When Ron gets off the plane he's going to call a press conference and announce his resignation." I think it had all got to him, and he wanted to go out on a high. His professional status had been questioned, and I don't think he enjoyed that.'

Keegan quickly called a council of war in the aisles of the chartered jet. England were back in with a realistic chance of reaching Spain, and yet the manager was about to announce he was stepping down. Around half a dozen of the elder statesmen of the team – including Keegan, Brooking, Mick Mills and Ray Wilkins – went to see Greenwood. Keegan and Phil Thompson were among those who said they would pack in playing for England if Greenwood resigned; they had turned the situation around for him as much as for themselves and the country. The deputation worked, and by the time the plane touched down Greenwood had promised to stay and take the team to Spain the next year.

Trevor Brooking says the incident tells you everything about the esteem in which the manager was held: 'Training was enjoyable, fun, and the Liverpool lads enjoyed their time on the training ground with Ron, somebody different, somebody they thought was knowledgeable and tactically astute. You mustn't underestimate the strength of the Liverpool connection. When you think of the success they had, their influence was massive and Ron was more relaxed than Don Revie. Ron wanted the players to express themselves.' A measure of Greenwood's popularity is that word of the aborted resignation did not get out until after he had left the job, following the World Cup.

This England team, though, were determined not to do things the easy way. Just three months later, at the start of the 1981–82 season, England lost ignominiously in Oslo to Norway, 2–1, to throw their World Cup dreams back in the balance. The result of 9 September 1981 spawned one of the most famous commentaries in history, one that has been copied a thousand times since. Norwegian commentator Bjørge Lillelien let rip at the final whistle, screaming:

Bert Williams looks on in dismay as Joe Gaetjens's freak goal condemns England to a shock defeat in Belo Horizonte in 1950. (© Getty Images)

Tom Finney scores a penalty with his left foot against the great Soviet goalkeeper Lev Yashin in 1958. (© Getty Images)

Ron Flowers challenges for the ball against Brazil, but England go out to the eventual 1962 winners in the quarter-finals. (© Getty Images)

In the 1966 final, the on-rushing Roger Hunt says the angle at which the ball rebounded after Geoff Hurst had hit the bar meant he couldn't put it in the net. (© Getty Images)

Alan Mullery and Martin Peters both scored in the sweltering heat of Leon in the 1970 quarter-finals, but West Germany stormed back to win 3–2. (© Getty Images)

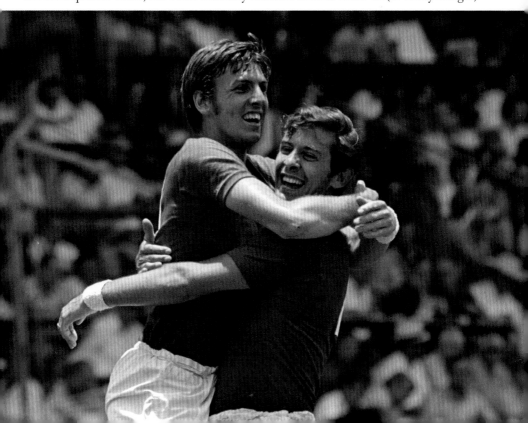

Paul Mariner is marked more closely by the Spanish police than by the French defence as England finally return to the World Cup finals in 1982. (© PA Photos)

His hat-trick against Poland in 1986 belatedly sent England on their way and changed Gary Lineker's life both on and off the pitch.
(© Getty Images)

'The Hand of God,' said Maradona. 'The hand of a rascal,' retorted Bobby Robson. (© Getty Images)

Chris Waddle says if he had scuffed his penalty in the shoot-out in Italia '90, it would probably have gone in. (© Getty Images)

After David Beckham's red card against Argentina in 1998, Tony Adams responds with a Herculean display. (© Getty Images)

World Cup quarter-final 2002, Shizuoka, and Michael Owen puts England 1–0 up against Brazil. It wasn't to be. (© Getty Images)

Paul Robinson had done his homework in 2006, but Ronaldo put his penalty in the opposite corner and England lost a shoot-out yet again.
(© PA Photos)

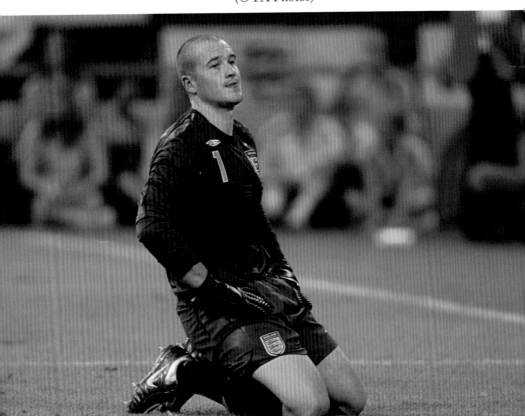

This is truuuuly incredible! We've beaten England, England the fighters' birthplace: Lord Nelson, Lord Beaverbrook, Sir Winston Churchill, Sir Anthony Eden, Clement Attlee, Henry Cooper, Lady Diana, we've beaten you all. Maggie Thatcher, as you say in your language in the boxing bars around Madison Square Garden: Your boys took a hell of a beating!

Ron Greenwood had warned that 'the bunch of part-timers' would present an awkward problem, and as centre-forward Paul Mariner sat in the dressing room after the humiliation, he recognised the desperate situation England now found themselves in: 'It was the lowest point of my career. It was highly embarrassing for everybody, and there was a massive fall out from it. People will never forget the quotes from that commentator. I remember the scene in the dressing room afterwards really well. People were distraught; it was such a low moment. Missing out three times in a row would have had a terrible impact.'

With six games remaining in the group, Hungary and Romania were the favourites to go through, but the latter suddenly ran out of steam, and when they sensationally lost at home to Switzerland in October, England were presented with a gift. Switzerland won 2–1 in Bucharest on Saturday, 10 October, a result that was broadcast around the football league grounds, and I clearly remember Ray Clemence saying on *Sports Report* on Radio 2 that he heard the score as he took a goal kick at White Hart Lane and immediately understood its significance.

Romania took just two points from their last three games, which meant that when Hungary, who had already guaranteed their qualification, came to Wembley on 18 November 1981, a draw would mean England joining their visitors in Spain. A decade of hurt, punctuated by failed campaigns, hooliganism, one manager sacked and another walking out, was poised to come to an end on a filthy night at the home of football. Ninety-two thousand people were packed into Wembley as the rain made the surface even quicker. Paul Mariner was to play a pivotal role: 'The build-up was full of fever and very passionate, and although we were sort of insulated from it, we were fans too and it did affect us – and it was extremely nerve-racking.'

After 14 minutes, Trevor Francis shot and Mariner reacted sharply: 'Trevor screwed it wide, and I had to adjust my feet a little bit and redirect it, so the old striker's instinct came in. You still know where the goal is, and in it went. I remember Terry Mac and everybody going crazy.' The forwards had done their bit in nudging England in front; now the defenders had to keep the back door bolted. Phil Thompson was the organiser-in-chief again: 'It was probably the nerviest international I ever played in. You never feel in charge, but we got there. I can remember the emotion on the pitch at the end was just immense and the crowd absolutely fantastic.' At the final whistle, I remember that, aged 13, I was, at long last, going to watch England in the World Cup finals. It was a novel feeling.

The country's excitement was mixed with enormous relief. Mariner was photographed in a sombrero and playing a guitar, and *The Times* summed up the manner in which England had staggered, like a suffering marathon runner, over the finishing line: 'England have reached the World Cup finals in Spain,' wrote football correspondent Stuart Jones. 'These nine words cannot begin to tell the tale of the last tortuous 14 months.' Bearing in mind they were hosts in '66 and holders in '70, England had actually come through qualification for the first time in two decades. Like their predecessors in 1970, they made a record – 'This Time (We'll Get It Right)' – and when they appeared on *Top of the Pops* they pushed Kevin Keegan and Mick Mills to the front.

In the run-up to the tournament, all the critical analysis centred on the defence. There were no problems in the striking department: Kevin Keegan dovetailed smartly with the target man Paul Mariner, and Trevor Francis and Tony Woodcock were both fine forwards. The finesse of Trevor Brooking underpinned midfield; the youth of Bryan Robson gave it drive. Ray Wilkins brought balance and experience, Graham Rix and Steve Coppell the natural width. But as Phil Thompson read all the pre-tournament supplements, one topic kept cropping up: 'Everybody who was dissecting our team always had a question mark over the back four. Was it good enough to keep out the best in the world? One paper said, "Phil Thompson is the right centre-back because there's nobody else." And I thought to myself, "Is that a compliment or a kick in the teeth?" And we answered all the queries, as we conceded only one goal in the whole tournament.'

Thompson's main partner in central defence in the qualifiers had been 35-year-old Dave Watson, whom he described as a 'fantastic warrior', and alongside him for the Hungary game at Wembley was West Ham's Alvin Martin. Watson had been talked out of retiring from the international game by Greenwood after Euro '80, and a month before the party for Spain was announced Greenwood assured him he was in. Then, a week before, Watson was told he hadn't made it. 'I could have cried,' Watson admitted to me. 'I would have gone to West Germany and Argentina, but we didn't qualify, and then, having played the qualifiers, when I was fit, Ron left me out for Steve Foster. I couldn't believe it.' No one has won more than Watson's 65 caps and not played in a World Cup finals.

Also included, at centre-half, was a 23 year old from Ipswich Town: a very good friend of Mariner's called Terry Butcher. Thompson liked the cut of his jib: 'Terry would listen and learn. His passion was fantastic. Going out onto the pitch with him and Marrers [Paul Mariner] gave you the belief you were going into battle, and I loved that. We had that at Liverpool. Terry was a kicker. We had a blend, and we worked off each other and it was a great partnership.'

There is always one player who comes up on the blind side to make the cut – Martin Peters in '66, Michael Owen in '98, Theo Walcott in Germany – and Terry Butcher was the 1982 version. He had two caps to his name when, in January, he collided with Luton's Brian Stein in an FA Cup tie and was in hospital for five weeks, after fracturing his nose. Butcher lost a stone and a half and had two operations on his nose, his battle for fitness coinciding with the last few months of his wife Rita's first pregnancy. Alvin Martin started the final friendly in Helsinki against Finland, but Butcher had proved his fitness by then and had done enough – he was going to Spain. 'The older element scared you in a way,' he recalled. 'Keegan, Brooking, Shilton, Corrigan. I felt like one of the kit boys there just for the ride. It was an incredible experience. To be called up, to be on the plane out there, was a dream come true. It meant the world to me and my family. We had had such a rocky time in January and February. To be in the party was priceless.'

Butcher was in dreamland as he flew off, but the England party had two enormous shadows hanging over them. Neither of their most influential players was fit. Kevin Keegan had a back injury, and Trevor Brooking hurt his groin in the last few minutes in Helsinki. It was an injury he had suffered before, so he knew what to do: 'Our West Ham doctor was called Brian Roper, and he was an orthopaedic surgeon. And he used to give me a really deep cortisone jab to disperse it. I told Ron [Greenwood] that I needed to see Brian, but he said, "Ethically you can't; you need to see Vernon Edwards, the England doctor." But, unfortunately, Vernon gave me the injection with a little needle, and it didn't go deep enough.'

Brooking was in Spain for about ten days before he got the injection he really needed, and that delay cost him any chance of playing a more meaningful role in the tournament. He was cross with himself as much as anything: 'Ron did everything the right way, but I should have been more pushy. I should have gone to Brian to get my cortisone jab before we flew to Spain, and I'm sure I would have been fit earlier. I was initially frustrated out there, and then I got angry, because I knew I should have tried to dig my heels in. I got the injection ten to twelve days later than it should have been. They would probably be horrified nowadays, but Brian had a really long needle and he put it almost under the crotch really, to a deep-seated area, which dispersed the problem. It got really sore for about 36 hours, and that's how I knew he had got the spot. The biggest frustration was that I was feeling very sharp and felt I was going to have a good tournament.'

While Brooking was trying desperately to recover from his groin injury, Keegan was secretly flying to Germany to see someone about his back. Approaching the opening game with France, Keegan hadn't trained for a few days, and Phil Thompson thought he might well be England captain – as he often was in Keegan's absence: 'Ron never mentioned anything to me about the captaincy, which I thought was strange, and he pulled me aside the day before the France game and said, "I just want to say to you that I'm going to make Mick Mills captain. You've probably got another World Cup in you, and it's going to be Mick's final one." I thought Phil Neal had a chance of playing right-back. I was devastated. I knew at 28 that the World Cup might not come around again, and it didn't. I believe Ron made the wrong decision in going with Mick, but I had a job to do.'

Another decision Greenwood had to make concerned the goalkeeping position. There wasn't a cigarette paper between Peter Shilton and Ray Clemence, and they had been alternating in goal. Clemence was given the number one shirt for the tournament and his rival Shilton number twenty-two, but if that pointed towards the Tottenham man being the favourite for Spain, that's not the way it turned out. Greenwood decided the time for swapping had ended, and Shilton was installed as England's leading goalkeeper, much to Clemence's understandable disappointment.

With Mills as captain, Brooking and Keegan injured, Butcher alongside Thompson at centre-half, Shilton preferred to Clemence in goal and Mariner and Francis up front, England finally re-entered the World Cup finals. It was a stiflingly hot day in Bilbao, the grass so warm as the players took off their flip-flops that it felt as if there was under-soil heating. Admiral supplied the strip, and the kit man had spent the previous night ironing on the numbers, which peeled off during the course of the 90 minutes, littering the pitch like discarded confetti at a wedding.

England didn't creep back into the World Cup. They scored after 27 seconds, then the fastest goal in the tournament's history, Butcher flicking on Steve Coppell's throw for Bryan Robson to volley in. As Paul Mariner said, 'It's no secret. You put Mariner and Butcher on the near post, get Coppell to throw the ball to a couple of Blackpool Towers, then get a runner going into the back post: Bryan Robson, one of the bravest players I have ever played with. He would go through his grandmother to score a goal, and all of a sudden the only people who didn't seem to know about it were the French defence. We were absolutely ecstatic.' It was only the day before the game, after the team had finished practising the move with Kenny Sansom throwing in from the left, that Coppell told coach Don Howe he could do a similar job on the right.

Terry Butcher's first touch in the World Cup had led to a goal: 'It was an unbelievable feeling. There was a big screen behind the goal, and you saw the replay and thought, "Wow."' Butcher quickly found out about the flipside of playing at this level as he was responsible for the French equaliser through Soler, but as the temperature dropped in the second half England took control, wrapping up a 3–1 win with a second from Robson and one from Mariner, who lost 11 lb in weight. Mariner remembers that, off the pitch, the dynamic Robson was such a Pac-Man aficionado that he had to have his thumb strapped at one point by the physios because he had a blister on it.

Mariner's injury problems that year had been much more serious, a ruptured Achilles in January causing him to wonder if he would ever play again, let alone reach a World Cup – making his achievement of a sixth goal in five games all the more laudable. The last England player to score in five games in a row was his boyhood hero, Jimmy Greaves, for whom

Mariner had fallen when he saw Tottenham at Bolton as a child: 'I will never forget it to this day. I have the image imprinted on my mind. They came out in white shorts, white socks and this fantastic royal-blue top, and Spurs won. And Greaves just glided round Burnden Park that day. He had an incredible touch, skill, pizzazz and elan. His finishing was remarkable, and to be spoken of in the same breath as that guy is an incredible honour.'

The England team and FA officials went back to their hotel in Bilbao and wound down with fish stew and steaks, wine and beer. A boombox and a few cassettes sorted out the music, and some players stayed up till the sun rose. At midday that following day, there was golf for those who wanted it, using buggies, and a few beers and some sangria on the clubhouse patio after the round. It was a completely different era, as Terry Butcher accepts: 'We had had a good night the night before, and we had been drinking all day – you wouldn't do that now – and in the foyer of our hotel there were these big armchairs. Ray Wilkins came in and fell asleep in one, curled up like a dormouse, and Ron held his press conference round him. Ray was snoring away, and all the press were round him. It was so different from today it's not true. There was a fantastic atmosphere among the squad.'

Winning the first group game in the World Cup has always been important for confidence, and even in the continued absence of Brooking and Keegan the team tackled Czechoslovakia in very good spirits. A Trevor Francis strike and an own goal saw England through to a comfortable 2–0 win. Francis had had to wear the tag of being the first million-pound player when he signed for Nottingham Forest, and he scored the winning goal in the European Cup final in 1979. In Keegan's absence, he was leading the line with Mariner, Francis being a mobile, quick striker who worked the channels very much in the style of his stricken captain.

Terry Butcher vividly recalls the manager getting hold of the microphone on the team bus on the way back to the hotel: '"Well done, lads," he said. "Magnificent performance again. Great result, we've qualified; just go and get pissed!" He was such a gentleman, Ron. I called him "the Pope" – not to his face – because he looked like the Pope. If he had had a mitre and staff, he would have been the Pope!'

Greenwood was a man for whom the squad had enormous regard and respect. 'Everything nice you could say about a human being you could say about Ron Greenwood,' maintains Paul Mariner. 'He put me at ease and told me all I had to do in the white shirt is what I had been doing for my club. He put players in a comfort zone, and when you join up with the national team, you're out of your element. Tactically, he was fantastic. When he lost his best two players, he came up with 4–4–2. The players were highly motivated, and I can't speak highly enough of Ron.'

Qualification for the second phase guaranteed, Greenwood tinkered with the team for the final group game against Kuwait, which was won thanks to a Trevor Francis goal. England topped the group and moved to Madrid for the second phase, a three-team pool involving Spain and the European Champions, West Germany. Spain were in terrible form and had been beaten 1–0 by Northern Ireland in Valencia – Gerry Armstrong's goal setting up one of the most famous wins in the province's history – but the hosts had scraped through as runners-up of Group Five, while the West Germans won Group Two amid enormous acrimony and controversy.

The Germans actually lost their opening game to Algeria 2–1, but come the last match, against their neighbours, Austria, both countries knew a narrow German win would ensure the two of them squeezed through at Algeria's expense. Horst Hrubesch scored after ten minutes, and thereafter the teams went through the motions, aimlessly meandering through the remainder of the ninety minutes as the appalled Spanish crowd screamed 'Fuera, fuera' (Out, out) and Algerian fans gesticulated angrily, suggesting money was involved. This shameless stitch-up, known as the '*Anschluss*', forced FIFA to alter the rules so that, from 1986, the final two games in each group would be played simultaneously.

France were runners-up to England in Group Four, and, ironically, by losing the opening game in Bilbao, they looked to have the easier passage into the last four – as their three-team Pool D contained Northern Ireland and Austria. It was the era of Giresse, Tigana and Platini, the golden midfield of Gallic football, and France won both games, comfortably reaching their first semi-final since 1958.

Scotland had just failed to progress from Group Six through to Pool A, losing out on goal difference to the Soviet Union, who were then, in turn, denied by the same differentiating factor from reaching the semi-finals. Poland went through as Pool A winners, a goalless draw with the Soviets enough in a game heavy with political undertones: just months earlier, Poland's then-Communist government had imposed martial law to quash internal dissent and deter any threat of a Soviet invasion.

The real drama was in Pool C. Italy had drawn all three of their Group One games, going through as runners-up to Poland; an enthralling Brazil had their best side since 1970 and had scored ten goals in winning Scotland's group; and the defending champions, Argentina, had made hard work of qualifying from Group Three, coming in behind Belgium, to whom they had lost in the opening match. Italy beat Argentina 2–1 in the first game, Gentile dominating the fast-emerging Maradona – who was then sent off in the meeting of the South Americans. Brazil's fluid, one-touch football was far too good for the waning champions, and a 3–1 win meant it was now between Italy and Brazil for the semi-finals.

Their meeting in the Sarrià Stadium in Barcelona was undoubtedly one of the best World Cup matches of all time. Paolo Rossi had been welcomed back into the Italian fold after his part in Italy's match-fixing scandal, but the striker hadn't yet scored in Spain. Finally, he came alive on a pitch mown in a strange fashion. A draw would have sufficed for Brazil, and twice they equalised Rossi goals – first through the great Socrates and then Falcão, whose joyous and extravagant celebration, like Tardelli's in the final, was one of the abiding memories of the three weeks. With 16 minutes remaining, Brazil were going through, but they failed to clear a corner and Rossi's striker's instinct saw him in the right place to complete his hat-trick and his rehabilitation. Brazil were out, and that generation has always been known since as Brazil's best team never to have won the World Cup.

In truth, Pool C sequestered all the highlights, because Pool B saw only three goals – all of them in the same game. Hard as they tried, England were ultimately undone by the failure of Kevin Keegan and Trevor Brooking to get fully fit in time. Don Howe had played in the 1958 World Cup and was now Ron Greenwood's coach: 'Kevin and Trevor were outstanding players, the type of players you need in your team. Kevin was one of the best runners off the ball you could have, as well as his ability to stick the ball in the net. Trevor was a playmaking goalscorer. He could manipulate the ball and put players through. He was a box-to-box man. You miss those types of players.'

Real Madrid's cavernous Bernabéu Stadium played host to the matches, but so abject had the Spanish been in their group games that the Madrileños had long since ceased believing their team had any chance of winning the World Cup for the first time. England's injured two players were getting closer to selection, but they were not fit enough for the first game against West Germany, in which the European Champions put safety first. Karl-Heinz Rummenigge of Bayern Munich hit the crossbar late on, and Paul Mariner was marked by a beast of a man, Hans-Peter Briegel, who had swapped sports: 'He was a decathlete and a heptathlete who, unfortunately for me, then turned his sights on football. It was one of the most difficult nights I have ever had. He was not only quick but strong, but 0–0 wasn't the end of the world.'

Three days later, Spain were finally put out of their misery, a 2–1 defeat against the Germans ensuring they could go no further and spelling out for England, most advantageously, what they had to do to reach the semi-finals. A 2–0 win against a poor Spanish side with nothing but pride to play for would see England meet France once again in the last four. Now both Keegan and Brooking were, at long last, available. 'Steve Coppell got injured, and the day before the Spain game we had a training match,' Sir Trevor told me. 'Keegan came into the team and played through the middle with Marrers [Paul Mariner], and Trevor Francis moved out to the right wing to replace Coppell. The shadow team won 1–0, and I scored. Most of us went to bed the night before thinking that side would start against Spain – that Keegan would play.'

When the team was announced the next day, Francis was playing wide right but with Tony Woodcock up front alongside Mariner. Keegan was left on the bench, mortified. Don Howe told me he doesn't remember a big debate among the coaching staff as to whether Keegan should start. But did England get their tactics wrong? Were they too timid? Spain were out, even if they won 6–0, and Brooking feels England should have been more positive: 'The onus was on us. We were a little bit cautious the way we approached the game – be patient, 90 minutes to get the goals – but I think if we had gone for the jugular in the first 20 to 25 minutes and got a goal, Spain were there to collapse.' They were widely regarded as an exceptionally ordinary side who had managed just one win in four games during the tournament: a team who seemed cowed by home advantage and depressed by it, not energised.

The crowd were fired up in the Bernabéu that night, 5 July, but Terry Butcher thinks it wasn't the football that was the reason but politics and war: 'Spain made it tough for us, and the crowd were very hostile because of the Falklands conflict, which had ended on 14 June. They were chanting "*Malvinas, Malvinas*". It was a nasty crowd, and those Spanish were clearly supporting the Argentinians.'

The conflict in the South Atlantic had been on Butcher's mind since he arrived in Spain: 'The Falklands War being on was quite sobering for a lot of the players. It wasn't all hilarity, because there was a serious undertone with what was going on out there. Playing football matches in a tournament was nothing compared with what those boys were going through down there. There was a subplot, if you like, with the Falklands, which kept everybody really grounded.'

Keegan and Brooking watched from the bench as the game reached the break goalless. England were in need of them, not just individually but what they brought together as a combination, perhaps never better illustrated than by the one-two that resulted in Keegan scoring an outstanding goal against Scotland at Wembley in 1979. 'We were room-mates, and the physio Fred Street called it the untidiest room he had ever seen,' said Sir Trevor. 'Kevin was really untidy, and he blamed me whenever he saw my wife. We were two different types of character but got on really well on and off the field and had a great understanding. One of my strengths was to try to be a creative passer. Kevin was a relentless worker, a fidget from the moment he woke up, and he was like that on the pitch, always an option for me. He was strong and wiry. He knew if he made his runs he would get a pass from me, and I knew when I twisted and turned he would be offering himself up. Our relationship evolved with mutual respect for each other's ability.'

The cavalry was let onto the field with 25 minutes remaining. After 108 caps between them, Trevor Brooking and Kevin Keegan were finally playing in the World Cup. Keegan soon had a great headed chance but put it wide and sank to his knees in disappointment. Paul Mariner dragged him up off the ground: 'I remember saying clearly, "Wee man, never mind. Come on, we'll get another chance." He was always "wee man" to me, even though to everyone else he was the god of English football. On the field he was just my mate Kev, and I felt heartbroken for him.'

Mariner spoke passionately about everything Kevin Keegan had been through: 'People don't understand when you're injured and you're flying back to Germany to get treatment on your chronic back problem. And you're not training, and then you get out on the biggest stage in the world, the biggest game England's played for donkey's years, and the saviour comes on [and] everyone's asking, "Is he going to get the goal?" And he's presented with the opportunity, which for him, if he's playing regularly, goes into the back of the net for fun. And because your timing's not right and you're slightly off – and you only need to be off by a little bit – and he misses, you really feel for your mate.'

Terry Butcher crashed a left-footed shot just wide, and Brooking himself was denied by the Spanish keeper, Arconada. But the breakthrough would not come, and the game finished goalless. England were out of the World Cup. They were unbeaten, they had conceded just one goal but they were going home. 'It was devastating,' admitted Phil Thompson. 'I can remember trudging off after playing Spain. It was as low as I've ever been, because you knew you had done well enough to qualify. We were better than the other two teams. We should have been going through.' According to *The Times*, 'The last to leave the arena was Mariner, a red Spanish shirt draped over his naked shoulder like some soiled and unwanted garment.' The former Ipswich striker says, 'I was heartbroken at the end of the game. It was a really bitter pill to swallow at the hotel, and we couldn't wait to get out and get home the next day.'

FIFA changed the format of the World Cup after 1982, reverting to a straight knockout system after the group phase – not that that was any consolation to Mariner, Thompson and Brooking, for whom this was the one and only shot at the trophy. West Germany went on to beat France on penalties in a thrilling semi-final in Seville, the German triumph tainted by an outrageous, unpunished assault committed by the goalkeeper Harald Schumacher on Patrick Battiston. Schumacher's cowardice ensured that the neutrals wanted Italy to win the final, the Italians having beaten Poland thanks to a Rossi brace in the other semi-final in Barcelona.

Rossi was suddenly on a hot streak, and he opened the scoring in the final in Madrid. Further goals from Tardelli and Altobelli made it comfortable for the Italians and rendered Breitner's late goal a mere consolation. Italy's third World Cup triumph cut little ice with those frustrated England players, like Phil Thompson, watching back home: 'We had a fantastic opportunity, because nobody had an outstanding team that year. With a little bit of luck we could have won it. How daft is that? We came through the sort of qualifying we did, and yet in the finals we were just a couple of goals short of going through.'

They had played all but twenty-five minutes of the World Cup without two of their best players, and Bryan Robson was struggling towards the end, as well, with injury. The issue of Keegan's and Brooking's fitness was the backdrop to which this whole campaign was played out, and in the end their absence was just too much to overcome. 'It was destabilising, but at the same time, without them, it did galvanise us,' recalls Phil Thompson. 'People were questioning the team, saying without the pair of them we didn't have a chance. Players like Mariner, Woodcock, Francis thought, "Right, we'll show them." But when you're playing the top boys, that's when you need your top players, especially Kevin being the striker he was and Trevor with his creativity. I was in awe of Kevin. His energy, his will to win, was absolutely top-class, and you clung to his enthusiasm and his passion and his immense belief in his ability. When we needed that bit extra, that creativity, we missed them.'

Neither Brooking nor Keegan ever played for England again, and Ron Greenwood stepped down – to be replaced by Ipswich Town's Bobby Robson. Just as with Alf Ramsey, the question was: Could the manager of Ipswich Town bring his success from Portman Road to the international stage?

8

MEXICO 1986

In the manner of Sir Alf Ramsey before him, Bobby Robson had turned Ipswich Town from an unfashionable team in an unfashionable part of England into one of the pre-eminent forces in the country. A World Cup player himself, in Sweden in 1958, Robson's first foray into management ended when he was sacked by Fulham. The club didn't tell him; the headline on an *Evening Standard* placard outside Putney Bridge Tube station let him know in the most shocking manner. Robson arrived at Portman Road in 1969, and, relying on the club's youth programme, he gradually improved the team. In 1978 they deservedly won the FA Cup, against the head, as they were underdogs to the city slickers of Arsenal. It was the start of a golden four-year period. Ipswich won the 1981 UEFA Cup and were twice runners-up in the old First Division, the Dutchmen Thijssen and Mühren gilding the lily of British talent like Mariner, Wark, Brazil, Butcher, Cooper and Mills. Mariner is not alone from that Suffolk team in feeling they should have emulated Ramsey's team and won the League itself.

Ipswich chairman Patrick Cobbold offered Robson a ten-year deal to keep him out of the FA's clutches, but just two days after the 1982 World Cup he succeeded Ron Greenwood as England manager, taking a pay cut in the process – from £72,000 a year to £65,000. Robson immediately dropped Kevin Keegan for the opening Euro '84 qualifier against Denmark, and the same Geordie fans who were later to worship Robson hurled abuse and spat at him for having the temerity to omit their hero. It was a sign of what the next eight years would be like.

England drew 2–2 in Copenhagen but lost the return at home, and as the players were jeered off the field, a section of the crowd turned on the manager. The chances of reaching Euro '84 were disappearing fast. The tabloid press poured scorn on Robson, and he said, 'Even the Prime Minister does not get the pressure and criticism of an England manager. Some of the things written and said are completely out of order, but you just have to bite your tongue and take it.' *The Sun*, in particular, was vicious and handed out 'Robson Out – Clough In' badges as they tried to lever the Nottingham Forest manager into the hot seat, and, indeed, Robson offered to resign so that he could take over. But such was the FA's disdain for the outspoken Clough that Robson kept his job. Denmark duly qualified for the finals at England's expense, and the *News of the World* called Robson 'the most vilified Englishman since Lord Haw-Haw'.

So, when qualification started for the 1986 World Cup, Robson was under huge pressure to justify the FA's faith in him. Four wins and four draws saw England win their group relatively comfortably, although they were grateful to Northern Ireland for winning home and away against Romania, a team England twice failed to beat. The game in Bucharest in May 1985 signalled the end of the international career of one of Robson's boys from Portman Road, Paul Mariner: 'I remember my last kick as a national team player. Glenn Hoddle got to the byline, and I just made my run a little too early and the ball went the wrong side of the near post. I fell in a heap and saw the ball go just wide, looked up and saw my number was up. Gary Lineker came on to replace me, and I knew that day I wouldn't get to Mexico.

'Thirty-two was a tipping point for a striker, because you must remember in the old days you had defenders like Tommy Smith [of Liverpool] who went through you for fun. When you could tackle from behind, it was a licence to kill. They killed all right, and my Achilles tendons took too much stick. It was the end of me.' The final group game took place at Wembley between the two Home Nations, and an inspired display from Pat Jennings in the Northern Irish goal ensured a 0–0 draw that meant both qualified at the expense of Romania – who cried 'foul' and 'fix' without a scrap of evidence.

Colombia were supposed to host the 1986 World Cup – the Colombia of violence and drug dealers – but with the tournament a now enlarged 24-team extravaganza it became clear the country would struggle to afford it. In November 1982, the authorities admitted defeat, and the choice fell to one of Canada, the United States or Mexico. The US included Henry Kissinger in their delegation and lobbied FIFA at its World Cup Committee meeting in Stockholm in 1983, but they would have to wait until 1994 as Mexico were chosen to pick up the baton for the second time in 16 years.

England went on a tour of Mexico in 1985 with a team who, naturally enough, showed a few modifications from the previous World Cup. Gary Stevens of Everton was now at right-back; Terry Butcher was the linchpin at centre-half, with Terry Fenwick, Alvin Martin and Mark Wright all contending to be his partner. Chelsea's Kerry Dixon and Gary Lineker, whose goals had just earned him a move from Leicester to Everton, had both scored 24 times that season in the old First Division and were vying to be the team's natural predator. Mark Hateley was the target man, then with AC Milan, and there were two natural, skilful wingers: John Barnes, born in Jamaica but now part of Watford's rise up the football ladder, had slalomed his way through the Brazilian defence in the Maracanã in the summer of 1984, a weaving run and goal that became something of a millstone round his neck; and Chris Waddle, whose insouciant gait belied his speed and skill, was about to join Tottenham Hotspur from Newcastle United.

It was in midfield that Bobby Robson struggled to come up with the right formula. In the middle there was the captain, Bryan Robson, brave, tough, determined and a goalscorer; Ray Wilkins, who had moved to AC Milan but whose detractors maintained his passing was more sideways than forwards; and Glenn Hoddle. The enigmatic Tottenham midfielder was supremely gifted but suffered the misfortune of being born an Anglo-Saxon. Therefore, however good he was on the ball, he was expected to do his share of the midfield dirty work: tackle, track back, help out, dig in.

Hoddle made his England debut in the autumn of 1979 and scored with a sumptuous volley, but too often it seemed he was regarded as a luxury and not a necessity. Chris Waddle played with him for both club and country: 'He was Paul Scholes when it came to tackling, but his range of passing was second to none. I don't think even Glenn realised how many players in the squad respected him as a footballer. I used to see him do it in training at Spurs – outside of the foot, beautiful balance, volley left foot that way, right foot that way – and the other players would say, "Wow, I've never seen anyone train like that!"'

England flew to Mexico City in the summer of '85 under an enormous cloud, figuratively speaking. The spectre of football hooliganism hadn't gone away, and attendances had continued to fall. Crowds for the 1985–86 season were the lowest since 1922, with the aggregate of the top four divisions 16.5 million. Nine million watched First Division matches, a figure that was set to fall by over a million. In March there had been a massive riot at Kenilworth Road as Luton and Millwall fans clashed before, during and after an FA Cup tie. The Luton chairman, Tory MP David Evans, banned all away supporters from Kenilworth Road from the start of the following season and introduced a scheme that would require even home fans to carry membership cards to be admitted to matches. Margaret Thatcher's Conservative government set up a 'War Cabinet' to combat hooliganism, and the nadir of football trouble came in May as a decade of crowd disorder came to a horrible head. At the European Cup final in Brussels, 39 Juventus fans died after a group of Liverpool fans rioted. English clubs were immediately banned from European club competitions indefinitely.

Just over a week after the Heysel disaster in Brussels, England found themselves playing Italy in Mexico City. 'The Animals Are Coming' was the none-too-subtle headline in *El Sol*, Mexico's equivalent of *The Sun*. The Italian-based Mark Hateley scored in a 2–1 defeat. England then lost 1–0 to Mexico, which meant for the first time since 1959 they had lost three games in a row. The *Daily Mirror* ran a front-page headline that demanded, 'Robson must go!'

At a press conference in Mexico City, Robson showed that the barbs did pierce. Asked about the pressure he was under, he exposed just how thin-skinned he could be on occasions: 'Pressure? What pressure? You people provide the pressure. If you didn't exist, my job would be twice as easy and twice as pleasurable.' It was Robson's misfortune to be caught in the middle of a circulation battle between the two leading tabloids in the land, *The Sun* and the *Daily Mirror*, and his dignity was one of the casualties of their sales war.

A year later, England's pre-World Cup base was a military complex in Colorado, a very American-type set-up that boasted fabulous facilities and great attention to detail. Training was more pre-season than end of season as the players – and their lungs – were put through their paces at altitude, but the elephant in the room was the fitness of the captain. Bryan Robson had suffered shoulder problems during the season, and three months previously Bobby Robson had wanted him to have an operation to ensure he was fit for the tournament. Ron Atkinson, the Manchester United manager, instead kept playing him, hoping his shoulder would not dislocate.

Bryan Robson did get through the domestic season, but the shoulder popped out for the third time in a friendly in Los Angeles against Mexico, just two weeks before the World Cup started. Bobby Robson denied it had happened, later confessing that his declaration was 'a white lie'. The England doctor, Vernon Edwards, made it clear that taking the player was a big risk – that the shoulder could go at any moment. However, in his autobiography, Bryan Robson says, 'I fell on it, and there were obvious concerns in the camp, but the shoulder went back in and I came through a series of rigorous fitness tests.' He had no doubts over his fitness, whatever Dr Edwards's thoughts on the matter, and Bobby Robson was ready to gamble.

His coach, Don Howe, knew to what extent the captain was being patched up: 'Bryan had to have this strapping around his shoulder, and then it came down and was wrapped around again. You can't really find anything that is strong enough to play in a game, and if Bryan Robson couldn't play, nobody else could. You thought – this leather strapping that went round him – "I wonder how long that will last?"' Trussed up, Bryan Robson was declared fit for the first game against Portugal in Monterrey, on 3 June 1986.

If the World Cup is all about magnificent stadiums, huge crowds and a great atmosphere then this town provided the antithesis. Gary Lineker and Peter Reid had joined up with the squad a few days late after playing in the FA Cup final, and Lineker had repaid Everton's outlay on him by scoring 38 goals in 52 games. Monterrey, the desert town with its sandy pitch and crowd of under 20,000, wasn't what he had been sold in the World Cup brochure: 'I was full of anticipation and expectation. It was a little bit anticlimactic in the sense that the conditions were so awful. The pitch and the fact there was nobody in the stands seemed a bit weird for the biggest games you've ever played in, and the heat was unbelievable. It was over 40°C, and we had to play at midday and 4 p.m. because of the demands of TV. So when you walked out I remember thinking "Crikey, I just want to get through this," rather than being excited about the game.'

The squad had been training on pitches where the grass was cut short, and then, suddenly, in their opening game, they were faced with a longer, thicker surface that made running with the ball harder. Terry Butcher thought he had stumbled into some sort of private establishment: 'There were these little box hedges, these privet hedges around the pitch. There were grass banks, and it didn't look like a World Cup stadium at all, more like a gentlemen's club. It felt like someone's garden.'

Tottenham's Terry Fenwick played alongside Butcher at centre-half, and Bobby Robson tried to get a quart into a pint pot by including Bryan Robson, Wilkins and Hoddle in midfield – which meant the man who pulled Tottenham's strings from a central position had to play out wide on the right-hand side, to his disappointment. Hoddle has always sympathised with Liverpool's current captain when he has been forced to play out of position: 'I was frustrated, and I have always related to what Stevie Gerrard has to do for England, because it was happening to me all the time.'

Chris Waddle played wide left, which meant no place for John Barnes, and the Hateley–Lineker partnership up front was the typical English one of a target man alongside a quick, smaller goalscorer. From the bench, Peter Reid watched the two teams cancel each other out: 'Glenn being on the right-hand side just wasn't his best position. For me it was a question of square pegs in round holes. I just thought, tactically against Portugal we didn't get it right. Our game is all about squeezing, but you can only squeeze in certain areas when it's 100 °F, and I thought we weren't cute enough. Instead of dropping off, we tried to play too high up the pitch. The balance in midfield wasn't right, and Portugal played through us.'

The Portuguese had been on the verge of anarchy before the tournament, the players arguing with the board over sponsorship money and accusing them of not arranging proper friendlies. With 14 minutes remaining they would have regarded a goalless draw as an excellent result, but then Diamantino evaded Kenny Sansom to reach the byline and Carlos Manuel scored from the resulting cross. Sansom admitted to BBC Radio 5 Live, 'It was my weak tackle. I made a poor tackle, and Terry Butcher had to come across, and the fellow laid it across the six-yard box for a simple tap-in.' England had lost their opening game, a big setback that they acknowledged as they retreated to the hotel in Saltillo, which they were sharing with some of the press and broadcasters – so the players were very aware of the level of stick they were receiving back home.

Three days later, in the same ground, England could have crashed out of the World Cup, and had they done so they probably would have taken

Bobby Robson down with them. The day before playing Morocco, Dr Edwards stuck a thermometer in the ground and back came the same reading of 40 °C. England kept the same team, but just before half-time Bryan Robson ran into the box and a Moroccan pulled him back by his right shoulder, dislocating it again. Chris Waddle was amazed by his captain's reaction: 'Bryan was the hardest player I ever played with and against, and you knew anything could happen with him. When his shoulder popped out he was standing there saying, "It's a bit painful, this," and trying to get it to click back in. It was like Rambo! If that had been me, it would have been, "Stretcher, ambulance. I'm away." To him, it was like, "Let's try to get it back in."'

Robson was replaced by Aston Villa's Steve Hodge, but another massive setback hit the team five minutes before half-time when Ray Wilkins was sent off after getting a second yellow card, as he uncharacteristically threw the ball in the referee's direction in frustration. Like the millions watching, I couldn't believe it – calm, methodical Ray Wilkins getting the red card? As Chris Waddle says, 'You wouldn't think Ray Wilkins would get sent off in a million years, would you? And then you start looking at it and think, "Where are we going now?" It's not meant to be. Whatever you do, we can't get it right. People say you make your own luck, but you don't. We were cursed from day one.'

A more adventurous and confident team than Morocco would probably have condemned England to the most humiliating of exits, but the ten men saw the game out without conceding a goal, and now the team had to change through necessity. With Bryan Robson and Wilkins unavailable, and the players unhappy, Bobby Robson stripped the team down, paring it back to what was essential. Hoddle moved to the middle, from where his range of passing and creativity could be most effective, and Peter Reid came in to do a straightforward job: get the ball and give it to Hoddle – echoing Stiles and Bobby Charlton 20 years previously. Trevor Steven of Everton came in to play on the right-hand side, Steve Hodge on the left and Waddle dropped out as the manager went for a more formal 4–4–2 formation, with Mark Hateley replaced by Peter Beardsley up front. The Newcastle striker had made his England debut just six months earlier, but his ability to drop off Lineker and find space between the opposition's midfield and defence was priceless. The balance looked good on paper, but the acid test was yet to come.

Before the final group game against Poland, the squad went up into the hills to a monastery to have a barbecue and a few beers. Bobby Robson was being savaged in the press, and morale was low. 'There were lots of long and sad faces, and the atmosphere wasn't great,' Terry Butcher recalls. 'You thought the whole thing was coming crashing down round our ears. We were very down, we had been hit hard and we were a long way from home.'

Bobby Robson held a meeting with the players. Always a good talker, he had a flip chart with him. 'In this meeting,' Gary Lineker remembers, 'Bobby said, "We know what we need to do. There are all sorts of permutations and combinations, but as long as we beat Poland we are through to the next round. Get that into your mind; now go ahead and do it." And when he finished, we thought, "That's the shortest meeting ever."' But in typical Bobby Robson style, it wasn't over.

'Then he flipped the chart over, and there they all were, the permutations,' Terry Butcher smiled at the memory. 'He didn't mean to be funny, but the lads just burst out laughing. It was like a bookie's board: if this happens and this happens! "I'm not going to explain it all, lads," he said. "Just go out and win."'

All the players I spoke to about the 1986 World Cup emphasised how good Bobby Robson was at this time. Phrases like, 'very good at getting everyone together', 'confidence in those playing' and 'making tough decisions' kept cropping up. Robson may have dithered at the start of the tournament about his formation – with Hoddle wasted out wide – and taken a big gamble over Bryan Robson's fitness, but now he acted decisively. Bryan Robson and Wilkins stayed with the squad, which was good for team morale.

A win would take England through on goal difference, and how Gary Lineker needed a goal, both for himself and his country! He hadn't scored in the six previous internationals, and his record up till then was six goals in fifteen games, five of them in two matches. His lucky boots had not yet come good in Mexico: 'I had a pair at Christmas-time that I couldn't stop scoring in. I had about a goal-a-game record in them, and we [Everton] had to win the last three matches to win the title, and the boots were accidentally left at the training ground when we went to Oxford United. I had to borrow a pair, and I missed a couple of chances, hit the post, didn't score and we lost. These boots had holes in them everywhere, but I had them repaired before the World Cup.'

Peter Reid wasn't concerned about his teammate's barren run: 'Gary not scoring didn't faze him. Knowing Lineker as I did, he wasn't afraid to miss. He didn't worry about not scoring, and sooner or later a chance would come along.' The game was played in a different stadium in Monterrey – one with a roof, stands and proper terraces – and on the 45-minute drive to the ground the team anthem blared out: 'Alive and Kicking' by Simple Minds. Everyone was about to find out if they were.

By half-time, the worrying was over. The changes, forced upon them by injury and suspension, had indeed produced a better-balanced and more cohesive England side – who raced into a 3–0 lead. Lineker had scored a hat-trick by the 34th minute – first converting Stevens's cross and then Hodge's centre before profiting from a goalkeeping fumble after a corner. Things would never be the same again for Lineker: 'That game changed my life in all sorts of ways. Prior to that, I had gone half a dozen games without scoring, and the whole team was under pressure. I was fortunate that Bobby kept faith with me. I could have gone. He left Hateley out and brought in Beardsley, and we immediately struck up a partnership. The hat-trick gave me worldwide fame. I went on to win the Golden Boot, off the back of my success I got a move to Barcelona and those goals had a drastic effect not just on my professional life but life in general.'

The England fans celebrated by doing a conga round the ground, and Chris Waddle came on with fourteen minutes to go, bearing gifts on a boiling-hot day: 'Bobby must have given me about forty-six bags of water – I think three of them had goldfish in them! I have never carried so much water. And I saw it later on telly, and I'm running on as if I'm holding a baby. Loads of the bags fell out of my arms and burst!' The Polish star of the day was Zbigniew Boniek, part of the side who had come third in Spain four years earlier and by now at Juventus, where he had won the European Cup. He was desperate for a goal against England and so jokingly sought the help of the man marking him: Terry Butcher. He should have known better. 'Boniek said to me in the second half, "Please give me one goal; you win 3–1." He was having a laugh, but all I said was, "Why don't you just fuck off!"'

England had been given a second life; a defeat and a draw in the first two games would normally mean the end, but they were fortunate their group was so tight. They moved to Mexico City for the knockout stages, but in a World Cup of setbacks Terry Butcher remembers another mishap that occurred when they checked into their hotel: 'The first one was right on a crossroads; it was like the M25 on a bad day. The noise was awful, and the boys didn't like the beds. It was horrific. We were there 24 hours and then went to the Holiday Inn by the airport. Italy were staying there, but the hotel was so big they could accommodate both squads. It was really humbling walking past the Italians – who were World Champions remember – and they looked so immaculate. When you looked into their rooms they had wine in there.'

The Italians went out in the second round, beaten by France 2–0, but neither Scotland nor Northern Ireland made it that far. Shorn of Kenny Dalglish, Scotland managed just one goal in three games and just one point after a scoreless draw with an out-of-control Uruguay – and Northern Ireland were unable to repeat their heroics of four years earlier. Billy Bingham's side also came home with a solitary point after a 1–1 draw with Algeria.

Paraguay were England's second-round opponents at the famous Azteca Stadium – a fabulous arena, even if the pitch was terrible – and with the setting, the crowds and the altitude, England felt like they had arrived at the centre of the World Cup. Alvin Martin came in for Terry Fenwick at centre-half. As the team ran out at the Azteca they couldn't miss a huge sculpture that hung above the pitch and threw a spiky shadow over the halfway line and, footballers essentially being overgrown schoolboys, they tried to hit it with the ball in the warm-up.

In front of just under 99,000 – over four times the size of the crowds in Monterrey – Gary Lineker's sudden scoring streak continued with two goals and Peter Beardsley got the third, but not before Terry Butcher had caused his defence to have kittens with a sloppy back pass at 0–0: 'I made a suicidal back pass, but Shilts [Peter Shilton] blocked it well. That stimulated us well. Gary got smashed all over the place by the Paraguayans, but he was so hot. We were saying, "Just get the ball to Gary and he'll score." I had an assist, a right-foot shot that the keeper saved and Beardsley scored. The pitch was wet and spongy, and whenever you took a divot they replaced it with footprint-sized divots so that the pitch looked like footprints on the moon.' Lineker had to endure some very physical provocation from the Paraguayan defenders, at one time being hit across the throat, but answered the bully boys in the best fashion: with goals.

He now had five in two games and was enjoying playing with Beardsley, the Newcastle striker's mobility, intelligence and unselfishness helping to create space for Lineker: 'Two small men went against everything British football had stood for – big man and little man – but the fact was that he dropped deep and left the penalty area to me, which was my strength. I used to hate [having] lots of my teammates in the area, because they would always get in the way and not know where they were going, but because Beardsley did all his work outside the area, it left it as a free zone for me.' Just as Beardsley brought out the best in Lineker, so Peter Reid helped Glenn Hoddle. 'Peter Reid was a holding player ahead of his time,' said Lineker. 'He was a Claude Makélélé type, if you like, and that released Glenn a little bit from the burden of having to track back. This was more natural, and the set-up released Glenn as much as any time in his international career.'

After struggling through the group, England were now flying and stayed in Mexico City to face Argentina in the quarter-finals. But just two years after his wonder goal against Brazil, John Barnes had yet to play any part in the World Cup. Chris Waddle feels the nature of that goal, and the system Bobby Robson employed, made it hard for the two wingers: 'To follow that for John was very difficult, because every time he picked the ball up and ran with it everybody thought he was going to do it again. That, though, was a one-off. We found it hard to play 4–4–2 with England, because we were supposed to help the full-back at one end and then head in each other's crosses at the other. Physically, it was impossible, but at times I don't think Bobby Robson could see that. We put a shift in at altitude. When he joined Liverpool, John wasn't expected to help out his full-back, and I wasn't expected to be on top of mine at Spurs, but with England I always felt I had Gary Stevens wanting me to help him out.'

England against Argentina in Mexico City was always likely to be a flammable affair just four years after the Falklands conflict and with the older Argentinian supporters still nursing grievances dating back to Alf Ramsey's infamous 'animals' remark in 1966. Centre-half José Luis Brown said in Brian Glanville's book *The Story of the World Cup*, 'We all had cousins, fathers, nephews in the Falklands and some of them didn't come back. Lamentable things, but we shan't be thinking of them.' Peter Reid described England's renaissance: 'The phoenix rising up from the ashes. The change of atmosphere in the camp was quite incredible. The Argentina game was hyped up out of all proportion. The atmosphere was quite unbelievable. I've played in big games in club football, but I can't tell you what the atmosphere was like that day. We were the enemy, without a doubt.'

And standing in their way that day was Maradona, the man who would become synonymous with this World Cup for the best, and worst, of reasons. This was Maradona at his peak, a player with an astonishing left foot, strength, speed, supreme balance, control and passing. After Argentina eased through their group, the Napoli star had been central to the second-round win over Uruguay, and how to contain him was number one on Bobby Robson's list of priorities. 'I've got 24 hours to devise a way to stop Maradona,' he declared at a news conference. 'Other teams have already tried everything. Let's just say that without Maradona Argentina would have no chance of winning the World Cup. That's how great he is.'

Argentina were not just skilful. Peter Reid knew they were savvy and streetwise as well: 'They weren't just technical. It's easy to forget how physically strong they were, and tactically they were cute. They man-marked some players and let others have it. We all knew about Maradona, of course, and I had seen him play for Barcelona at Manchester United in a Cup Winners' Cup tie. It was a question of staying on your feet and working him onto his right-hand side more than anything else.'

Gary Lineker didn't just have Argentina and their rugged defenders to think about. His scoring spree had reawakened interest in him from the team Peter Reid had seen at Old Trafford that night: 'Before the tournament, [Everton manager] Howard Kendall called me in and said they had an offer from Barcelona, which they were interested in. That surprised me a bit, considering how many goals I had scored, and I thought Everton might endeavour to keep me.

'Then it went quiet during the World Cup – very quiet after two games! – but after the hat-trick the interest was rekindled and my agent called me. I had discussed with him beforehand that I didn't want any talk of transfers during the World Cup – I didn't want to be distracted – but he called me after the Poland game and said he was being put under pressure by Barcelona, that if we wanted to do the move we had to say so now [or] otherwise forget the whole thing. I said I wanted to concentrate on the World Cup and if it goes away, it goes away. I said if they wanted me now, they'll want me at the end of it, and that's how we left it. It was quickly wrapped up after the tournament had finished.'

Lineker was not only scoring goals; he was showing his adeptness at poker as well: 'Ultimately, if I had had to stay at Everton that would have been fine. They were certainly the best team I had played for, and in an ideal world I wouldn't have minded an extra couple of years there anyway. But obviously Barcelona is Barcelona, one of the great clubs of the world. It was a bit of poker, but it wasn't like I didn't have a good hand anyway.'

Perversely, for such a massive match, FIFA entrusted the officiating to a little-known referee from Tunisia: Ali Bin Nasser. Terry Fenwick came back in for Alvin Martin, and in front of a gigantic crowd of just under 115,000 the first half was relatively quiet. The team were unanimous that the best way to deal with Maradona was not to man-mark him but to ask the player nearest to him to deal with the danger whenever he picked the ball up. Beardsley shooting into the side netting was the nearest England came in the first 45 minutes.

Five minutes into the second half, Maradona dribbled towards the England penalty area and passed to Jorge Valdano. The striker couldn't bring the ball under control, and Steve Hodge hooked it up into the air and backwards to his own goal. Maradona continued his run, and as Peter Shilton came to claim the ball, the Argentinian captain jumped with him and pushed the ball into the net with his hand. Ali Bin Nasser gave the goal, and the linesman, a Bulgarian called Bogdan Dotchev, gave no indication that any infringement had been committed.

The reactions of the England players depended simply on who had seen what. Glenn Hoddle saw it clearly: 'Still to this day, I can remember my gut feeling, chasing the referee. What those officials were doing at a World Cup quarter-final, I just don't know. Psychologically, that's the worst game of football that's played on my mind. I had to come back to England and go on holiday straight away. I just couldn't deal with it; it was literally giving me sleepless nights. I just couldn't deal with the injustice of it all. I was due to wait two weeks before going on holiday with the family to Spain, but in the end we just had to get out of the country, so we went somewhere else for a week before going to Spain. It was very difficult to overcome that.'

Gary Lineker knew from Peter Shilton's reaction that it was definitely handball, and Lineker sensed Dotchev's flag twitch – but, crucially, he did not raise it. Over 20 years later, the linesman tried to absolve himself of any blame:

A European referee would never recognise the validity of such a goal. European refs take charge of at least one or two important games per month and are used to big-match pressure. What is there for Bin Nasser to referee in the desert where there is nothing but camels?

He sounds like a charming man, doesn't he?

Dotchev then seemingly tried to hide behind the regulations he claimed were in existence in 1986: 'With the ref having said the goal was valid, I couldn't have waved my flag and told him the goal wasn't good – the rules were different back then.' Keith Hackett was, until recently, the general manager of the referees' governing body and was an international referee at the time. He said that Dotchev would have been well within his rights to alert the referee to Maradona's handball.

Terry Butcher had been keeping his eye on Valdano, Real Madrid's tall and elegant striker at the apex of Argentina's forward line, and so didn't see Maradona's indiscretion: 'It was only when Hoddle and Fenwick rushed past me saying, "Handball, handball," that I followed suit – but without any real conviction, because I didn't see him handle it. Some of us did and some didn't. The ones that had seen it were very angry, the ones that hadn't, well, we didn't know. If we had all seen it as blatant handball, then we would have all been really fired up, but because he did it so well it lifted them more than us.'

Down on the England bench, Don Howe remembers virtually everybody shouting in unison: '"Handball, handball!" Then you wanted to see the slow-motion replay. We were asking, "Did he reach up with his hand or what?"'

Chris Waddle was among the subs watching England's players pursue the hapless referee: 'To be fair to Maradona, he did it really well. Everyone says to me, "He's this and he's that. He's a cheat." Yes, of course he's a cheat, but I have to say if Gary Lineker had done it at the other end I would have been up clapping and saying, "That's clever isn't it?" How Maradona disguised that was fantastic. For all that it was breaking the rules and whatever, you've got to say it was very, very clever how he did it. If Gary had done the same, I wouldn't have been saying anything.'

An unrepentant Maradona later claimed it was the 'Hand of God' that had scored, and it wasn't until August 2005 that he admitted he had punched the ball in. Bobby Robson was not impressed by Maradona's claim of divine intervention: 'It wasn't the Hand of God. It was the hand of a rascal. God had nothing to do with it. That day, Maradona was diminished in my eyes forever.'

If the first goal was the hand of a cheat, of an urchin, the second was simply brilliant and came from the foot of a genius. 'Maradona turns like a little eel and comes away from trouble,' was how Bryon Butler on Radio 2 described the start of the Argentinian's coruscating run from inside his own half. England lost the ball, and Peter Reid tried to close Maradona down: 'I went to try to shut him down, and he turned me, and he's gone, and I'm trying to get back. I still have recurring nightmares about it. I didn't get near him, to tell the truth. His ability to run with the ball at pace was incredible, and it wasn't a great surface.'

Now midway inside England territory, halfway between the centre spot and right-hand touchline, Maradona came up against England's number six, Terry Butcher. He, too, still wrestles with the memory: 'I still have nightmares about the second goal, even today. It was a great piece of skill. I showed him inside to Reidy, but his tank was empty.'

Reid was trying to get back, still confident Maradona would be stopped: 'I did think someone would get him. As I'm chasing him, I know he's still got to get past our back four and someone's bound to hold him up and I'll get a tackle in on him. When you're in that heat, in those conditions, his strength, pace and ball control were unbelievable.'

Just outside the penalty area on the right-hand side, Maradona was now faced by Terry Fenwick, who, crucially, had been shown a yellow card earlier in the game. Peter Reid insists that made a big difference: 'Terry had already been booked, and if he had been Italian he would have blocked Maradona off, but then he would have been shown another yellow card and sent off.' Maradona, running at full tilt with the ball stuck to his left foot, eased past Fenwick into the penalty area. Gary Stevens rushed across from right-back to try to cover, and Terry Butcher was charging back trying to catch Maradona. Peter Shilton came out to narrow the angle, Maradona went past him on the right and Butcher was now in a position to put in a challenge. He tried but failed: 'I tell people he beat me twice. Everyone says it was an own goal, and I would love to claim it. But, no, I didn't get the final touch. His body was in the way. I couldn't see the ball, and I just lunged to try to block it. If I had done, I would probably have got a move to Italy as a brilliant defender. I was just inches away from stopping one of the greatest goals ever in the World Cup. I could have been a million miles away, but it still hurts one hell of a lot, because I almost stopped it. You can see me banging my hands on my shins after he's scored.'

Watching helplessly from the halfway line was Gary Lineker: 'It was the one time in football, especially considering the importance of the game, that I was tempted to applaud. It was unbelievable what Maradona did, especially considering how bad the surface was. It was just loads of pieces of turf stuck together, and every time you put your foot down the whole thing moved. How he scored that goal defied belief. He was just a genius.'

Down on the subs bench, John Barnes and Chris Waddle appreciated what they had just seen: 'As Maradona scored, John and I looked at each other as if to say "Wow!" and the stadium just went up. Ray Wilkins walked down the dugout and said to us, "I'm telling you, you'll never see a better goal than that live." There was just this buzz around the stadium for about 15 minutes, and you get that at football matches after great goals. You could hear people talking about the goal for minutes afterwards.'

First Waddle and then Barnes were thrown on, as England tried to claw their way back into the game, and with ten minutes remaining Barnes beat Giusti on the left flank and crossed for Lineker to head in his sixth goal of the tournament. Suddenly the impetus of the game changed, and even though Tapia hit a post, Argentina were hanging on. With three minutes left, Barnes centred again and Lineker, at the far post, was poised to take the game into extra time. 'I've worked out now how it happened,' he said. 'I saw the cross all the way. I knew I was going to score. I headed it, and from somewhere their little left-back dived up from below me and it hit the back of his head as it was going in.'

It was England's last chance, and as the players came off the field Steve Hodge ran after Maradona, wanting his shirt. Kenny Sansom was confused: 'We said, "Why do you want that cheat's shirt?" But it's now worth about £250,000, so I wish I had got it!' Back in the dressing room, some of the players asked the FA officials present to demand the game be replayed because of Maradona's handball, and when some of the Argentinian players wanted to change shirts, Ray Wilkins gave them short shrift. Sansom, Gary Stevens and Terry Butcher were selected for doping, and Maradona was among the Argentinians picked out. It was Butcher's chance to find out the truth: 'I gestured to him *Was it hand or head?*, and he tapped his head. I didn't say anything, because I didn't then know for sure that he had definitely handled it. If I had seen it clearly I would have been right at him in the doping area. It's one of the most blatant forms of cheating ever, and the goal should never have stood.'

After a game played in the midday heat, the drug-testing procedure inevitably took some time for Butcher and his teammates to complete: 'We had to drink lots of water, and it's hard when you've just lost a World Cup quarter-final in that way. A noon kick-off at altitude in the searing heat of Mexico City: how bizarre is that? You're spent, and the last thing you can do is have a pee.'

In November 2008, Diego Maradona's first game as Argentinian coach was at Hampden against Scotland, whose assistant manager was the same Terry Butcher. He refused to shake Maradona's hand: 'I will never forgive him. It was cheating, the act of a cheat, and I can't accept that. All that "Hand of God" bollocks.'

At a press conference, when the media pressed him on Butcher's stance, Maradona sniffily and provocatively asked, 'Who is Butcher?' That, in turn, riled Kenny Sansom: 'Maradona had wonderful balance, [a] low centre of gravity and great acceleration. I have forgiven him. It doesn't matter now. It's gone, but when he was up at Hampden and said "Who's Butcher?" that gave me the hump.'

Maradona scored twice more, marvellously, in the semi-final against Belgium – the first with the outside of his left foot and the second after another mesmeric run past four defenders. As Glenn Hoddle left the country to forget about the trauma of the quarter-final, Chris Waddle settled down with friends to watch Argentina play West Germany: 'I watched the final in a social club in Gateshead with a few mates and a few beers. They were all praying Argentina got beaten because of what had happened, but I wanted them to win. I said it would be good for football if Maradona wins it, because he deserves it. He was the best player in the world. Why did he need a right foot when he had a left foot like that?'

Maradona didn't score in the final. Nonetheless, he played a pivotal role, his sweet pass with seven minutes remaining releasing Burruchaga to slide in the winner against a West German side who had valiantly fought back from two goals behind. If England had been unlucky in Mexico City, there was more heartbreak to come in Turin four years down the line.

9

ITALY 1990

Between the end of the 1986 World Cup and the start of the European Championship in West Germany two years later, England lost just two of the seventeen matches they played. There was an experienced, hard spine to the team: Shilton in goal, Butcher at centre-back, Bryan Robson in midfield, Lineker up front, and Barnes and Waddle on the wings. Others emerged organically – like Arsenal's young tyro of a centre-half, Tony Adams, appointed club captain at the age of twenty-one, who made his international debut in Madrid in February 1987 and became one of many victims of Bobby Robson's famous ability to mix up players' names: 'I remember the snow the night before the game. I thought it was going to be [called] off. Bobby Robson called me into his bedroom and said, "Sit down, Paul," and I thought, "This is a good start." Paul Adams was an apprentice at Ipswich. "Good luck, Paul," he said. I didn't put him right! He called Luther Blissett "Bluther"!'

Gary Lineker scored all four goals in the 4–2 win that night, and after qualifying comfortably for Euro '88 Bobby Robson thought England had a good chance – but the tournament turned into a complete nightmare. Terry Butcher was missing with a broken leg, Chris Waddle was recovering from a double hernia operation and Gary Lineker had been suffering from hepatitis. He missed a couple of chances in the opening game: a shock 1–0 defeat against the Republic of Ireland in Stuttgart.

Marco van Basten then destroyed Adams in grabbing a hat-trick as the Dutch won 3–1 in Düsseldorf, and although the young Arsenal player scored in the subsequent 3–1 loss against the Soviet Union, he learnt about the unforgiving side of the England fan: 'Glenn Hoddle took a great free kick, and I banged this header in, a great header, and ran to the

159

fans. They gave me the finger. They booed. It was a disastrous tournament. I had a Fiat Uno, which I had won as Young Player of the Year, and when we flew back into London there were three or four coach-loads of supporters there. And they chased me through the airport, and I had to leg it. I just bombed off in my car.'

As Tony Adams fled irate fans, Glenn Hoddle was leaving behind his international career. The most gifted Englishman of his generation had won 53 caps since his debut in 1979, but, at the age of 30, he would never be chosen again. He was playing in France with Monaco, by then under Arsene Wenger: 'His control was superb, and he had perfect body balance. His skill in both feet was uncanny . . . I couldn't understand why he hadn't been appreciated in England. Perhaps he was a star in the wrong period, years ahead of his time.'

Chris Waddle also moved to France, to Marseille, a year later, in July 1989, and says Hoddle's moderate England record was not his fault: 'Yes, Glenn Hoddle underachieved at international level because of the system England played. All flair players have. Gazza shone in 1990 – but he was a box-to-box player who played in the English system very well – but flair players like me, John Barnes, Alan Hudson, Tony Currie, Frank Worthington: we couldn't really get on because of the way we played. We suffered, and Glenn definitely suffered, because he was a central midfield player and so the onus on him was to do his shift. He wasn't frightened to say his piece and always believed in his ability. People like Peter Reid in Mexico were happy to do his running.

'If he was Italian or French, Glenn would have won 100 caps. Glenn was like Dan Marino at the Miami Dolphins, and I was the wide receiver; I made the run, and he just hit it. Now the way the game's changed you could use Gary Lineker up front on his own and Glenn in the hole, like we did at Tottenham with Clive Allen up front. We told Glenn to go play. Like Bergkamp did for Arsenal; just go and play.'

Hoddle was history and so, very nearly, was Bobby Robson as well. Sandro Mazzola, the former Inter Milan striker, remarked: 'This is incredible. What future can England have now? If they go on with Bobby Robson, it means that they won't win anything.' *The Sun* yelled, 'Plonker!', and even in the House of Commons they asked questions. Robson later admitted to *FourFourTwo* magazine that this was the worst time of his whole reign:

I went to Bert Millichip, who was the FA's chairman and a wonderful man, and said, 'I'll walk.' Bert said, 'Why would you want to do that?' I replied that we'd played poorly, the press were on my back and it might be best if I go. 'If you can stick it, so can we,' he said, so I stayed and that was that.

Robson's decision to carry on ensured he would remain the focus of enormous media scrutiny. England began qualification for Italia '90 with a goalless draw against Sweden at Wembley before flying to Saudi Arabia for a friendly in Riyadh. The game finished 1–1, prompting the *Daily Mirror*, who had begged earlier during his reign 'For God's Sake, Go!', to make a virtue of where England were playing by imploring 'Go, In The Name Of Allah, Go!', while *The Sun* joined in by yelling 'England Mustafa New Boss'. England had won just one of their last six games, and when the *Daily Mirror*'s Nigel Clarke landed in Athens for the friendly with Greece, he claimed, 'I am here to fry Bobby Robson' – an ambition that he might have succeeded in when England were 1–0 down.

England came back to win, and in the penultimate World Cup qualifier, away to Sweden in Stockholm, a player who had grown up with Robson at Portman Road provided one of the most iconic images of the age. Early in the game, Terry Butcher went up for a ball: 'I was ready to melt this header back 30 to 40 yards, really give it everything, and the guy just stuck his head up and flicked it on. I smashed the back of his head. It was a real sickener, and I knew I had done real damage. When you put your palm over your head and you take your hand away and the whole of your palm is covered in blood, you think, "Oh-ah. This is a good one." I never touched the ball.' Butcher had a huge V-shaped cut in his head.

The physios, Fred Street and Norman Medhurst, bandaged Butcher's head up, and at half-time the England team doctor, Dr Crane, inserted between seven and nine stitches in the gaping wound. When the bell sounded for the second half, there was an inch-long cut still open. There was never any suggestion Butcher was going to be replaced: 'It didn't hurt at all when I headed it. It just squelched. I could feel it was starting to coagulate and get sticky. Everybody's jersey had a bit of my blood on it. If that happened now, everybody would have to go and get a new kit.'

England held on for a goalless draw, and the photographs of a bloodied Butcher, his bandages completely soaked in blood and his shirt smeared with it, were flashed around the world. After England beat Denmark in Japan at the 2002 World Cup, I was having a drink with Terry in Niigata when several England fans came in. They saw him, dashed into the gents and reappeared minutes later with loo paper tied round their heads: an homage to Stockholm with which he has no problem. 'I still get sent loads of stuff up in Inverness to sign. [At my] first game at Caley Thistle, lots of fans wore bandages with red on it. I find it quite flattering. When I got back to Rangers on that Friday, though, manager Graeme Souness didn't say, "Well done," or anything like that. He just said, "I saw you on TV. Don't even think you're not playing on Saturday." I felt very dizzy and faint and went to sleep that afternoon right the way through to Saturday morning and then played as we beat Aberdeen 1–0.'

The result in Stockholm meant England needed just a draw in Poland to qualify, but they very nearly didn't make it. Peter Shilton had a fine evening in goal, but even he could do nothing about Tarasiewicz's long shot in the last minute, which smashed into the crossbar. With a lucky goalless draw, England just about slipped through the door to Italy before it slammed firmly shut.

By the time the World Cup came around, Bobby Robson already had a new job lined up. Lurid details about his allegedly hectic private life had contributed to the FA announcing that they would not extend his contract, and, wanting to safeguard his future, Robson agreed to take over at PSV Eindhoven in Holland later in the summer. Some labelled him a deserter, and one tabloid columnist said, 'He should be sent to the gallows for treason': a ludicrous overreaction, as Robson was about to become unemployed and had every right to seek a new post.

The X-factor in his last England squad was provided by the inclusion of the hugely promising, and highly strung, young Newcastle midfielder Paul Gascoigne. Exiled out to the left wing when he played for the England B team, Gascoigne booked his place in the World Cup party with a fabulous performance for the senior side against Czechoslovakia in April. Robson, his fellow Geordie, heaped the pressure on by implying this was his last chance, and Gascoigne responded by scoring one and having a hand in two others in a 4–2 win. Czech coach Josef Venglos praised him in a roundabout way: 'Gascoigne does not look like an English footballer.'

Despite his heroics in Stockholm, Terry Butcher was not sure of his place in the starting 11 with the emergence of Nottingham Forest's Des

Walker and Mark Wright of Derby County. Even though he had led Arsenal to the title just a year earlier, Tony Adams was left out. Playing in the final warm-up game in Tunisia, Butcher, on the eve of his third World Cup, lost it: 'I didn't play well. I head-butted their centre-half, and when I was subbed I got to the end of the very long bench – with the gaffer at the other end – and threw my shirt down in disgust. The headlines the next day said I threw my shirt at the England manager, which I would never do. I didn't think I was fit to wear it. When we got to our base in Sardinia we saw a clip of my headbutt, and Bobby berated me in front of the whole squad. He had been defending me. "I put my neck on the line for you," he said, "and you're as guilty as anything. Look what you've done!"'

England were scheduled to play all their group games in Cagliari, because the Italian government felt it would be easier to control the hooligan element on a small island like Sardinia. English clubs were still banned from Europe, and the Conservative government hadn't yet made up their minds as to whether to give their blessing for a return. Relations between the England squad and the media were not good, either. Bobby Robson was clearly unhappy about the intrusion into his private life, even if the sports journalists were largely not to blame. That kind of story was the domain of the news reporters.

For the players the run-in to the first game, a repeat of their Euro '88 opener with the Republic of Ireland, dragged by. They trained, they ate, they slept and they rested. Terry Butcher grew a beard out of boredom, and about three days before the Irish game he formed an escape committee: 'About ten of us went, including Chris Woods, Gazza and Waddler. After the team meal, we went out in formation past the restaurant, down to where the cars were waiting and into the local town. We had a couple of beers, bit of a sing-song, bit of karaoke, some of the lads were arm-wrestling with the locals and we got back about one or two in the morning – everyone putting their fingers to their lips, trying to be as quiet as possible.' Their rooms were on the ground floor, and the committee went to sleep feeling pleased that a successful mission had incurred no casualties.

At eight o'clock the next morning, the players were woken by an insistent knock on the door. Bobby Robson wanted a team meeting. Butcher thought someone had squealed: 'When we got there, Bobby

Robson went absolutely apoplectic. He shouted, "It's three days before the World Cup opener, you're representing your country and your captain's about to be sent home with an injury." I said Bryan [Robson] was with us the night before and he was fine. What happened was that Bryan had gone to Gazza's room – and Gazza was in bed – and he wanted to get him up, because he [Gazza] had got us up the past few weeks. So Bryan lifted the bed up, and because it was a tiled floor, the other side of the bed slid towards him. He was wearing flip-flops, and the edge of the bed ripped off his toenail – pinged it off – and there was blood everywhere. Gazza reacts quickly, gets Bryan into the bathroom and puts his foot in the bidet and turns on the hot water. That makes it even worse! At that stage they had to call the England doctor, who reports it to the manager. Bobby was shouting at us, "You're a disgrace. I know who you are, but I want you to come to me and have the decency to admit you've let your country down.'"

Butcher went along to the manager's room to take his medicine: 'When I opened his door, he looked at me and said, "I knew it would be you, Butcher. It's always you. You're a disgrace. You did this to me every preseason at Ipswich. You think more of alcohol than you do your football." By now my beard was really big, and I had my head down, really apologising, but behind Bobby were Gazza and Chrissie Waddle, who had come in earlier, and he made them stand there. Gazza is pulling these faces, and I start laughing, and now Bobby is going berserk saying, "It's no laughing matter. I should send you home on a plane right now. You're a disgrace to your country, to your family and to me." The more Gazza made faces, the more I laughed, and Bobby then said, "That's it. That's enough. I've had it. One last thing, Butcher . . ." – and I really thought "I'm going to get sent home now" – and Bobby looks at me and says, "Butcher, you're fucking ugly!" And Gazza and Chrissie are on the floor laughing now, and Bobby realised what was going on and chased us out of his room!'

The next thing Chris Waddle saw was Butcher chasing Gascoigne round the swimming pool, trying to beat him up. 'We had so many laughs, and that's very important,' said Waddle. 'Don't get me wrong, Gazza got on everyone's nerves – in a nice way. Six a.m. every morning he would ram the doors open, run across the grass to the swimming pool, do forty lengths, then have fruit for breakfast, because he was so obsessed about his fitness at the time. The amount of times Terry wanted to kill him! Gary

Lineker was starting to turn to the media, and he kept interviewing me and Gazza, and we basically did comedy sketches. We called him 'Junior Des'. We kept taking the Michael.' As Gary Lineker told me, 'I figured if I could learn to interview those two, who never took anything seriously, then I could cope with anyone.'

England went one better against the Irish in Cagliari than they had in Stuttgart and came away with a draw from a dire game played on a slippery pitch. Bryan Robson had an injection in his toe to kill the pain and played, and even though Gary Lineker scrambled home the opener, a mistake from sub Steve McMahon allowed Kevin Sheedy to drill in the equaliser.

'No Football Please, We're British,' ran the pithy and accurate headline in one Italian newspaper. *The Sun* wearily led with 'Send them home'. It was as if they couldn't sum up the effort to endure another disheartening championship. Next up for England were the reigning European Champions, Holland, although, in truth, the 1990 version was nothing like the vibrant, attractive side who had won in West Germany two years earlier. The Dutch camp was not a happy one: Ruud Gullit was struggling with a knee injury, and Marco van Basten was listless.

What happened on the training grounds of Sardinia between the Irish and Dutch games has been the subject of much conjecture in the past two decades. England had played 4–4–2 against the Irish, the formation Bobby Robson always favoured. As Chris Waddle said, 'It was fine against Ireland, in what was the worst game ever. No disrespect to them, but it was their Cup final. We were badgering Bobby to change the shape for the Holland game, and we sent a deputation to him via the captain, Bryan Robson. He was pushing for it. One day we went training and Bobby set up a little practice game and we did 3–5–2.'

Bobby Robson had never wanted to play with a sweeper, feeling it was a system that was foreign – in more ways than one – to English players, but he always denied it was pressure from his own players that made him change: 'I made the switch, not them. I had no intention of allowing van Basten and Gullit to rip holes in us.'

Don Howe was now at his third World Cup as England coach: 'We had one session with a sweeper, and it wasn't wonderful. I didn't think he would do it in the end, but he did. He had a mentor somewhere he talked to, and I have a feeling that someone chatted to him about the effects it would have on the general run of the team and Bobby said, "We're going to play with a sweeper." It was his own decision.' As Gary Lineker said, 'Top managers will listen to their players, but ultimately it's their decision.'

So England went in with a sweeper, Mark Wright, and Paul Parker of Queens Park Rangers replaced Everton's Gary Stevens to make a back five of Parker, Wright, Walker, Butcher and Pearce. Des Walker had been in the team for just under two years, his lightning speed the perfect foil and cover for the yeoman centre-half that was Butcher.

'No one can really know how big an event the World Cup is until you get there,' said Walker. 'The pressure steadily built, and I never realised how much [pressure] I was under until I got in my car and drove back up the M1 afterwards and I got that sense of relief!' Walker felt playing with a sweeper made perfect sense: 'Holland made the pitch very, very big, so if you stay rigid it's very difficult to stop them passing the ball around. With Paul Parker and I, we were very versatile and we could mark out wide or in the centre. Barnes and Waddle wanted the flexibility not to stay out wide, and with this system we had that flexibility and mobility.'

Barnes was playing in support of Lineker with Waddle, Robson and Gascoigne the midfield three, and England thrived on their new system, playing wonderfully well. Gascoigne was a revelation, at one stage executing a classic Cruyff turn that neatly took him away from his Dutch marker. As Chris Waddle remembers, at this stage of his career, his room-mate Gascoigne was no respecter of anyone's reputation: 'You would say, "You're going to play against Rijkaard." And he would say, "Who? Who's he?" He didn't care who he was playing against, and it wasn't an act. He would say, "I'll introduce them to Paul Gascoigne." And Gazza was a hard tackler; he could get stuck in. He was capable of anything, because he had no fear. He didn't care if he lost the ball 100 times; he would have it 101. I don't think you could coach him. If you were working on a system, you might as well leave him out and tell him to go and play keepie uppies. When he got to the World Cup, he thought, "Wow, this is unbelievable." He was like the kid in the sweetshop.'

The game finished goalless, which was the very least England deserved after Stuart Pearce had thundered in a last-minute free kick only for the referee to insist the kick was indirect. The only real downer was that for the second successive World Cup Bryan Robson broke down in the second

game when he tore his Achilles tendon. In the final group match against
Egypt, who were very negative opponents, Bobby Robson reverted to a
flat back four. It was a pragmatic decision and one that was justified by
a 1–0 win after Gascoigne's free kick found the head of Mark Wright
for the only goal.

In a group heavy on draws and light on goals and entertainment,
England had done just enough to come out on top. 'You just need to get
through the first stage,' said Des Walker. 'Your thoughts aren't on winning
the thing, just qualifying. As soon as we got through, we looked back and
knew we were in good shape. Everybody wanted the ball, because there
was always someone to give it to. The team had bags of moral courage.
Everybody wanted to do their bit; no one thought, "I don't want to make
a tackle in case I give away a penalty." Everyone said, "Let me score it; let
me tackle him." No one hid, and when you've got that in a team you've
got a chance of winning. Everybody respected the ability of the others.
As a unit, it was the best team I played in and everybody on the pitch
was world class.'

And the atmosphere off the pitch seemed to be just as good. One night
at dinner, Chris Waddle and Terry Butcher decided to do everything in
reverse, as Butcher told me: 'We put our clothes and glasses on back
to front, flip-flops on the wrong way round and walked backwards into
dinner. We had already told the waiters we wanted coffee, dessert, main
course and then starter. They loved it and walked backwards to the table
to serve us. The night before the Egypt game, Woods, Waddle and I wore
our England blazers, shirts and ties, gelled our hair, put our sunglasses on
and shoes and socks and jockstraps – but no trousers. We got in early and
arranged tablecloths around us and told the waiters to put wine bottles
on the table but fill them with water.

'Bobby [Robson] and Don Howe came in and went mad thinking we
were getting stuck into the wine and getting drunk. We were making
toasts. "Come on England, Good luck tomorrow, chaps," all that sort
of thing, all based on the International FA Committee. Then who came
through the door but the International FA Committee themselves! Bert
Millichip and all these people. Bobby put his hands over his face as if
to say, "Oh my God, look at our players." The lads loved it; it was so
different. After main course we said, "Right lads, a toast." And as we
stood up and the tablecloths fell away, they saw we had no trousers on,

and we proposed a toast. As we walked up the steps out of the restaurant, we bared our arses to the International Committee. When we came back in, we got a big round of applause!'

For the second-round match, England travelled to Bologna to face Belgium and Robson switched back to the sweeper system, with Mark Wright the libero. McMahon replaced the injured Bryan Robson in the midfield three, and England rode their luck as Belgium twice hit the post. At the other end, John Barnes, who was playing just off Gary Lineker, had an excellent goal wrongly ruled out for offside.

After 71 minutes, McMahon was replaced by David Platt, whose industry, timing of runs and goalscoring were to be enormously important. There were no goals at full-time, but Chris Waddle was loving the system: 'Suddenly there was space. We could get the ball and enjoy it. Wrighty was the free man who could cover at the back. We had players who could handle and look after the ball, players who could run with it. We had pace up front, Gary could get in behind, John Barnes could link the play up in the hole, Gazza and I could run and pass, Platty could join up with Links [Lineker] in the box for the crosses. I remember saying to Barnesy, "This is how we should have been playing for the last five years." Everyone believed in the system. It was flexible, and if it wasn't working you could slip into a four at the back or it could be 4–5–1.'

With the game about to drift into penalties, England won a free kick on the left-hand side and Gascoigne lifted it into the box where Platt swivelled adroitly and hit a perfect volley across the goalkeeper, Preud'homme, and into the net. The England players fell deliriously upon the Aston Villa midfielder. In 2007, Platt told *The Times*:

> It was the timing that made it special. It was synonymous with the change in the relationship with the media. There had been a stand-off between them and the team. We weren't playing well and there had been problems off the pitch with our supporters. It changed the mentality. It kick-started us into playing good football and peaking at the right time.

The England fans, some of whom had been caught up in trouble in Rimini beforehand, celebrated by singing, 'Let's all have a disco,' and Butcher and Waddle spontaneously joined in, jigging along to the supporters' chants in celebration – Waddle wearing a shirt of their vanquished opponents.

With the sweeper system bedded in and England now into the last eight, the team genuinely started to believe they could win the World Cup. Argentina were a cheap imitation of four years earlier, Italy were progressing without pulling up any trees and only really West Germany had impressed, scoring ten goals in the group games and then beating Holland 2–1 in the second round. Scotland had slipped quietly out of the reckoning at the group stages, a 1–0 defeat by Costa Rica adding to their list of unwanted defeats, but the Republic of Ireland were having a World Cup debut to remember. They won a penalty shoot-out against Romania in Genoa before losing narrowly to Italy in the quarter-finals.

It was Cameroon who were fast becoming everyone's favourite second team. Immensely strong and quick but fatally ill-disciplined, they caused a massive shock in the first game of the whole tournament, beating Argentina 1–0 – even finishing with nine men – and in Roger Milla they had the competition's unlikeliest star. Lured out of retirement by the country's president, the 38 year old's impact off the bench was undeniable, and his two goals against Romania meant Cameroon could afford barely to raise a sweat in their last group game against the Soviet Union. In the second round, in Naples, Milla scored twice more, the second making a fool of Colombia's vainglorious and extrovert goalkeeper Higuita – whose hubris led him to think he could dribble past Cameroon's super-sub 40 yards from goal. Milla simply dispossessed him and knocked it into an empty goal.

Now Cameroon met England in the quarter-finals in Naples. David Platt's match-winning performance in Bologna meant he started instead of McMahon in midfield – along with the room-mates and Geordies, Paul Gascoigne and Chris Waddle. Dinner for the team was set at half past seven, and Bobby Robson's obsession with the players drinking enough water was such that every night, when the players left the restaurant, the waiters would give each of them two bottles of water, one fizzy and one still.

'One night back in our room, Gazza said, "Come on, let's have a glass of water,"' Waddle remembers. 'He was always the first to moan about these things, so I didn't understand what he was up to. He insisted and took the top off the first bottle, and it was full of a yellow liquid. I said, "Gazza, this water's off. Let's take it back." But he wanted to open the second one, and that was full of a red liquid. So I said, "What the hell's going on here?" And Gazza looked at me and said, "Ah, I've paid the waiter, so we've got a bottle of red wine and a bottle of white wine. And the gaffer's told us to drink our bottles – so let's have a party in our room!'"

With the papers banned, and the days of saturation 24-hour news coverage still in their infancy, the players were insulated from the growing sense of excitement and anticipation back home. Having just finished my university exams, this was a World Cup from heaven for me: I could watch every minute without feeling guilty at all. One day we organised a football match between the boys and the girls, who promptly lined up with a sweeper system, pointing out that not only was it now de rigueur but clearly the way forward in order to win important matches. I like to think it was my future wife who was putting across the tactical points.

The last eight was the furthest any African team had ever made it at the World Cup, and Des Walker soon realised the Cameroonians had absolutely no inferiority complex: 'We came out of the tunnel, and we were both lined up, and Butch [Terry Butcher], the captain, was giving it the ra-ra. I looked across at their captain, who was about 6 ft 3 and about 4 ft wide, and he mimicked Butch's English accent, and you could see on their faces they had no fear of us at all. They were naive and went out and enjoyed it. They were a big, physical team. They started knocking us about, and, to be fair, they had us on the run.'

England took the lead through David Platt's header, but Cameroon then started to play with real fluency and turned the game around on the hour mark. First, Gascoigne fouled Milla in the area and Kunde scored from the penalty spot. Then, just minutes later, Milla set up the substitute Ekeke to put Cameroon in front. It was nothing less than Cameroon deserved. Bobby Robson knew he had to change things, and he brought on Trevor Steven for Terry Butcher in the 73rd minute as England reverted to 4–4–2. Cameroon promptly let England back into the game.

'We knew technically they would be better than us, but what they didn't have was discipline, and they threw it away,' said Chris Waddle. 'They would do silly tackles, leave spaces and lose concentration. When they got the ball, they would love to show off, and the crowd took to them. They gave us a lot of help, but that's football and we took it.' The first act of charity came in the 83rd minute, when Ebwelle brought down Lineker in the area. Thinking of his brother, Wayne, and all those watching in his bar in the Mediterranean, Lineker himself calmly equalised from the spot. In extra time, Lineker was again fouled in the 18-yard box, and again he scored from the resulting penalty.

Despite being second best for much of the match and indebted to Peter Shilton's efforts in goal, England scraped through to their first World Cup semi-final since 1966. 'Let's all have a disco,' chanted the England fans again as they relished the prospect of West Germany in the last four. 'A flat back four saved us,' said Bobby Robson the next day. 'We've got here. I don't know how.'

Terry Butcher knew that his England career was coming to an end. World Cups bookended his international days, and in Turin he was going to lead his side out for the biggest England game in 24 years. He was the archetypal warrior centre-half: 'I was fantastically proud of playing for England. Gary Lineker always talked about caged tigers, and that was my speech before a game. "We're all caged tigers," I would say, and I would prowl around. As soon as the whistle went, that's the cage being unlocked: let's get out there and rip them to pieces. Stuart Pearce and I would be up and growling and kicking. Gary was so laid back he was almost horizontal. I loved every minute of it.'

Butcher was responsible for organising for the wives and families to come out to Italy as the country revved up for the most anticipated match in a generation. Flags appeared on balconies, on cars and hung out of windows – commonplace enough now but not as much then. England were going to start with a sweeper. John Barnes's injury meant that Peter Beardsley was now going to partner Gary Lineker, who admired the enormous strides one player in particular had made in the tournament. Back in April of that year, Paul Gascoigne was probably not even going to be in the squad, but he was now an integral part of the side, and Lineker paid tribute to his rapid progression: 'Gazza was incredible. He had such amazing talent, but he was irritating, even on the pitch. I never had arguments with any player like I had with Gazza. Lots of times we fell out, even for a few minutes, and then it was OK. He was so good with the ball that he wanted it all the time and the only time he would actually release it really was when he knew you had no other alternative but to give it straight back to him. That's how good he was at times. He wanted to run the show.' Gascoigne was irrepressible off the pitch as well, Bobby Robson taking him to task for playing tennis against an American tourist on a blazing hot afternoon, after a full morning's training, in the days running up to the Belgium game.

'I'm Scared Of Gazza,' was the headline in the *Daily Mirror* on the day of the semi-final as West German coach Franz Beckenbauer respectfully paid lip service to what the Tottenham midfielder had done. 'There is no reason why with Gascoigne and Gary Lineker England cannot win the World Cup,' he said at a press conference. Gascoigne's blossoming had blotted out the potentially devastating absence of the injured captain Bryan Robson, and the England team were confident. 'The supporters get far more nervous and build it up far more than the players do,' says Chris Waddle. 'It was the best squad and team since '66. We knew we were playing a team favourite to win the whole thing, but the Germans looked at us and thought, "We're going to have to play well to beat these."'

The teams matched each other in terms of systems. Lothar Matthäus of Inter Milan stoked Germany's engine room from midfield, and Völler and Klinsmann were strikers who complemented each other. 'If we had played 4–4–2, they would have beaten us,' said Waddle. 'As it was, it was man for man. If we won all our individual battles, we would have a great chance – and we did cause them problems. Walker and Parker knuckled down on Klinsmann and Völler and hardly gave them a kick. Gazza did really well on Matthäus. We were cruising. As the game went on, I was thinking, "If we can just get that goal, that little bit of luck, a deflection or something like that . . ."'

The luck, though, fell Germany's way. On the hour mark, Brehme's free kick deflected off the charging Parker and looped, agonisingly slowly, over a back-pedalling Shilton and into the net. With eighteen minutes remaining, England switched to a flat back four as Trevor Steven replaced Butcher, and ten minutes from time Gary Lineker took advantage of some hesitancy in the German defence to drive England level after Parker had crossed. The celebrations in Turin were matched by the pandemonium up and down England – and in number 6, Flass Street, Durham City, where, on our last night as students, a full house, with a supply of beer close to hand, was desperately hoping for an evening to remember.

In extra time, Buchwald hit the post for Germany and Waddle went equally close to putting England into the World Cup final: 'I hit it across the box, it hit the post and people don't remember where the ball came back to. It came straight back to me. I was standing on the corner of the box when I hit it. It went across the keeper and hit the post with Gary and Platty running in. If it had hit the post normally, as it were, either one of Gary or Platty running in would have scored or it would have gone in on the other side.'

In the first period of extra time, Gascoigne, who had been shown a yellow card against Belgium, was booked as he tried to win the ball back from Thomas Berthold, whose rolling around on the ground did the Englishman no favours. Gascoigne dissolved into tears, realising he would miss the final if England made it, and Gary Lineker famously mouthed, 'Have a word with him,' to the bench. In three short weeks, Gascoigne had become immensely popular, and the watching public felt the lovable Geordie's dismay. There was a touching boyishness, a naivety almost, about the way he so easily and quickly started crying.

When the game had to be settled by penalties, Gascoigne's yellow card was to have a far-reaching effect. 'I thought I was out of it, because Gazza was the fifth penalty taker,' recalls Chris Waddle. 'But he was in a state, so Bobby asked me if I would take it on. I said, "Yeah." I had really enjoyed the game. I had passed it well, run with it well, my confidence was high, so you don't think about what might happen if you miss. So Bobby said, "You're down as the fifth."'

The first six kicks were all successful: Lineker, Beardsley and Platt scored for England; Brehme, Matthäus and Riedle for Germany. Then Stuart Pearce stepped forward – England's first choice penalty taker till Lineker took over for the tournament – and on the bench Bobby Robson was certain England would be going 4–3 up. But Pearce's penalty, hard, low and straight, hit the trailing leg of Bodo Illgner and flew to safety.

Olaf Thon scored for Germany, meaning Chris Waddle had to convert his to keep the shoot-out alive. Everybody in England was either hiding behind the sofa or, like me, watching through the cracks in their hands. On a beautiful afternoon in Rome ahead of the Champions League final, Waddle talked me through it: 'I could see their goalkeeper diving right all the time, so I thought I would place it to his left. Then Stuart smashes one down the middle, and the goalie kicks it away, and I'm thinking, "You've got to make sure, so it's power. Definitely power."

'Everyone says, "On the walk from the halfway line to the penalty spot what goes through your mind?" Well, nothing! I thought, "If he saves it, it's going to hurt him. If I hit this hard, he's not going to save it. And these balls fly as well. I am really going to give this a right go." I could never ever have struck the ball better. A lot of people have said that if I had scuffed it it would have gone in. That was my plan: really leather it. I couldn't have hit the ball better or harder. Maybe I hit it too hard or leant back a bit, and then you see it sail and you think, "That's it." And you know it's over. I went and kicked the post, and I remember Matthäus coming straight up to me and saying, "Sorry, that must be really horrible." And that was really nice of him, especially as all his teammates were jumping over one another.'

An overcome Gascoigne was in tears on the pitch. His crumpled face, as he mopped it with his sodden England shirt, was to become the enduring and endearing image of Italia '90. With his effervescence and enormous talent, Gascoigne had made people feel that they could be proud to be English again.

There were plenty more tears in the dressing room as the players reflected on just how close they had come to a World Cup final. 'Sometimes it's meant to be, and it just wasn't meant to be,' is the philosophical way Gary Lineker looks upon it. Our last night at university was ruined as we dragged ourselves to the local nightclub, the wonderfully named Q Ball, and shuffled around the dance floor without any enthusiasm at all. Talk about a wake.

Des Walker wanted to look out for his room-mate, Stuart Pearce: 'He got drug-tested, and it was three hours before he got back to the hotel. I knew he wanted to be left alone to collect his own thoughts. I wish anybody else had missed the penalty rather than Stuart, because he's my mate and I knew how hard he would take it. But, having said that, looking back, he's probably the best one to miss, because, along with Bryan Robson, he had the most moral courage and they would use it as a driving force rather than [letting it] pull them down. I was the happiest man in the world for him when he scored against Spain at Euro '96. It said he had no fear.'

Chris Waddle's miss didn't break him: 'I was quite fortunate, because I was playing in France, so I was well out of the way, but I have to say it made me a far stronger player character-wise. I went on to win leagues with Marseille [and] played in the Champions League final. Unfortunately, my England career ended under Graham Taylor, but I came back to Sheffield Wednesday, won Footballer of the Year and played in two Cup finals, so my career wasn't hindered – in actual fact it went up a level. There are two ways of going: you either go and hide and curl up in a corner and say "I don't want to do that any more" or you come forward. I saw Maradona miss a pen, I saw van Basten miss a pen, I saw Baggio miss a pen in America, I saw Baresi hit it higher than mine. All great, great players. I wasn't the first, and I won't be the last.'

'It's the one thing I look back on in my career and think, "If only . . ." You knew that Argentina in the final were there for the taking,' said Gary Lineker. And so it proved, as the most egregious match was settled, ironically, by a penalty in West Germany's favour as Argentina imploded and had two players sent off. Bobby Robson left the England job after losing the irrelevant third-place play-off to Italy; and *Guardian* writer Dave Hill said he had endured 'the most sustained campaign of press humiliation the national game has ever seen'. Even so, Robson left on a massive high, the most successful England manager since Sir Alf Ramsey, despite the crushing disappointment of Turin that lived with him forever after that.

Robson was, according to Gary Lineker, 'terrific, hugely enthusiastic, always taking training, very supportive of his players but demanding a certain performance from them and never swayed by any of the media'. He was also, unintentionally, hilarious. 'He put Glenn Hoddle's boots on one day in Mexico for training,' recalled Chris Waddle, laughing. 'Afterwards he told Glenn to send them back because they were too small. He hadn't taken the paper out of the toes! We also had four Steves on the bench one day: Steve Bull, Steve Hodge, Trevor Steven and Gary Stevens – something like that – and he looked at the subs and said, "Steve, warm up!" And suddenly everybody got up and started running up and down the touchline. I think he put Kerry Dixon on instead!'

Bobby Robson might have been lost to the national manager's job, but his dignity, Pearce's penalty, Platt's volley, Lineker's goals, Waddle's and Butcher's dancing and Gazza's heart-rending tears had helped change the face of English football. Forever.

10

‖‖

FRANCE 1998

England returned home from Italy to a rapturous welcome. One hundred and twenty thousand supporters camped out at Luton Airport to greet the team, and Paul Gascoigne, the centre of attention, wore a giant pair of plastic breasts. Bobby Robson and Gary Lineker missed the extraordinary homecoming, because they stayed on in Italy to receive the FIFA Fair Play Trophy.

'After the penalties in Turin, Bobby was gracious, humble, proud and just fantastic,' said Terry Butcher. 'He would have loved to have seen the crowds at Luton. What a momentous day that was: Gazza and the false breasts. I was nearly decapitated by a low bridge at one stage. I was wearing a stewardess's hat and glasses, and I had to be pulled down physically before a bridge threatened to take my head off.'

On my five-hour drive home from university in my trusty Ford Fiesta, whose radio you had to kick intermittently to make it work, the news was all about England's glorious failure. My first words to my father were, 'Dad, it will take me till Christmas to get over this.' But although it was a defeat for the England team, it was lift-off for football.

After the tragedies of Heysel, Hillsborough and Bradford, the violence that scarred the '80s and the debacle of Euro '88, England's thrilling run to the World Cup semi-finals – and the visceral rawness of Gazza's tears – caused a sceptical nation to fall in love once again with the national game. Attendances steadily started to grow, and when the Premier League began in 1992, BSkyB won the right to screen the majority of live matches. Gradually, viewers were able to see more and more live football, and the players – and their agents – were enriched, as the amount of money pouring into the game increased. No longer was football the wayward son of the sporting family but the shining example of how to market a game domestically and globally.

Ironically, one of the tenets of the Premier League when it started had been to help the national team. It certainly did not have the desired effect in the short term. England endured a disappointing Euro '92 in Sweden under new manager Graham Taylor and went out after losing the pivotal game against the hosts 2–1. 'Swedes 2, Turnips 1', was one of *The Sun*'s more creative, if biting, headlines – and one that was to dog Taylor.

When it came to qualification for USA '94, England were up against Norway, Holland and Poland for the two places on offer. A 1–1 draw with Norway at Wembley in the opening game meant the two matches against Holland were always going to be pivotal. England led the Dutch 2–0 at Wembley after 23 minutes, but by half-time Dennis Bergkamp had halved the deficit and Jan Wouters's stray elbow had fractured Paul Gascoigne's cheekbone. With England hanging on, Marc Overmars turned on the afterburners to get clear of Des Walker, and it was the beginning of the end of the Nottingham Forest defender's international career: 'People build it up that you're invincible. They think, "He doesn't make mistakes." And as soon as I made one they thought, "Oh, he's not as good as he once was." If they don't expect you to make a mistake and you do then they come down harder on you.'

Five minutes were left at Wembley when Overmars got clear of Walker: 'Over 15 yards he is as quick as anyone. He was lightning, and the mistake was he got under my arm. I knew it was my mistake.' Desperately trying to recover, Walker brought Overmars down in the area – and Peter van Vossen equalised from the spot. It was two points lost, and after another stalemate, in Poland, Graham Taylor fiddled fatally with the formation as England produced a wretched performance in losing 2–0 in Norway in June 1993. Poland had faded out of contention by now, but England needed a result in Rotterdam in the autumn to edge out the Dutch.

Graham Taylor suffered horrendously at the hands of some erratic refereeing, and his frustration boiled over. Five minutes after he should have been sent off for a professional foul, Ronald Koeman scored from a retaken free kick. Taylor ranted at the linesman: 'Hey! Hey! Tell your pal that he's just cost me my job.' It was a prescient outburst. Bergkamp got a second, England failed to qualify and Taylor was sacked. I have worked with Graham for the best part of a decade now, and you couldn't wish to meet a more thoroughly decent and honourable man. He takes the responsibility for not qualifying, and it has lived with him ever since.

Taylor's last game in charge was in San Marino, and it turned out to be Des Walker's valedictory match as well. New manager Terry Venables declined to add to his 59 caps, even though Walker was just 27: 'Some players think playing in the Champions League is higher than representing your country. Not a chance, not in a million years. Not only is playing for your country the pinnacle, but you have to adjust a lot more. With your club you have the safety net of your fans, the respect of the rest of the players and your status at that club. When you go into the international arena it's a level playing field, and that's difficult; to get everyone's respect is difficult. That's a massive step up. The Champions League cannot give you as much, as it cannot give you the three lions on your chest.'

Euro '96 saw football mania sweeping the country just as it had six years previously, with exactly the same denouement. In the group stages, England drew with Switzerland, saw off Scotland, beat Holland gloriously 4–1 and edged past Spain on penalties. They then went out in the semi-finals to the Germans in the same way.

Throughout it all, England's captain, Tony Adams, was managing to keep himself away from the drink as he very slowly started to come to terms with his alcoholism: 'In Euro '88, I was still weeing the bed and the maid was coming in and going, "Pee, pee, pee, pee." And I remember Viv Anderson, who was rooming with me, going down and telling all the lads, and it was excruciatingly painful.

'Arsenal won the League in '89 and '91, and in between I didn't go to the World Cup. I must admit my drinking was getting in the way of the big events, and I think it did cost me a lot of games and tournaments. It was very evident to me that my alcoholism had me, and the summer periods were really tricky, because I just wanted to go and get smashed.

'I remember when Dave Rocastle, Alan Smith and I found out we weren't going to Italia '90. I dragged them down the pub, and we got smashed. I drank through all that summer. Pretty well every game was pizza and oblivion. I was on standby in a bar, very drunk, in Rhodes, AWOL. By 1994 there was a lot of drunken behaviour in my life. I kicked down a door in a drunken oblivion, and there were periods it was really dark.

'By January '96, I wanted to be sober more than drunk. The wife had gone, the kids were with the mother-in-law, my sofa was the park bench. I was getting pissed. There were more injections, more morphine, more booze. Then, I thought enough is enough. I tried to do it my way for those eight months, and I found that football could help me not drink. As soon as the football [Euro '96] was finished, I went on the bender of all benders.' In September 1996, Adams publicly admitted he was an alcoholic, and, in time, he founded the Sporting Chance Clinic, designed to help all sportsmen and women who struggle with addiction.

England had a new manager for the World Cup qualifiers: the former Chelsea boss and England midfielder Glenn Hoddle. Like Terry Venables, Hoddle liked to play with five at the back, but he had a slightly different tactical approach, which Adams felt changed the system into a more defensive set-up: 'I wish there had been some kind of continuity and that Terry had talked to Glenn. Under Terry, we used full-backs to play centre-halves as part of the three and some rotation in the wider areas where we would use forwards. When Glenn came in we went to a back five. There was no rotation in the wider areas. It was centre-halves and wing-backs. Under Glenn it got into a 5–3–2 that wasn't fluid enough.'

Despite losing at home to Italy, by the time the return came around in Rome in October '97, England knew a draw would see them qualify automatically for the World Cup and force their hosts into the play-offs. The England team hotel was perched upon one of Rome's famous seven hills, and the Arsenal captain, fourteen-months sober by now, relaxed by immersing himself in a book that mirrored his own life, the story of one person's spiritual awakening during a transitional period: 'It was such a peaceful, beautiful day on the outskirts of Rome. I was reading *The Celestine Prophecy*, and I was floating. I was so spiritual I was untouchable. I was in such a peaceful place. I could do my job, I could step out onto the pitch, I knew the difference between going and kicking someone and wanting to win and actually living my life in a useful, peaceful, humble kind of way. I knew where I was, and early recovery can be like that for some people.'

The players rose to the challenge and played outstandingly well as a 0–0 draw assured them of their passage to France. Ian Wright hit the post late on, and Christian Vieri had an even later chance to win it for Italy. The only downside was the overreaction of the Italian *carabinieri*, who were seemingly determined to treat every English fan as a thug. Paul Gascoigne had an exceptional game in midfield, and captain Paul Ince's cut head had to be bandaged up in the same way as Terry Butcher's eight years earlier.

Ince was skipper on the night in place of the injured regular Alan Shearer. Tony Adams was overlooked. 'Tony was getting over injuries at the start of my reign,' said Glenn Hoddle, 'and in international football Alan was our biggest star, respected in world football and by referees. I didn't know whether Tony would be fit all the time, and I needed continuity. Alan was our focal point.'

Adams disagreed and still does to this day: 'I thought I had done a good job in Euro '96, but Glenn had his reasons for taking the captaincy away, and one was that he thought Alan Shearer could get more penalties at competitions – which I didn't buy. I thought Glenn made a mistake. I felt I could do a bit more. I thought they played too much golf in France. I think I might have even put my foot down, but I didn't feel like I could because I wasn't the captain. But there was no problem at all between me and Alan Shearer. Simply, I should have been captain, but I wasn't, so you get on with it.'

The huge decision Glenn Hoddle had to make about his squad was whether to include the talisman of 1990, Paul Gascoigne. The years since his starring role in Italy had not always been kind ones. He was so overhyped for the 1991 FA Cup final that he ruptured the cruciate ligaments in his right knee in a wild challenge on Gary Charles and, as a result, had to postpone his move to Lazio. During his time in Rome, his form was inconsistent and a broken leg forced him to miss the best part of a season. His personal life was in limbo as well. He had had a high-profile wedding to Sheryl in 1996, only for them to divorce two years later as she accused him of beating her. On his day, Gascoigne was still a fine player. His ball retention and passing were excellent, as he showed in Rome, but, crucially, he was struggling to stay fit. This was the conundrum Hoddle was wrestling with when he went to see him at his new club, Middlesbrough.

'Paul's story goes back eight, nine months before the World Cup,' Hoddle said. 'I sat him down and said I was concerned he was getting so many injuries. I gave him the warning sign in a nice way: "Come off the drink." He looked me in the eye and said, "Yes gaffer, yeah, yeah." But not having him every day, I did think, "Has the penny dropped?"

'I wanted a fit Paul Gascoigne in my squad, and I was prepared to go to the last minute, because a fit Gazza could unlock the door – even if I used him in the last 30 minutes of a game. But he just wasn't fit, and in the penultimate friendly game against Morocco he got injured after 20 minutes and we had to take him off. It was the saddest decision I've ever had to make as a manager, but it was the right one. I couldn't trust that he wouldn't get injured in the first game.

'I remember from my own experience, of '82, two players [Keegan and Brooking] who weren't fit going and taking up places. I also knew that if he wasn't playing he wouldn't be a happy bunny, and that played a part in the balance of the squad. I gave him every opportunity. I said this was Gazza's stage. There were so many reasons to get your body and mind in shape.'

Just a week before Hoddle whittled down his squad to the final 22, Gascoigne was photographed eating kebabs in the early hours in central London after a night out. The squad were in Spain, in La Manga, when Hoddle had to make the final decision, and he called the players up one by one to his room to tell them of their fate, with the soothing strains of Kenny G in the background. When Gascoigne learnt he wasn't going to France, he went berserk, leaving Hoddle's room trashed, with glass strewn everywhere and chairs overturned. Tony Adams backs the manager's decision unequivocally: 'Gazza was in no fit state to go, and I understood 100 per cent why Glenn didn't take him. I wasn't fit in 1990, such is the illness of addiction. It would have been an unbelievable gamble to take him. A fit and sober Gazza would have been fantastic.

'You're taking a practising alcoholic away to La Manga, where there's booze and sun, and it was inevitable he was going to get smashed. I would have done if I was still drinking. He had no tools; I had tools at that stage. I was making phone calls, I had people around me [and] I knew how to stay stopped [sober]. Stopping's the easy bit; staying stopped is the harder part.'

Chelsea's Graeme Le Saux had missed Euro '96 because of a broken ankle but was a regular in Hoddle's teams. An intelligent, thoughtful footballer who received ridiculous abuse for daring to be different – reading *The Guardian* and having a degree are not exactly criminal offences – he had to endure scurrilous and unfounded allegations about his private life during his career. He questions the way Gascoigne was told he wouldn't be in the squad: 'I think the situation was handled very poorly. We were all getting called up individually to Glenn's room. It was like going to see the headmaster. Then everyone was waiting for that man to come down to see if they had passed or failed, and the pressure there was immense. I wasn't surprised Gazza didn't go. He was in freefall at the time; he was desperate. I remember being in the piano bar and Gazza singing songs and being the centre of attention socially.'

Hoddle maintains telling the players face-to-face was the only way, that a phone call or a message under the door just wasn't on. Gascoigne was one of six players left out by Hoddle, and as the hero of Italia '90 was forced to face the reality of the end of an unfulfilled international career, a teenager was just starting his. Eighteen-year-old Michael Owen of Liverpool had just scored eighteen goals in thirty-six Premiership games, his first full season, and when he was chosen to go to France he had five caps behind him, not that he was fazed: 'You take it in your stride at that age. You think it's normal until you arrive and recognise the scale of what you are about to embark on: the buzz about the place, the hype, the attention. The atmosphere is charged.'

Owen and the England squad were based in La Baule, a resort on the western coast of France, in the Western Loire, that boasts a beach 12 kilometres long. From there they were to fly to their matches – the first of which was in Marseille against Tunisia – but the backdrop to England's first World Cup finals match in eight years was a grim one. There was trouble the night before the game, rival fans fought as they came out of the metro on their way to it and violence broke out down on the beach, where thousands were watching on a giant television. Tear gas was used to restore order, and the disturbances were the most serious involving England fans in five years. A decade later, Hoddle was told somebody had planned to blow up the England bench.

The subs on that bench included Michael Owen and David Beckham, left out of the starting line-up even though he had been picked to start every qualifier. Hoddle insisted Beckham wasn't focused enough in the warm-up matches and that he seemed a bit vague in training. The manager then allowed Beckham to talk to the press about his omission, an approach that Sir Alex Ferguson criticised in the Sunday papers, saying Hoddle was not protecting the player. Southgate, Campbell and Adams were the centre-halves for the opening game, with Le Saux and Anderton the wing-backs; Ince, Batty and Scholes were the midfield three behind Sheringham and Shearer. England eased to a 2–0 win, the goals coming from Alan Shearer's first-half header and a late curler from Paul Scholes.

Part of the backroom staff that Hoddle assembled for this World Cup was Dr Yann Rougier, who had worked with Arsenal during the 1997–98 season when they had won the Premiership–FA Cup Double. Each England player had been screened and prescribed specific mineral and vitamin supplements on the basis of his recommendations. They were also given creatine, which was to kick in just before the tournament.

The vitamin injections were not obligatory, but Graeme Le Saux found the whole process somewhat unsettling: 'We had all these glass vials with antioxidants in them in liquid form, and you had to snap the top and bottom of the glass to release it. The first day about five people came down to breakfast with bits of tissue paper round their fingers where they had tried to snap the glass and cut themselves. We had injections on the day of the game, and it was a huge trust issue. There were quite a few Arsenal boys there, and they had just won the Double, and we had to take their word for it that they had had a second life [given the stage of their careers]. No one held a gun to your head, but there was peer pressure and you felt that's what you had to do. That was a big deal for me, because you ended up relying on it in a sense. I took all these tablets before the first match and we did well, so you feel you had better take them again.'

Glenn Hoddle says the idea to bring in Dr Rougier was to cover all bases: 'The injections weren't obligatory. Some players were interested, and some were not. I should have brought on board John Syer, a sports psychologist I knew from my Tottenham days. Because of the lack of time together with England, the squad could have done with that team building. He was with us at Spurs in '81, '82 and '84, when we had a very successful time.'

Against the top seeds, Romania, Owen and Beckham were on the bench again and Gary Neville came in for the injured Gareth Southgate. Glenn Hoddle had a sense of foreboding about the game that he just could not shake off, and after half an hour he had to make a change when Paul Ince hurt his ankle. Beckham replaced him, rotating smoothly with Darren Anderton down the right-hand side. Poor defending from a throw-in allowed Viorel Moldovan to put the Romanians ahead at the start of the second half, and Hoddle could hear the England fans chanting for Owen: whether to start with him or not had been one of the great talking points.

Tony Adams feels Hoddle's approach with the Liverpool striker was correct: 'I didn't see anything wrong with the way Glenn did it: Michael coming off the bench, impact player, very quick as the game's spread out later on.' With 17 minutes remaining Hoddle made the change. Owen came on for Sheringham, and six minutes later the teenager equalised from close in, reacting sharply to a half-chance and becoming England's youngest ever scorer in the World Cup. Hoddle would have settled for a point, given his unease all day, but in the last minute Dan Petrescu got the better of his Chelsea teammate Graeme Le Saux and squeezed in the winner from a narrow angle.

'Dan wandered infield, and I started tracking him but didn't want to mark him 100 per cent, because he was going out of my area and I thought someone would take him off me,' Le Saux recalls. 'But they didn't and a gaping hole opened up. I realised the ball would be played into the channel, and I'm now playing catch up as I'm a couple of yards the wrong side of him. I got a clout off him in the face, which knocked me back a bit, and I was shepherding him away from goal thinking he's going to come back on his right foot, because he had no angle. But he never did. He hit the ball with his left foot, and it went through Dave Seaman's legs.

'I got slaughtered for it – and this was one of my biggest gripes afterwards. It was very much, "It's your fault." And Glenn and John Gorman pointed the finger. It wasn't a case of, "It happens. Let's analyse it." It was a case of, "What were you doing? You weren't strong enough." I read the situation wrong, and we never really went over how it happened. The next game I felt under so much pressure, because I had been slaughtered in the papers. I really felt like I was on my own. I think if Glenn had had another left-sided player out there he wouldn't have played me in that Colombia game. That's certainly how I felt. I was clearly culpable for part of that goal, but it wasn't just my mistake.'

Hoddle told the team, in no uncertain terms, that they couldn't afford to defend like schoolboys at international level, and, having lost to Romania, England needed at least a point against Colombia in the final group game to ensure they qualified for the knockout stages. During training the day after the Romanian game Hoddle recognised that morale among the subs was low, a problem with which he empathised: 'I pre-empted the situation by saying that those not playing were the most important in many ways. I sat on the bench for most of the 1982 World Cup, so I told them I knew what it was like.'

Graeme Le Saux also sensed something was wrong with those unlikely to see much action on the field: 'For the squad players, there was definitely an undertone of dissatisfaction, and players and managers have to take a responsibility for that because those are players you have to rely on. You could definitely tell there was a 'Them and Us' scenario developing, and that all added to this underlying sense that the tournament wasn't managed as well as it could have been. Some of the players who didn't play didn't feel they were part of the squad.'

There is no doubt as to what Graeme Le Saux thinks of Glenn Hoddle as a coach. He calls him 'fantastic, tactically very brave and very committed to his philosophy'. But Le Saux's regret is that he wasn't able to enjoy fully the experience of playing in a World Cup: 'I didn't ever feel I was part of this huge tournament. It wasn't made to feel special for me, and I would want the players to embrace it. You get more out of them that way, because they would realise how privileged they were and go out and show it. I didn't get that sense. There was a huge controlling element, and that was overbearing from my point of view.

'I was speaking to the Danish, Italian and Dutch boys from Chelsea. The Dutch lads were down in Monaco in a beautiful hotel and had their wives with them all the time, and their families; I was in touch with Frank Leboeuf and Marcel Desailly. For us, it was so intense and overbearing. One night we met the wives in a hotel in the north of France. My wife Mariana was pregnant and couldn't come up and nor could a couple of the other lads' [wives], and we felt like gooseberries. It made you feel like you had no responsibility. There was lots of control, and we were very isolated in La Baule. It was all done with the best of intentions, and I got a sense that Glenn must have felt security and comfort in putting into place all these things.'

In the run-up to the Colombia game, Hoddle spoke to Eileen Drewery, the faith healer he had known for over two decades since going out with Drewery's daughter as a teenager. Hoddle had introduced her to the England players, to help those struggling with injuries, and he wanted her to be in France with the squad, but prior engagements meant that wasn't possible. Their relationship drew much criticism, and for that Hoddle blames the media: 'That was a distraction caused by the press. I would have been wrong not to have offered it to the players, and that's all it was: an offer. Even if one player gets over an injury quicker, then it's good. It was just an extension to the medical team and a service that I knew worked, and it was open, that's all.'

Graeme Le Saux holds up the example of Eileen Drewery as saying a lot about the regime: 'You weren't forced to go and see her, but you pretty much felt you had to. It was quite subtle, but was it the sort of thing that you were going to say was nonsense, like some did? No one wanted to go into press conferences, because all the questions were about her and we were exposed. Darren Anderton and Sol Campbell, who had seen her, were really dragged through it in the press, and players shouldn't be exposed to that.'

Ray Parlour had just finished an outstanding season, as Arsenal won the Double, and had been man of the match in the FA Cup final, but his form was not enough to win a place in the World Cup squad. He suspects the reason might have something to do with his visit to see Drewery when he had a calf injury. Drewery put her hands on his famous tumbleweed curls, and Parlour couldn't resist a quip: 'Short back and sides, please.' Within days, the story was in *The Sun* and Arsene Wenger warned Parlour he might not play for England under Hoddle – and he was right.

Darren Anderton was picked instead: a player with a history of injury problems who had been to see Drewery for help with a hamstring injury. Despite his nickname of 'Sicknote', Anderton played on till his mid 30s, and towards the end of his career he told the *Daily Mirror*:

> People used Eileen as a stick to beat Hoddle with, which was unfair on her because she didn't do anybody any harm and helped me . . . My hamstring turned to rock after the first day of pre-season training at Tottenham, and I knew I was struggling. Glenn read about it on holiday, rang me up from his sun lounger and gave me the phone number of a lady who might be able to help. Looking back I think Glenn preached too much in public about Eileen and he left himself open to ridicule by sending other injured players to see her.

Anderton kept his place for the Colombia game, and David Beckham started for the first time – with David Batty dropping out. There was a change up front as well, with Michael Owen replacing Teddy Sheringham. Hoddle says he always intended to play Owen in this game, whatever Sheringham did against Romania, because Owen's pace was perfectly suited to Colombia's very flat and square back four. England began well and were ahead after twenty minutes when Anderton volleyed a fine goal, and ten minutes later Beckham scored his first for his country, a curling free kick, and then sank to his knees and celebrated in front of the cavorting England fans. 'I don't think Glenn knew at that stage what sort of player David would develop into,' says Tony Adams. 'I don't think we knew the extent of the talent that was unfolding.'

Those early strikes were enough to see England through to victory and a second-round date in St Etienne with Argentina: an opponent who periodically crops up in England's World Cup travels. For Graeme Le Saux both the venue – the Geoffroy Guichard Stadium – and the opposition had great resonance: 'The atmosphere at the stadium was really intense, and for me it was very special, because my wife Mariana is from Argentina. Some of her side of the family had come to the game, and they were there supporting me and maybe the extended family were watching in Argentina. It was such a massive game historically. St Etienne were a team I liked, growing up in Jersey. My maths teacher, Mr Kavanagh, was a big fan of them, so just playing there was a big thing for me. He supported them because that's where Michel Platini started. And we used to be able to pick up some French TV in Jersey, so I watched them on the TV a few times. And even the green-and-white kit I remember well.'

The night of Tuesday, 30 June 1998 is one no England football fan will ever forget. The game started at breakneck speed. In the sixth minute, David Seaman brought down Gabriel Batistuta in the area and then very nearly saved the striker's penalty. Four minutes later England equalised with a penalty of their own, Shearer converting after Michael Owen had gone down under a challenge from Ayala.

Just past the quarter-of-an-hour mark, Beckham found Owen inside the Argentinian half in the centre circle. Owen controlled the ball and was off, his pace and persistence too much for Argentina's Chamot and also for his own teammate, Graeme Le Saux, whose job it was to be an outlet on the left-hand side: 'I remember getting to halfway and thinking, "I'm not going to get there." And then it was like watching a horse you've backed, and you're saying, "Go on, go on." And the flow of that run is amazing. That's Michael Owen at his best. He was always at his best when the opposition were diving in and committing themselves. When he was in full flow he was great at getting people off balance and using his pace to go the other way, and he had such a low centre of gravity.'

Owen shrugged off Chamot but was now faced just outside the penalty area with Roberto Ayala, a central defender of immense talent who had just been bought by AC Milan. Now in full flow, Owen went to his right-hand side, something that Glenn Hoddle does not think would have happened if he had not been an unknown: 'Three or four years later, Ayala, the last man, would probably have sent Michael on his left. They didn't really understand him then. As soon as I saw Michael up against the last man, I thought he was going to score. Ayala was squared up, and I knew he couldn't stop him. He might have brought him down, but Michael was too quick for him.'

Owen took the ball to the defender's left and actually into the path of Paul Scholes, who would have had an excellent chance himself, but nothing was going to stop the teenager now. 'That goal he drifted past people, used their imbalance to go past them, and he even did it with the goalkeeper,' says Le Saux, who was just watching with admiration by this stage. 'He completely wrong-footed the keeper. When he hit it I couldn't believe it. The shot was a low one, and he went high and to the keeper's right. There was nothing we could offer him in support; we couldn't do anything for him. It was incredible; the movement and action flowed, and it had its own momentum. That person is reacting to the environment around them, and they're not even thinking about it. They are so in tune with what's going on they are just rolling with it.'

Owen's stunning goal, in reality the launch pad of his career, put England 2–1 up. As he admitted to me, he was simply too young and inexperienced to be cowed by the magnitude of the occasion: 'I was completely fearless at that age, and if anyone was in the way between me and the goal, I would find a way of getting round them. These days, teams have employed specialist defensive coaches, attacking coaches, coaches for almost everything, so the game has come on leaps and bounds and the importance now is the skill in finding that space and, when you have it, to take maximum advantage of it. Ultimately, that's my job. Over the years my statistics show I'll take one out of every two chances.'

England, though, couldn't hang on to their lead until half-time as Argentina equalised just before the break with a wonderfully constructed free kick from just outside the area. Batistuta looked as though he was going to take it, but instead Verón slid the ball down the left-hand side of the England wall to Zanetti, who had crept out from behind it, and Zanetti's firm left-footed drive made it 2–2.

Two minutes into the second half, Simeone barged Beckham to the ground, and as the England midfielder lay prostrate, he flicked out his right leg and caught Simeone behind the right knee. It wasn't done with enough force to bring the Argentinian down, but Simeone fell to the ground theatrically and Verón, Almeyda and Batistuta – who started waving an imaginary card – sensed an opportunity and surrounded referee Kim Milton Nielsen, urging him to take drastic action. Simeone was booked, and Beckham's life was turned upside down when he was shown a red card.

Glenn Hoddle saw the incident clearly: 'I thought it was a bit petulant, and when the ref went for his card, I thought it was going to be yellow. I was as shocked as anyone, and as a manager that horrible feeling comes into the pit of your stomach, but you have to detach yourself from the emotion, the injustice to the team, the injustice to David, and you have to literally think on your feet. What's the next decision? Because that's what the team needs, and I had to deal with that pretty quickly.'

Beckham trudged off dejectedly past his manager, who didn't give him a second glance, but Hoddle denies that he blanked his player: 'I didn't snub him. I never dreamt it was a red card, and the bottom line is my mind was going at a million miles an hour as to whether I was going to take a striker off and put a midfielder on with so long to go. I wasn't upset with David; I was fuming with the ref. My responsibility was with the team, and that's where my focal point was. I sent Terry Byrne, the masseur, down to the dressing room to see how David was.' It was the start of a great friendship, with Byrne later becoming Beckham's personal manager.

Hoddle decided against taking off either Shearer or Owen and instead asked them to share the duties of playing on the left-hand side of midfield. They took it in turns. England switched to a 4–4–1 with Neville and Le Saux slipping into full-back roles, and it was the sort of backs-against-the-wall, they-shall-not-pass scenario that Tony Adams loved: 'My own performance got better when we were down to ten men. We got a bit stretched, but it makes you gamble a bit more: a bit more shit or bust. You go for a tackle or a header you might not do with 11. I thought we were exceptional when down to ten men. We had to wait for a free kick or a corner to try and nick it; other than that, it was keep it solid and let's go to pens. The crowd were unbelievable; they were inspiring. You could hear the bugler playing [the theme from] *The Great Escape*. It was like being in a war film, and nothing was going to get past me.'

The noise from the England support, which included Mick Jagger, was phenomenal as they got behind the team, but Graeme Le Saux couldn't last the distance. He has always wondered whether the vitamins he had taken had ultimately had a detrimental effect: 'The cramp in my calves was horrific, and I couldn't run, and I had never really suffered cramp before. Yes, there was pressure and tension, but if you've taken something that maybe has unbalanced you slightly that might result in dehydration.'

Southgate and Merson replaced Le Saux and Scholes, and with nine minutes remaining England thought they had won it. Sol Campbell headed in powerfully from a corner, and several players rushed off to celebrate with the defender, unaware that the referee had disallowed the goal for a foul by Alan Shearer on the goalkeeper, Roa. Argentina quickly moved the ball up the field, and with England seriously undermanned it took a brave tackle from Gary Neville to keep them out.

So it came down to penalties. Afterwards, Hoddle was criticised for not practising them enough in training, but he says they did do a certain amount: 'Excluding David Seaman, we only had nine men, and four players came to me and said they didn't want to take one. Those who didn't want to were right to say so; some people have missed before they've even started their walk to the spot, and you just can't recreate the atmosphere in training. So we only had five left, and Batty said he was up for it along with Ince, Michael, Alan and Merse [Merson].' Tony Adams says, 'Most of the penalty takers do practise them at the end of training. My defence of Glenn is that you can't put 20,000 in the stands and recreate the situation.'

Berti scored first for Argentina, and Shearer followed suit. Then David Seaman dived to his left to keep out Hernán Crespo's kick, but England couldn't take advantage; Paul Ince's shot was at a comfortable height for Roa to save. Verón, Merson, Gallardo and Owen all converted their kicks to make it 3–3.

Graeme Le Saux was watching it all with the subs: 'That was proper head-in-your-hands stuff, rubbernecking it from the bench. You want to look but you don't, and if you don't look at one and you score, then you think, "I had better not look at the next one."' When Ayala put Argentina ahead, David Batty had to score to keep England in it. Hoddle still thought England were going to win, but Batty's strike was easily kept out by Roa and England went out, yet again, in heartbreaking fashion. It transpired later that it was the first penalty Batty had ever taken as a professional.

Tony Adams was the first England player back to the dressing room: 'I stuck my arm around David Beckham, and he was a mess; he was crying. I said, half-jokingly, "I've had one opportunity to win the World Cup, David, and you fucking blew it!" I told him, "It happens. Move on." I was early in recovery after 18 months, and at that stage I was crying for fun after never crying for the first 29 years of my life. At that time, *Watership Down* would have made me cry. I saw a man in a lot of pain: a wonderful man, one of the most emotionally intelligent fellows that I've ever met. He was crying to his mum and dad afterwards. David Batty wasn't. He shrugged his shoulders and was in a bit of denial.'

Graeme Le Saux was dragged off to be drug-tested: 'I had to sit in a neutral room with Ortega and one other, and I understand Spanish, so I knew what they were saying. And they were so elated, and I was so mortified. I remember coming into the dressing room after that, and David Batty was there. I was trying to think of something to say but couldn't. I didn't blame him.'

Glenn Hoddle addressed the players as a group in the dressing room that night in St Etienne, deciding to wait till the next day to talk to David Beckham. Tony Adams says he would have played it differently: 'Glenn was gutted, and we all react differently. I think if I was manager I would have gone over to David and said something, but I can imagine Glenn was in a lot of pain himself. David wrote to me later, which was really kind, and I wrote back. I put, "To the second best England captain of all time, from the best England captain of all time."' Hoddle told Beckham the next day that the red card was an abysmal piece of refereeing.

The night wasn't quite over for the distraught England players. 'I remember getting on the bus, sitting there for ages, and the Argentinian bus nearby was absolutely rocking,' says Graeme Le Saux. 'There was a bit of name-calling and jeering, and they were rubbing it in a bit. Paul Ince was getting very wound up and wanted to get off. I was crushed; I didn't know where my brain was. You're exhausted, and you're physically and emotionally shot to bits.'

It was all downhill after the World Cup for Glenn Hoddle and England. His decision to publish his World Cup diaries, written in conjunction with the FA's David Davies, was 'a huge mistake and lost him the dressing room', according to Graeme Le Saux. 'In the Euro qualifiers, you could sense the players were very disappointed by that.' The friendly against the Czech Republic that November was Hoddle's last game in charge, and he was sacked in February after making comments about disabled people to *The Times*.

Tony Adams reflects upon Glenn Hoddle's tenure as England coach: 'Right place, wrong time. It was too early for Glenn. I think he's an outstanding coach, and I think he's got a lot to offer. And maybe this country has chewed him up too early, and we do that with people. He needed people around him who had been to a World Cup before, someone with experience, someone like Don Howe, as an advisor or something.'

I put these two points directly to Hoddle, bearing in mind that he was only thirty-eight when he led England in France. He accepts that, 'Another two to three years as a manager would have been helpful. I did wonder whether I was too young, but I thought if I turned them down, this opportunity might not come around again and I was confident of my ability.' And what of Adams's feeling that he would have benefited from a right-hand man of more experience than John Gorman? 'It didn't work for Steve McClaren, did it? I wanted people I could trust, feel confident with and who understood what I wanted. With John, we had done that at Swindon and Chelsea. Someone else might have tried to persuade me to play with a back four.'

Glenn Hoddle was such a fabulously gifted footballer that Graeme Le Saux feels his ability may well have caused him problems when it came to getting his message across: 'There were some communication issues with players – that they took things one way when he didn't mean it. When the game comes easily to someone I think it's very difficult for them to appreciate how hard it comes to others. He was so natural, technically so gifted, he made space for himself so easily, that therefore he probably presumed the others could. He maybe didn't appreciate how good he was compared to other players. International management is all about one-to-one and the ability to communicate with people you don't spend a lot of time with. You don't build up the same relationship with them as you do with club managers.'

Hoddle was in the Stade de France to see France lift the World Cup against Brazil, and he sums up his World Cup odyssey as one of frustration: 'Big games turn on little decisions, and a poor refereeing decision has put us down to ten men. And then a 50–50 goal has been chalked off, so there's frustration but a lot of pride, too, in the way we played.'

David Beckham fought back from the ignominy of being sent off in France to become one of the most famous men on the planet four years later. We still don't know where Glenn Hoddle's football story will end.

11

JAPAN AND SOUTH KOREA 2002

England's bid to reach the first World Cup finals ever to be staged in the Far East came down to a straight fight with their old rivals Germany to win Group Nine and therefore qualify automatically. Kevin Keegan's team could not have made a worse start. In the last game ever to be played at the old Wembley, which by now was looking decrepit, dirty and dismal, the manager had a tactical shocker, playing Gareth Southgate just in front of the back four in a 4–1–3–2 system. It didn't work, and England were beaten by a quickly taken free kick from Liverpool's Dietmar Hamann. The greater drama was to follow afterwards, though, when Keegan promptly resigned in the dressing room. The defeat followed hard off the back of a disappointing Euro 2000, where England had failed to reach the knockout stages, and, on quitting, Keegan said, 'I really just feel a little bit short of what's required. I just don't feel I can find that little bit of extra that you need at this level to find that winning formula.'

After Howard Wilkinson had held the fort for the next qualifier – a goalless draw in Finland – England broke with tradition and appointed their first foreign manager. Sven-Göran Eriksson's managerial spells in Sweden, Portugal and Italy came to a crescendo when he led Lazio to the Serie A title in 2000, and within a year he had become the new England coach. As he says in his book, *Sven-Göran Eriksson on Football*:

My intention had been to stay another year with Lazio, but when the offer from the FA came, I immediately felt, 'This is exactly what I want to do.' I have read the book, *The Second Most Important Job in the Country*, which is all about England coaches from 1949 through to Kevin Keegan. It shows that all of them have been declared idiots at some time in their career, so I know what to expect. I didn't take the job for the money and not for the weather, either! I took it because it's England.

The team and the supporters were in the dumps after the thin gruel of Euro 2000 and the poor start to the World Cup qualifiers, but not everyone was excited by the arrival of an exotic overseas coach. His CV or, more pertinently, his nationality enraged some, and Jeff Powell's polemic in the *Daily Mail* was the most memorable:

> So, the mother country of football, birthplace of the greatest game, has finally gone from the cradle to the shame. England's humiliation knows no end. All that is left for the football men of England is to pull the sackcloth up over our heads and let the grave-dancers pile on the ashes . . . In their trendy eagerness to appoint a designer foreigner did none of the Lancaster Gate Seven pause for so long as a moment to consider the depth of this insult to our national pride? As they preened themselves over yesterday's installation of Sven-Göran Eriksson, did they begin to realise how gleefully the rest of the world would be laughing at us?

Powell's grievances were that no country had ever won the World Cup under a foreign manager, that the decision by the FA was an indictment of its own system, as they were responsible for the development of coaches in England, and that Eriksson's CV was misleading, as his triumphs in Italy were underpinned by the millions of euros the Cragnotti family had pumped into Lazio.

I took over as presenter of *Sports Report* and *Sport on Five* that season, and my memory of the public's reaction to a foreigner becoming manager is that people were so depressed by the state of the England team that they didn't care if the new man came from Mars if it got them winning. It has always been the same in football. When a controversial appointment is made, the hullabaloo will quickly die down if the team strings a few results together. England promptly won the first five games under Eriksson, including three World Cup qualifiers, but his first big test was the reverse fixture against Germany in Munich on 1 September 2001. Sitting in the open stands at the Olympic Stadium, I remember very clearly the feeling of disbelief settling over everyone there, like a gentle mist, as England came from a goal down to win 5–1. Michael Owen was arguably at his peak, scoring a hat-trick, with Steven Gerrard and Emile Heskey getting the others. '5–1, even Heskey scored' is a chant born that night that is still, occasionally, dusted down and brought out.

Eriksson's status was rapidly being elevated from continental curio to miracle worker. 'I can't believe that we beat Germany 5–1 away. It seems like a dream; it's unbelievable,' he admitted. 'I said to the players, "I don't know what to say to you."'

Franz Beckenbauer, who as a player in 1970, and as a manager 20 years later, had ended England's World Cup hopes, went overboard with his praise: 'I have never seen a better England team. They had pace, aggression, movement and skill. It was fantasy football. Michael Owen was simply unstoppable.'

The media joined in, falling over themselves to eulogise about this most extraordinary of scores. *The Independent* reflected on 'one of the least believable results in international sporting history', and *The Sunday Telegraph* wondered if it hadn't all been a 'magnificent, ridiculous dream'.

A routine 2–0 win over Albania four days later meant England needed to beat Greece at Old Trafford to reach Japan and Korea or at least match Germany's result. Michael Owen and David Seaman were both injured for the game, and as England struggled to find any sort of rhythm, Seaman's replacement, Nigel Martyn, was beaten by Charisteas's low left-footed shot to give the Greeks a half-time lead. England were having a stinker, but with 22 minutes remaining Teddy Sheringham came on and immediately equalised with a looping header. The goal, though, failed to settle England down, and a minute later they were behind again as Nikolaidis got the better of Rio Ferdinand to fire in. By now, many England fans were keeping an ear out for the Germany–Finland game, which was goalless and running a couple of minutes ahead, and when that match finished 0–0 England knew a late equaliser would suffice.

The captain, David Beckham, was all over the pitch as he tried to make up for the shortcomings of many of his teammates. In the 93rd minute, England were awarded a soft free kick just outside the Greek penalty area, and, having waved away Sheringham, who wanted to have a crack at it, Beckham stepped up and curled the ball into the top left-hand corner before running off to celebrate wildly in front of the old Stretford End. John Motson summed it up in his commentary on the BBC: 'He deserves the goal, and he's virtually played Greece on his own.' Beckham's rehabilitation after France '98 was complete: from *persona non grata* to national hero in just over three years. It had been quite a renaissance.

About an hour after the match, I was still in the commentary box along with a dozen or so journalists when Beckham walked past us on his way up to one of the corporate boxes at the back of the South Stand. Something very unusual then happened: a spontaneous round of applause broke out among us. Beckham's performance had been inspirational, and without him England would have been in the play-offs.

If Beckham had been the key to England qualifying for the World Cup, then he was the centre of attention in the build-up as well when he broke his foot against Deportivo La Coruña in a Champions League quarter-final on 10 April. The tackle by Pedro Duscher fractured the second metatarsal bone in his left foot. There were just over seven weeks till England's first game in Japan, and suddenly the world and his wife became experts on toe injuries.

Just two weeks later, in the Champions League semi-final, Beckham's great friend and teammate Gary Neville suffered an identical injury, breaking the fifth metatarsal in his left foot. He was out of the World Cup. Leeds United's Danny Mills had started just once at right-back for England at the time of Neville's injury and stood to gain the most: 'I was out in Harrogate having a meal when someone phoned me and told me that Gary Neville had broken his foot. I'm not going to lie. My first reaction was, "Great, I might have a chance of going to the World Cup," which is awful, because someone has a severe injury, but that is the nature of the beast. You become very selfish, and you can't help it, and I defy any footballer not to think that when the situation arises.'

Mills, Wes Brown and Gary Neville's brother, Phil, were those vying for the right-back slot, and it was the unlucky Phil Neville who missed out on the squad for the second successive World Cup. Leeds were having a good season, and Mills was one of four players from Elland Road named in the twenty-three – along with Rio Ferdinand, Nigel Martyn and Robbie Fowler – but he was suspended for the last two games of the season after picking up two red cards, fourteen yellows and having to attend one FA disciplinary hearing.

He wasn't expecting what happened next: 'Missing those two games gave me a bit of a rest, but then Dave O'Leary did a huge article in one of the tabloids which said, basically, "He's in the England squad, but if he has another season like this one at Leeds, discipline-wise, he'll be on the transfer list." It was a kick in the teeth for me. I had the fantastic achievement of getting in the England squad, and now your club manager slates you. People were asking whether I could be trusted, and now your own manager sticks the knife in and you're thinking everyone's against you.' If Mills was worried about his club manager, then it seems that Sven-Göran Eriksson had no such concerns. Mills says the Swede never mentioned his aggressive, robust style of play.

With Beckham still some way off fitness, Sven-Göran Eriksson suffered another setback, as the team prepared for their pre-World Cup camp in Dubai, when the dynamic Steven Gerrard had to withdraw from the squad with a groin injury. His Liverpool teammate Danny Murphy was called up as a replacement, but Eriksson wanted to take West Ham's wide-man Trevor Sinclair on the trip as well, and so he phoned him up. 'It was a surreal situation from the start,' Sinclair recalls. 'I had never had a call from Sven in my life before. There were lots of hoaxes going around from various radio stations where people had called pretending to be him, and I thought it was a radio DJ taking the mickey. I honestly did. I said, "Hi, Sven. I'm playing golf. Give me a shout later. Get Claire at the FA to call me." I shoved him off in case it wasn't him.'

Eriksson didn't take offence at Sinclair's abruptness on the phone, and the winger went to Dubai and then on to the Far East, where England had two final warm-up matches. He won his fourth cap against South Korea knowing he wasn't in the squad for the World Cup, and after the game in Jeju he asked Eriksson for a meeting: 'I felt like a vulture waiting for one of the guys to get injured. It was uncomfortable for me. I'm a big team player; I'm patriotic. I wanted the guys to do well, but it was like a double-edged sword. I was really itching for the chance to get involved rather than be the 24th in a 23-man squad, so I was in a bit of a predicament.'

Eriksson and Sinclair agreed that he would return to England and train at West Ham's Chadwell Heath, on the proviso that if anyone was injured before the deadline for the squad being announced, he would be called up. He wasn't home for long: 'I was happy with that. I was ready to recharge my batteries. I had just had a baby, and my wife was pregnant. Even when I landed in Seoul for the transfer back to the UK there were rumours that Danny Murphy had got injured and could be struggling, but I continued with the journey, thinking I may be coming back in a couple of days.

'As I landed in the UK it was confirmed that Murphy was out and Adam Crozier of the FA and Sven had already guaranteed I would be the next cab off the rank. I had 24 to 36 hours in the UK and flew straight back out. We had already been away a month, and even that short break meant I went back with a spring in my step.' It was a very different Trevor Sinclair who faced Cameroon in Kobe in the last warm-up game. Compared with the anxious, nervous model who had played against South Korea, he now felt comfortable and worthy of his place among England's best 23 players.

As Trevor Sinclair battled for a place in the squad, Danny Mills and Wes Brown were vying for a spot in the starting line-up. Mills had been given the number two shirt and the number two kitbag, which he took as a positive sign, and when he outshone Brown in the two warm-up matches and had been given his instructions for set pieces during the last training session, he was confident of facing Sweden in Saitama in the opening game – but still refused to accept he was about to play in the World Cup: 'I walked into the team meeting, keyed up and ready to go, and sat there thinking, "Please be in the team." I was sitting there the most nervous I have ever been, sweaty, three to four hours before kick-off. And you do know the team but not officially, and you get so many kicks in the teeth in football that you never really want to assume, because managers can change their mind at the last minute.

'Players can get ill overnight or pick up a last-minute injury, and that can affect the whole shape of the team. I sat there with my wash bag on the floor, arms folded, fingers crossed under my arms, thinking, "Just please [let there] be a god." And then Sven said, "The team is David Seaman, Danny . . ." And that was it. I don't think I heard anything for the next two or three minutes. It was just like, "Jesus, calm yourself down, get relaxed and listen to the team talk."'

There was a huge England following in Saitama, just outside Tokyo, for the game. The ground was one of many revamped for the World Cup, and Sven-Göran Eriksson was faced with the oddity of managing a national team against his own country. David Beckham started, even though he wasn't 100 per cent fit. England took the lead after 24 minutes when Sol Campbell powerfully headed in a corner. Danny Mills was playing well in what was his first ever start in a competitive match, but just before the hour mark he made a mistake. As he chested the ball down in his area, it ran away from him slightly and his stretched clearance went straight to Niclas Alexandersson, who came inside Campbell and thundered it past Seaman. Given that England were in the 'Group of Death' along with Argentina and Nigeria, a 1–1 draw was not the ideal way in which to start the tournament, and it ramped up the pressure for the next game, against Argentina in Sapporo – as if it needed any more hype.

The change in David Beckham's status since he had been sent off in 1998 was absolutely extraordinary. That day he had been the player who let England down. Fleet Street, and the media in general, pointed the finger, the *Daily Mirror* screamed 'Ten heroic lions, one stupid boy' and angry England fans hung an effigy of him outside a London pub. The witch-hunt that followed was completely disproportionate to a mistake made by one man during a football match, albeit a high-profile one.

Four years on, Beckham – and his wife – were global brands, known and promoted all over the world, and his face was plastered across advertising billboards around Tokyo. Beckham-mania had well and truly caught fire in Japan. 'We just hung onto his coat-tails whenever he was mobbed as he got off the bus,' says Danny Mills. 'We were under no illusions: those thousands of Japanese fans weren't there for me or Nigel Martyn or Gareth Southgate or Martin Keown. They were there for David Beckham and a few for Michael Owen. We were fully aware of that and more than happy to go along with it. This was a good bunch of lads, a good mix of old and young. We weren't daft. We knew the situation, and we took the bonuses off the back of it. Becks could pull in all the sponsorship deals, and we were more than happy to go along with it.'

Argentina had won their opening game against Nigeria thanks to a header from Gabriel Batistuta, the same player who had been so insistent Beckham be sent off that night in St Etienne. This was the first World Cup I went to as a presenter, and for the game we left the concrete jungle of Tokyo for the northern island of Hokkaido and the city of Sapporo, where the 1972 Winter Olympics had been held. Hokkaido is the dairy capital of Japan, and on the train from the airport to the city centre we momentarily escaped the urban sprawl that suffocates so much of the mainland and spotted our first animals of the trip as cows grazed happily in the fields.

FIFA had decided to play the game indoors, in the Sapporo Dome, and the pitch was literally rolled in from outside, replacing the artificial surface on which baseball was played. Walking into the Dome for the first time was a shock to everybody: 'When we went to have a look it was 80 to 90 °F outside and baking hot,' says Danny Mills. 'We walked into the stadium and onto the pitch, and it was freezing. The air conditioning was on! We had been training in ridiculous heat, we were in T-shirts and suddenly we had to ask the kit man to get some jumpers out. It was very echoey when we trained there on our own, and you had the normal situation with footballers when, because it had a roof, you see who can hit it. No one got anywhere near.' Just like the 1986 team with the sculpture in the Azteca Stadium.

The England support in Sapporo that day was something to behold. Come kick-off I looked around the Dome and saw hundreds of Union flags, from all parts of England, draped from wherever they would hang. The level of England's support abroad is often staggering, and here we were five and a half thousand miles from home and for England it would feel like playing at Wembley. The atmosphere was very intense and heavy with revenge – revenge for the penalties and Beckham's red card at St Etienne and for Maradona's Hand of God goal. For the Argentinian fans, it was revenge for Rattín's sending off in 1966, for Ramsey's 'animals' remark and, maybe for some, for the Falklands conflict.

As far as Trevor Sinclair was concerned, he had come along to the World Cup for the ride and was determined to enjoy it. It had taken two separate injuries for him even to be in the squad, and he didn't expect to play much football in Japan, if any at all. Nicky Butt of Manchester United came into the team for Darius Vassell to play in central midfield along with Owen Hargreaves, but 19 minutes into the game the Bayern Munich man hurt his shin.

Eriksson looked at Sinclair and gave him the nod. It was an incredible sequence of events. First Gerrard was injured, then Murphy and then Hargreaves, and instead of watching the World Cup on the TV back home, Sinclair was about to come on against Argentina: 'I was trying to take it in, the whole experience. I was thinking that I couldn't let down all these supporters. It was one of the most memorable atmospheres I have ever had the pleasure of playing in. It was surreal at the time and a privilege to be a part of it. Sven got his tactics right. I was so psyched and focused when I went on. "Don't get too excited, and don't get too down" was his mantra. For me, that was a very important ethos and ambience to be around, and that brought out a better performance in me. Keep all your wits about you, go out there and do what you do.'

Michael Owen had already hit the post when, on the verge of half-time, he was brought down by Pochettino in the area and England were awarded a penalty. Nicky Butt knew what was going to happen next: 'As soon as we got the pen I knew Becks was going to score. He had been taking them in training and smashing them down the middle, and that's what he did.'

Watching the tapes now, it is noticeable how much Beckham concentrates on the ball as it is on the spot and ignores all the shenanigans going on around him, which included his Manchester United teammate Juan Sebastián Verón trying to put him off. Beckham ran up, and his right foot made contact with the ground before the ball, but he struck it firmly enough down the middle as the goalkeeper, Cavallero, shifted his weight to his right. Beckham sprinted to the corner flag, kissing his shirt as the England fans went bonkers. Later he said, 'I walked up to Michael Owen and he said he fancied it, but so did I. That finally puts to rest what happened four years ago, when my world was turned upside down.'

England threatened a couple of times in the second half, but the longer the game went on the deeper they defended, and come the last 20 minutes Argentina were pressing hard for the equaliser. Pochettino went close, and then had another effort well saved by Seaman. It turned into a Premier League-style game for England, with all hands to the pump and the fans increasingly vocal as they urged the team to a crucial and famous win. The noise bounced off the roof and so was 'multiplied by ten', according to Nicky Butt. 'Considering how far away it was and the amount of money it cost the fans to get there, it was probably the best atmosphere I've played in.'

England held on, and come the full-time whistle Danny Mills remembers that it was like the top being taken off a Coke bottle: 'There was a bit of unpleasantness on the pitch. The Argentinians refused to swap shirts and refused to shake hands. When we went into the changing rooms, they still wouldn't swap shirts, and then I realised that for those who had played them before it was really kicking in. It really meant something, and they were really overexcited – even players like Sol Campbell. The tension came out. It was a score settled – and revenge.'

Michael Owen told me, 'Different people experienced different emotions. It was a massive game but not knockout, and I think we would all have preferred to win the '98 game and progress. Though, of course, it was still a big match and an important one; they all are at international level.'

I went round the corner to a hotel with a few colleagues to unwind, and up on the 12th floor, with a fabulous view of the city, we were just coming back to earth over a few drinks in the piano bar when the resident singer decided it was time for an old favourite. The punters quickly recognised the first few bars of 'Don't Cry for Me Argentina', and a massive cheer rang out. It turned into a long night all across Sapporo, which had probably never seen anything quite like it, as England fans celebrated and partied in the city centre without any hint of trouble. I slowly made my way back to my hotel as the sun came up, and I could see the main park was filled with supporters sleeping off a highly memorable 24 hours.

Back in England, the scenes in Manchester were a microcosm of what was happening all over the country. Nicky Butt says in a funny sort of way it was disappointing to miss all the hoopla: 'You don't see all the hysteria back home, and when I spoke to my dad and my friends after the game they said Deansgate in Manchester was totally closed and there were parties on the streets and everything.'

Earlier that afternoon, Sweden had beaten Nigeria 2–1 in Kobe, and the two European sides now had four points each, leaving Argentina, with three, in serious danger of being squeezed out. England knew a point against Nigeria in the southern city of Osaka would be enough to take them through to the second round. For us, based in Yokohama, on the outskirts of Tokyo, it meant another trip on the bullet train, the *Shinkansen*. These were a delight to travel on, the most efficient and relaxing way to get about, and all the jokes you hear about Japanese trains are true. You can literally set your watch by them. You go to the platform, find the number plate of the carriage indicated on your reserved ticket, line up behind the white line, smile at the smartly dressed guards and get on. When on board, there is much more than a curled BLT or two-day-old flapjack to eat. Sushi, squid and gyoza – delicious dumplings – are just some of the things that come under the Japanese heading of 'fast food' on the bullet train.

It was 93 °F in Osaka, conditions that were almost unbearable for England's fair-skinned midfield of Scholes and Butt, and an unchanged team were clearly intent on a safety-first approach. Nigeria's goalkeeper, Enyeama, made a couple of fine saves, and once he had kept them out both teams seemed happy to settle for a draw. For England that meant qualification, and for Nigeria it signified dignity, as they could go home with a point. Surprisingly, joining them in an early exit were Argentina, who could only draw against Sweden 1–1. Coming second in the group, on goals scored, did leave England open to the likelihood of playing Brazil in the last eight, but, as Danny Mills admits, 'It never entered our thinking that it might be Brazil two games down the line. It was never an issue. The all-important thing was just qualifying.' The big news from elsewhere in the World Cup was that defending champions France were also out, having failed miserably even to score a goal in their three games.

England's base throughout the World Cup was on Awaji Island, a holiday destination in the south of the country, and Danny Mills is almost embarrassed at how well they were looked after: 'We were treated much [better] than we deserved as footballers. That's what playing for England meant. One day we went to the Hard Rock Café, and we were allowed a couple of beers. One night we turned up and the streets were closed; the fans were four blocks deep, and as Becks got off first it was stardom, flashbulbs were going off everywhere, and then our security guy, Ray, got off. Gareth Southgate shouted to him, "Don't worry, Ray. The rest of us will be alright; look after Becks." It summed up what it was like: he was the main guy, he was the star and we were the supporting act, but there was no resentment at all, because we were living off the back of it as well. The more he got, the more we got.'

England's scheduled second-round match was against Denmark in Niigata, a two-hour train ride north across the main island of Honshu. The authorities ran extra services late into the night so that England fans staying in Tokyo could get back after the game, but it was the supporters back home that had, for the first time, come to the England players' attention. The squad had seen the pictures of pubs packed at breakfast time, when the games kicked off, of the scenes when England scored and of people jumping into rivers in celebration.

Seeing those images and hearing the stories made the players realise that, despite the distance and the time difference, the whole country was right behind them, but it didn't make Danny Mills feel responsible: 'God, no. We wanted to win the World Cup for ourselves. In that situation, you want to win for you and the team, and you can turn round afterwards and say it's great for everyone else. Fans might not want to hear this, but they come a distant second really. You are so focused and so into it; you have blocked out the rest of the world. You win, you have a glass of beer, a massage and think about the next game. You are so focused that nobody else matters apart from you and the rest of the team.'

The England team picked itself by this stage, with Trevor Sinclair on the left-hand side of midfield and Nicky Butt having an outstanding tournament in the centre alongside Paul Scholes. England were benefiting from the fact the pair of them had played together there for Manchester United since they were youngsters, and Butt puts his excellent form in Japan down to a medial ligament injury he picked up in the April: 'I think there's a lot to be said for resting players, a lot to be said for a Christmas break. I got injured in April. I didn't play, I didn't train, I was out for six weeks and just ticked over, kept my knee OK, and when I came into the Argentina game I was so fit I felt I could run all day. And looking back I think it was a massive bonus that I got injured.'

David Beckham was getting through games on the right, without being at his best, and the Liverpool pair of Heskey and Owen were the strikers. Both were looking for their first goal of the tournament. Denmark had helped put out the World and European Champions France in the group stages, but on a rainy night in Niigata England got off to a flier. After just four minutes, Rio Ferdinand headed David Beckham's corner back across goal and Danish keeper Thomas Sorensen made a hash of it, fumbling it over the line. It looked a clear own goal, but, in its quaint and idiosyncratic way, FIFA decreed it was the defender's, as 'there was sufficient positive impetus from Ferdinand's action that he should have the goal'. On a slick surface, England were all positive impetus, passing the ball well, and by the midway point of the first half they were two up.

Sinclair's pass to Butt then deflected kindly into Owen's path, and from just outside the six-yard box he scored his first goal of the 2002 finals. Ebbe Sand missed Denmark's best opportunity, and by half-time it was all over, Beckham setting up Emile Heskey, who shot powerfully into the net. Owen and Scholes had to come off with injuries, but as England cruised through to the quarter-finals hundreds of fans spent the second half doing a massive conga around Niigata's Big Swan Stadium. The locals loved it. It was the night the England fans spotted Terry Butcher in a bar with Alan Green and me and rushed off to the loos to bandage their heads up in tribute. It was a very long, very noisy and very enjoyable evening.

England now had the most attractive-looking of all of the quarter-finals to anticipate. Brazil had won their group at a canter, scoring 11 goals, and had then eased past Belgium 2–0 in the second round. Luiz Felipe Scolari had taken a team who at one stage were struggling even to qualify for the World Cup and moulded them into a very fine side. The attacking three 'R's – Ronaldo, Rivaldo and Ronaldinho – were the crown jewels. Gilberto Silva and Kléberson were an immensely tough screen, with Roberto Carlos and Cafu allegedly full-backs but in practice more quasi-wingers. One hundred and twenty-five miles down the coast from Tokyo, the city of Shizuoka waited for one of the most glamorous matches in world football and the first World Cup meeting between these two countries for thirty-two years.

Nicky Butt now found himself in an unusual position. This most unassuming of footballers was praised by Pelé as one of the best players of the World Cup, and his name was up in lights. Butt says, 'It was obviously unbelievable that somebody of his stature says that, and it's something you will tell your kids and grandkids. I don't know if he got me and Scholesy mixed up as we've both got ginger hair! People were knocking on my mum's door, and I'm not really a superstar, and my mum wasn't used to it, so I knew something big was happening at home. She got a bit upset, and she didn't know what to do. My dad was in his local pub one day, and this bloke came in to buy him a drink, and it turned out to be a reporter. Those were things my family weren't used to.'

With the kick-off time 7.30 a.m. back home, the morning rush hour was turned on its head. As the *Coventry Evening Telegraph* reported on 21 June, 'roads were deserted and the city centre almost free of shoppers as families, workers and drinkers gathered for the massive quarter-final tie'. The scene at the Chestnut Tree pub in Craven Street, Coventry, was repeated up and down the country. More than 300 packed in, and landlord Dave Kilcoyne reported that some fans had been waiting outside since

5.35 a.m: 'They were waiting to get in for their breakfasts and to take their lucky seats.' Thousands of workers at the nearby Jaguar plant, who originally voted against taking time off to watch the game, did a U-turn overnight after holding a re-vote, and the Browns Lane plant in Allesley ceased production for the day.

In a World Cup of huge upsets, the other quarter-finalists were Germany, the US, Spain, Korea, Turkey and Senegal. Everybody was looking at the England quarter-final as containing the potential champions. Danny Mills agreed with that: 'We knew if we won this game there was a good chance we could win the World Cup. The staff didn't mention it, but we talked about it as players. If we could win this one, there was nothing else left, and we were desperate to win.'

It was so hot in Shizuoka the England team did most of their warm-up inside in a gym and then a few runs outside for about five minutes in the shade near one of the stands. Michael Owen had been troubled by a groin problem, but he played and scored after 23 minutes. Emile Heskey's ball towards the England centre-forward was not cut out by Lúcio, and Owen calmly lifted the ball over the goalkeeper, Marcos, to give England the lead.

I asked Owen if there were any adequate way of describing the thrill of putting England 1–0 up in a World Cup quarter-final, against Brazil of all teams: 'Ha! No, not really. I suppose you only think about that after the event. You're so focused on the moment that when it happens you never think, "I've just put us 1–0 up against Brazil." You're obviously aware that some matches are closer than others and what it could mean, but if you lose your focus and become complacent, then that's when the problems begin.'

It was the perfect start for England, and the strategy, as outlined by Trevor Sinclair, was going well: 'Everything went to plan in the first half. That was our game plan. Get behind the ball, make sure they don't create too many chances and hit them on the counter-attack, and we did that really well. Michael scored. If we could have held out till half-time they might have sweated a little bit more and [worried] that our game plan was working.'

In the oppressive heat, England so nearly reached the sanctuary of the interval a goal ahead, but then the whole emphasis of the match shifted in stoppage time. Both Beckham and Scholes missed tackles in the Brazilian half, and the ball was quickly transferred to Ronaldinho, whose mesmerising step-over at pace flummoxed Ashley Cole. Campbell was backtracking furiously, and Ronaldinho's skill opened the tin can of England's defence just enough for Rivaldo to equalise with an accurate left-footed shot. The goal was a hammer blow, as Trevor Sinclair admits: 'It was a killer. Without it we would have been going in delighted. Everybody would have been geeing each other up, saying everything's going to plan. It would have given us extra belief.'

Back in the changing room, the sense of frustration was palpable after Rivaldo's goal. Later, Gareth Southgate was credited with saying that during half-time England looked to Sven-Göran Eriksson and 'were expecting Winston Churchill but instead . . . got Iain Duncan Smith'. Danny Mills says hindsight can be cruel: 'Players were trying to get drinks on board, trying to cool down. Your feet are absolutely screaming. Maybe we needed a bit of a lift, a bit of a rousing speech, some aggression to get us pumped up and go out and get over the disappointment and make a bigger impact than we did. I say this on reflection. At the time you are so wrapped up in trying to get cool, get a drink inside you, get your breath back, running over the last few minutes of the half and thinking ahead.'

Trevor Sinclair defends Eriksson's conduct, saying he was right to talk to the players the way he always did: 'He was quite calm, getting specific messages across to groups of players and individuals. He ticked all the boxes for me. He is not one of those who chuck teacups and pin lads up against the wall and scream and shout. That just wasn't his style. It wasn't when we were winning, and it didn't change: his ethos again. We had vocal players, so you don't need the manager to do that. There are leaders all over the field. I know he has been criticised for it, but you can't please all the people. You had your own little groups – me and Ashley Cole on the left-hand side – and you talk about different things.'

Five minutes after half-time, Brazil were awarded a free kick forty-two yards out on the right-hand side. Ronaldinho curled the ball goalwards, and David Seaman started to come for it and then back-pedalled desperately as the ball dipped over him into the corner of the net: genius or stroke of luck? The former, according to Ronaldinho: 'Cafu had alerted me to the fact their goalkeeper was standing off his line. As I was about to take the free kick, I saw where he was and was able to beat him.'

But, for the England players, it was a fluke. 'It was a freak goal that was a cross that ended up in the net,' said David Beckham. And Sol Campbell agreed: 'You can't defend against freaky goals. When he was putting the ball in, he was crossing it.' Nicky Butt is on the same wavelength: 'I don't care how good a player you are. The ball was curling away from the goal, and if you're going to try and shoot, you curl the ball towards the goal. I'm not saying he can't do unbelievable things, but that was definitely a fluke.'

Eight minutes later, Ronaldinho was given a straight red card for a challenge on Danny Mills: 'It was a late tackle, and a couple of lads just said, "Stay down, stay down. Don't get up; the ref's going to card him." Could I have jumped up immediately? Probably. Did it hurt? Yes, but that's OK. The adrenalin's pumping: they could have cut my arm off and I probably wouldn't have noticed. That's gamesmanship. After that, technically we weren't quite good enough. They kept the ball so well, and we didn't test their keeper really in the second half.'

The last half-hour was painful to watch from an England point of view, as Brazil played keep-ball expertly and Eriksson's team never threatened to equalise. 'I hoped we would do better eleven versus ten, but we were tired and Brazil were very good at keeping the ball,' said Eriksson afterwards. 'I don't think we had one shot on goal . . . Once it was 2–1 we were not strong enough to come back.'

Nicky Butt was left wondering what might have been had Brazil not scored on the stroke of half-time: 'I really do believe if we had gone in leading we could have shut up shop in the second half. The players we had could have done that. I could have sat in front of the back four. The back four was so strong, we had a great goalkeeper in Dave Seaman and Emile Heskey was working his nuts off in that sort of role in front of midfield. But we were nowhere [near] good enough in the second half.'

As the exhausted team made a slow and sad lap around the pitch, acknowledging the huge England support, David Beckham consoled his devastated goalkeeper. With his own memories of France clearly very much at the forefront of his mind, the England captain said, 'If anyone makes David Seaman a scapegoat, then I think that's an absolute disgrace. That can't keep happening to people.'

Danny Mills and Rio Ferdinand were pulled in for drug-testing straight away and so couldn't go back to the dressing room with the rest of the team. FIFA needed them to perform one more time in the World Cup, and Danny Mills remembers just how tough that was: 'We were in solitary confinement, we had just lost about a stone in weight in fluid and we were put in separate rooms and told to have a pee – and it's nigh on impossible. And it was all compounded by the fact that we walk into the drug-testing room and who's there? Cafu and Ronaldinho. Rio asked him, "Did you mean it [the goal]?" And he said, "Yes." And we both said, "Bullshit!"'

Suddenly England's oriental adventure was no more, and Danny Mills began to feel it: 'That night I sat there, tracksuit on, slowly getting drunk, thinking, "It's over." My feet were covered in blisters, and I was thinking, "Could I have made the next game?" Suddenly everything hurts, and the pain is compounded by the misery you are going through. Whereas before, when you're winning, you just get on with it, all of a sudden you lose, and all the cuts, bruises and everything hurt ten times more. Your room in Awaji was your life – kit everywhere, pictures on the wall. It was your domain, your wall, and within half an hour you've struck camp and you're off to the airport.'

As England sloped home, Brazil went on to win the trophy for the fifth time, beating Germany 2–0 in the final. Both goals came from Ronaldo, so there was a happy story for someone in Japan. He could now banish his own nightmare from the Stade de France fiasco four years earlier. England were left to regret the one minute in the oven of Shizuoka that had ended their dream.

12

GERMANY 2006

England came home beaten but certainly not disgraced. Brazil were worthy winners of a World Cup notable for the scintillating run to the semi-finals of the co-hosts South Korea, under the urbane Guus Hiddink, and the extraordinary number of upsets, with France, Argentina and Portugal failing even to make it to the knockout stages. There were surprises everywhere: Turkey came third and both Senegal and the US were quarter-finalists. Sven-Göran Eriksson's team for the European Championship qualifiers was augmented by the appearance of a brilliantly precocious 17 year old from Everton, Wayne Rooney, who played in the last six games, and when England travelled to Istanbul in October 2003 they needed just a point to qualify.

The build-up, though, was totally overshadowed by the row over Rio Ferdinand's missed drugs test. The Manchester United defender forgot to give a sample after a training session on 23 September, and, even though he passed a test 36 hours later, the FA banned him from the tie in Turkey. His absence would be keenly felt by both the team and the manager. The England players reacted with fury and threatened to boycott the game, and David Davies, then the FA's executive director, was not taken aback to hear who was behind the proposed action, as he wrote in his book *FA Confidential*:

> I was informed Gary Neville was leading the charge against the FA. Somehow, this news did not surprise me. Gary was a leader who cared passionately about those who sat alongside him in the dressing room . . . Some at the FA were stunned by the scale of the revolt stirred up by Red Nev. Paul Barber [the new director of

communications], went in to talk with Gary and was almost knocked back by the strength of feelings. No Rio, no game, came the message from Gary Neville.

The press reaction to the boycott was one of outrage: 'Who Do They Think They Are?' trumpeted the *Daily Mirror*. David James urged the players to consider the fallout if they did go on strike, and Danny Mills, who was still in the squad but had lost his place to the fit-again Neville after the World Cup, decided he had had enough when the media turned on the players: 'It came out that the vote to strike was unanimous, and I had to bite my tongue, knowing full well it hadn't been. It got to the point when we were on the front page of every paper, being called this and that, and getting abused on the street. And I thought, "I'm not having this." I said in the papers I knew full well it wasn't unanimous and there were a lot of people in that room who bottled it. They said they wouldn't play if Rio wasn't reinstated. He wasn't, and they played the game. Making idle threats is the sign of a coward really; if you're going to make strong threats like that, you have got to stand by it.

'I don't regret what I did. It possibly did count against me a little bit when it came to playing for England. It didn't do me any favours. At that time Beckham was all-powerful. Gary Neville was his best mate and was the ringleader, without a shadow of a doubt, and I was up against him. But that's how I am. I stick up for myself, I stand by my beliefs and I fight for them strongly. And that's why I don't regret anything I did to this day, even if it did cost me more places in the England squad.'

Ferdinand was not reinstated but told the players not to boycott the game, and England did play, a goalless draw in Istanbul seeing them through to Euro 2004, where they went out in the quarter-finals on penalties against Portugal. The qualifiers for Germany 2006 were reasonably straightforward for Eriksson's team, with the only blip a memorable win for Northern Ireland against England in Belfast. David Healy's goal was the difference on a raucous night at Windsor Park as Eriksson experimented with his formation and lost a qualifier for the first time. Playing Wayne Rooney out wide on the left and David Beckham in a 'quarter-back' role in front of the back four simply did not work, and the Irish celebrated their first win over England since 1972 – but the defeat didn't impede them for long on the road to the finals.

In a mirror of the situation of 1990, England went to the World Cup knowing that their manager would be leaving once it was over. Eriksson's relationship with the public was fine so long as England were doing well, but he had developed an uncanny knack of getting into the headlines for reasons other than those related to the national team. Ahead of the 2002 World Cup, the newspapers revealed he had been having an affair with a fellow Swede, the TV presenter Ulrika Jonsson, even though he was still with his Italian girlfriend, Nancy Dell'Olio. Then, in the summer of 2003, he was photographed going into Chelsea owner Roman Abramovich's house in London. Eriksson insisted they were just friends and that he wasn't being lured to Chelsea to take manager Claudio Ranieri's job. Whatever went on over tea that day, the FA reacted by handing Eriksson an extension to his contract till 2008 on a reputed £4 million a year.

After England had disappointed by reaching only the quarter-finals at Euro 2004, news broke of another Eriksson affair, this time with FA secretary Faria Alam. She had also been seeing the FA chief executive, Mark Palios, and he was forced to resign after it emerged that the FA's director of communications, Colin Gibson, had attempted to keep the chief executive's relationship with Ms Alam quiet in return for giving a newspaper more information on Eriksson's affair. Up before the FA Board, Eriksson survived after being told he had 'no case to answer', but when he was stung by the *News of the World* it was one story too far for the governing body.

The newspaper reported that he had told their undercover reporter – posing as a sheikh – that he could quit the England job after the World Cup, and he also divulged information about certain players. The following week the paper quoted Eriksson as saying that three unnamed English Premiership clubs were riddled with corruption, relating to illegal payments in transfer deals. It was all too much for the FA, who announced in January 2006, some six months before the World Cup, that Eriksson would leave his position after the tournament.

History repeated itself with one of England's key players as well. If the nation was obsessing over David Beckham's toes in 2002, then this time it was Wayne Rooney's foot that was the centre of intense focus. At Stamford Bridge at the end of April, Rooney broke the fourth toe on his right foot following a tackle from Chelsea's Paulo Ferreira. There were six weeks to go before England's opening game against Paraguay, and Rooney faced a race to be fit in time. It wasn't the first occasion a broken Rooney toe had thrown England into disarray. He had fractured a metatarsal during the quarter-finals of his first championship, Euro 2004, and the break had halted England in their tracks against Portugal.

Despite his injury, Rooney was always going to be in the squad, but Eriksson sprung one gigantic surprise when he included Arsenal's teenager Theo Walcott. The 17 year old had yet to make a first-team appearance for the north London club, and Eriksson had never even seen him play a match, but the Swede decided to include him ahead of Tottenham's Jermain Defoe and Darren Bent of Charlton. Eriksson admitted there was not a great deal of logic to his decision: 'Sometimes you do it on feeling as well, and I am excited about Theo Walcott. I thought we should pick him. At his age you have no fear and you do not feel pressure.'

Eriksson was taking a huge gamble. He had plumped for only four forwards in the party, and Walcott and Peter Crouch were the only fit ones at the time of the announcement in mid May. As well as Rooney being injured, Michael Owen was coming back from a broken bone in his foot, a case of yet another England player with a metatarsal injury. Steven Gerrard wrote in his book *My Autobiography* that Eriksson made two errors when it came to the forward line: 'A few decisions were wrong, like not taking five strikers. Eriksson certainly shouldn't have brought Theo Walcott to Germany. I almost fell over when I heard. One day he will mature into a very good player, but he had no right to be in Germany. None at all. I was gobsmacked to find him on the plane.'

Peter Crouch had made it to the pinnacle of English football via an apprenticeship at Tottenham and loan spells at Dulwich Hamlet and Swedish club IFK Hässleholm. At 6 ft 7 in. and with an engaging smile and personality, Crouch's honest and public struggle when trying to score his first goal at the start of that season for his new club, Liverpool, had endeared him to many. After he scored against Hungary in a warm-up game at the end of May, he performed a dance on the touchline that had been born at David Beckham's pre-World Cup party. Crouch told me how that had come about: 'I remember tapping Jamie Carragher on the shoulder at the party and saying that I was going to do something stupid on the way to the toilet. I walked through the dance floor and did the robot dance, and little did I know that Carra had tipped the camera crew to pan down on me exactly at the right time. A couple of weeks later, David Beckham said to me that it was brilliant and that they were going to have to keep it in the programme. I said, "Yeah, whatever, if you want to." And we were all watching the programme in the team hotel the night before the Hungary game and all of sudden my dance came on. I got a million phone calls and texts – all the lads were saying how brilliant it was – so I said that if I scored tomorrow [against Hungary] I would do the dance.'

Crouch did the dance again on his way to a hat-trick against Jamaica days later, and such was its sudden popularity that when the second-in-line to the throne came to visit the squad he insisted on being shown the moves. Unbeknownst to him on the dance floor at the Beckhams', Crouch had given birth to a craze: 'It just exploded. For me it was a bit of banter, a bit of release, but then I saw on CNN professional body poppers showing me where I had gone wrong. I've got a picture on my wall at home, framed, of me and Prince William doing it and all the lads around me laughing. I couldn't believe how big it had gone. People think it was inspired by the Arctic Monkeys and the single "I Bet You Look Good on the Dancefloor", but it wasn't. It was just something we probably used to do as kids.'

England travelled to Germany with a great deal of optimism. Former FA chief executive Adam Crozier had labelled this crop of players as the 'golden generation', a tag that would come to weigh heavily upon their shoulders, but they did have some very talented players in the team: Terry and Ferdinand in defence; Beckham, Gerrard and Lampard in midfield; and now Rooney up front with Owen. The portents were good. This England team were considered a serious challenger to Brazil's crown, even with concerns over the injuries.

Rooney travelled out with the squad to Germany on 5 June, but it was merely a symbolic gesture, as two days later he returned to the North West of England, and Whalley Range hospital, for a scan on his foot. Even though Rooney could have had the scan done in Germany, Manchester United wanted the X-ray performed at home, and there was clearly a difference of opinion between England and United on what part he could play in the World Cup. United's worries were based on history: Beckham's broken metatarsal had sidelined him for eight weeks and Gary Neville's for sixteen. The two camps couldn't agree on when Rooney should next play, and so two independent medical experts, the top men in the field of metatarsals, were brought in. Professor Angus Wallace and Professor Christopher Moran of the Queen's Medical Centre in Nottingham were, effectively, the referees in all this, asked to arbitrate between the two parties.

Jonathan Legard was the BBC's football correspondent in Germany and embedded with the England team in their hotel. He says Sven-Göran Eriksson never once wavered in his belief that Rooney would play some part in the tournament: 'We watched him arrive with the squad at the team hotel in Germany on the Monday before the opening game. We watched him leave two days later – destination a hospital in Manchester where doctors would decide his World Cup future. We watched the FA's David Davies smiling and joking as Rooney emerged in front of a gallery of cameras at Whalley Range. Then we waited. And waited. And waited. Until we encountered Sven, purely by chance, padding along one of the hotel corridors well into the evening. His expression and his response – "I think it's good news. I think he's coming back" – confirmed what he had said all along. Just before midnight local time in Germany, Rooney announced himself out of the darkness with the words, "The big man's back in town."'

The big man was back, but he had to be put in cold storage for a while. The two professors had agreed he could return to Germany but that he couldn't play in the opening game and that he was unlikely to be fit for any of the group matches. They would fly out to Germany to give Rooney the green light to start playing again.

Paraguay, Sweden, and Trinidad and Tobago were England's opponents in Group Four. As I walked to the ground in Frankfurt for the opening game against the South Americans, it felt almost as hot as England's last World Cup finals game in Japan. Paul Robinson of Tottenham had taken over as England's number one goalkeeper after Euro 2004, and he reflects on just how emotional it was in the dressing room: 'I remember watching one of the British Lions videos with everyone getting really pumped up, and it was like that beforehand. All 23 players stood in a big circle with our arms round each other, and everybody was shouting. And the adrenalin and the atmosphere were unbelievable. Everybody was so pumped up, and then during the national anthems we put our arms round each other again, really holding on tight to each other. You could feel the man next to you was really gripping, and it was such an intense 20 minutes before the game.'

With Wayne Rooney training but not yet fit enough to play, Peter Crouch and Michael Owen played up front. Owen had broken a metatarsal in his right foot on New Year's Eve, after colliding with Paul Robinson during a League game, and then needed another operation in March, so he had only managed four matches in total before lining up against Paraguay. In a forgettable game, England went into an early lead when Beckham's free kick skimmed off the head of Carlos Gamarra and past Justo Villar into the net.

Villar's match, and World Cup, ended when he was injured a few minutes later, but he did take a memento away from his brief appearance in the finals, thanks to his opposite number. 'He asked me for my shirt before the game in the tunnel,' Paul Robinson said. 'My sponsor, Nike, embroidered all the wristbands on my gloves for me, so I had three pairs of gloves for each game, both teams [and] the flags embroidered on the gloves with the game and the date. I gave him a pair as a gesture.'

England had not played particularly well, but the winning start was of more importance than the quality of the performance, and the squad returned contented enough to their hotel, a spectacular mountain-top retreat in the Black Forest in southern Germany. The Schlosshotel in Bühlerhöhe commanded a fabulous view across the Rhine Valley to the Vosges and was the former summer residence of the European aristocracy. It was 15 kilometres from the spa town of Baden-Baden, where the players' wives and girlfriends were staying in the Brenner's Park Hotel.

In Germany, the presence and spending power of the wives and girlfriends – known henceforth as the WAGs – became almost as newsworthy as what their partners were doing on the pitch. Frank Lampard's fiancée, Elen Rives, was seen dancing on a table at Max's nightclub, singing 'I Will Survive', as the WAGs drank £2,000-worth of champagne. One hour-long shopping trip, in which they splashed out £55,000, peaked with a ten-minute binge on shoes and shirts alone that netted some lucky shopkeepers £10,000.

The paparazzi quickly descended on the sunlit streets of the quaint old town, hitherto better known for the restorative qualities of its water. Some of the WAGs were dubbed 'hooligans with visas'. Even the foreign media took an interest. 'Between matches the British wives and girlfriends have their own championship – for the title of WAG queen,' reported Italy's *Gazetta dello Sport*. Baden-Baden's new mayor was so taken by the summer arrivals that he became very unpatriotic. 'I am meant to say that I want Germany to win the World Cup,' Wolfgang Gerstner said very sheepishly. 'But I want England to reach the final, because I enjoy seeing all the beautiful wives around town.'

Over two years later, on the eve of a World Cup qualifier in Belarus, Rio Ferdinand admitted that the whole thing had got out of hand: 'If I'm honest, we became a bit of a circus in terms of the whole WAG situation. We got caught up in the whole thing. It seemed like there was a big show around the whole England squad. It was like watching a theatre unfolding, and football almost became a secondary element to the main event. People were worrying more about what people were wearing and where they were going, rather than the England football team. That then transposed itself into the team. We were all caught up in the bubble. Walking around somewhere like Baden-Baden, there were paparazzi everywhere. It was a circus.'

The WAGs were never an issue in France in 1998 and, given the distance, were never going to be in Japan four years later, but Paul Robinson, whose daughter was two and a half at the time, maintains there is a balance to be struck: 'We didn't see the commotion that was going on at home with the WAGs, but it was the press that made it that way. You go away for any length of time and if you have young children you are going to miss them and your wife as well. But at the same time you realise you are away at work and there are people who spend a lot more time away than we do and at a lot tougher jobs than we do. But it is nice to get to see them and it does make it better. There is a time and a place for it, but maybe not as much as what happened there. A room on your own can be a lonely place if you have had bad training or [a bad] game or you're not playing. We are not hard done by, but it is nice to have the family close by.'

Peter Crouch insists the close proximity of the WAGs was not a distraction to the squad: 'Because we were going down to their hotel and being seen with them, it could be perceived as such, but it wasn't to us. It's not, though, something you want, and it won't happen again.'

England have effectively reverted to the 1998 rules for the 2010 World Cup in South Africa, with Fabio Capello adamant there will be no repeat of the sideshow of Baden-Baden: 'The players will have one day with the girls and friends. One day after each game. That is enough. If the girls do not want to come for the day, then they should stay at home.'

Peter Crouch is perfectly happy with his manager's approach: 'I don't think any of the lads would disagree with Fabio Capello's stance. If people talk and write about it so much it can become a distraction, so I think it's best for everyone if we don't have much contact with them. At the end of the day how many World Cups can you play in? You want to have every chance of succeeding.'

Nuremberg was the next stop for England and a game against Trinidad and Tobago, who were making their debut at the World Cup. It was a very frustrating afternoon, and, with time running out, it was on course to be one of the most embarrassing in England's history. Not only had they failed to break down the Caribbean side's defence, but they were indebted to a spectacular clearance off his own line from John Terry to keep the score at 0–0. Peter Crouch had shinned a volley wide in the first half when, seven minutes from time, Beckham crossed for him to get above the dreadlocked defender Brent Sancho to head in.

'I'll always be able to say that I scored in a World Cup, and I was ecstatic that I managed to get it,' said Crouch. 'The game was so tense you could feel it. If we had drawn would we have got through? We just had to win it. When Becks went down the right, I knew with his quality, as long as I got in the box, I had a chance of scoring. He whipped it in, and I had a few complaints that I pulled Sancho's hair – and maybe I did. I have no idea, but it wasn't intentional and I'm not bothered!'

Graham Poll was the British referee at the World Cup who gained notoriety for showing Croatia's Josip Šimunić three yellow cards in one game. He told BBC Radio 5 Live that the refereeing fraternity couldn't believe Crouch hadn't been penalised for tugging the defender's hair: 'The referee camp was horrified he had got away with it. It was highlighted to us in the debrief. They said that this two-metre-tall man wasn't a natural footballer, and it was highlighted for the referee in England's last [group] game. He [Crouch] was picked out.'

Steven Gerrard drove in a late second, but while England had two wins out of two, they were not playing with any real fluency. Almost as important as the result was the appearance of Wayne Rooney after an hour. Jonathan Legard said that once he had returned from Whalley Range hospital it was just a matter of time: 'The manner in which Rooney threw himself back into training from then on left nobody in any doubt that he was ready for the fray.'

Paul Robinson says they knew how close the Manchester United striker was to being ready before the game: 'There are 23 of you in the squad and you are away together on a camp, so you are in constant contact and conversation. You are with each other every minute of every day, so you find out regularly how he is getting on. Rooney was always going to play. He was nearer than people were led to believe just to safeguard him in case he wasn't. By people resting all their hopes on one player, Rooney, it in a way took the focus off the rest of the squad but then heaped it on him with the expectation it brought.'

Two wins out of two meant that a point against Sweden would see England through as group winners, but the game in Cologne started horribly when Michael Owen went down in agony in the very first minute with no one near him. Our commentary box was right above where Owen crumpled, and we could all see straight away that he was in serious trouble. He had ruptured his anterior cruciate ligament and was out of the World Cup. He had made a huge effort to get fit in time after breaking his toe and later conceded that he probably shouldn't have gone to Germany: 'Loads of people get metatarsal injuries, but they are normally not as bad as mine. Nobody's foot would not have broken in that situation. I then rushed my preparations for the World Cup. I played half a game for Newcastle. After being in plaster for so long, my leg was deconditioned, and, with hindsight, I should never have gone to Germany with England. It's easy to say that now, but if I had my time again I would still have gone, because it was a World Cup. I'm not thinking what could have been, but with hindsight my leg was half as strong as it should have been. Muscles support limbs, and I twisted my knee awkwardly – and that was it. All that came from someone landing on my foot, so I don't think it's my fault.'

England recovered from the setback of losing Owen by going in front after 34 minutes when Joe Cole volleyed in a brilliant opener from 35 yards. But they struggled at set pieces all evening, and the former Aston Villa forward Marcus Allbäck headed the equaliser from a corner early in the second half and then very nearly repeated the trick just minutes later. This time, Allbäck's effort came off Jamie Carragher's arm, and Robinson reacted brilliantly to tip the ball onto the bar. Olof Mellberg then clipped the top of the bar as another corner caused England problems, but Eriksson's team seemed to have won it five minutes from time when

Gerrard powerfully headed in Joe Cole's cross. In stoppage time, however, England failed to deal with a long throw and Henrik Larsson nipped in to make it 2–2. England still topped the group, but their discomfort at set pieces gave them plenty of food for thought when they got back on the training ground.

England's second round game against Ecuador in Stuttgart was, again, played in boiling hot temperatures. By now, it was obvious that England were doing enough to get by but no more. All the anticipation, all the excitement, had largely dissipated as we watched an England side splutter their way through 90 minutes. The Ecuadorian goalkeeper, Cristian Mora, had painted his country's colours on his cheeks, and he was very near celebrating a shock lead when John Terry's mistimed header fell to Carlos Tenorio. The striker was clean through, but as he shot, Ashley Cole bravely flung himself at the ball and deflected it onto the crossbar. Now playing 4–1–4–1, with Michael Carrick in the holding role, England had a better base from which to build – but struggled to support an isolated Wayne Rooney up front. On the other hand, Tenorio and Agustín Delgado, once of Southampton, were giving Terry and Ferdinand plenty to think about.

England's winner came on the hour, when captain David Beckham became the first Englishman to score at three different World Cups. Despite struggling with dehydration and heat exhaustion, Beckham curled in a free kick that beat a diving Mora. Frank Lampard was struggling to reproduce his fine Chelsea form on the international stage, and although he missed two excellent chances late in the game, England held on comfortably. They had reached the quarter-finals, but Paul Robinson acknowledged the reality of the situation: 'We got through without playing well and hitting top gear, without playing to our full potential. We hadn't gelled, but nobody could put their finger on it; something just needed to click to hit top gear. [It was like] we had got past the first few questions on [*Who Wants to Be a*] *Millionaire*, now this is where we want to be. One good performance and a bit of luck and you're in the semis and you start dreaming of the final.'

'I would be England manager if I could put my finger on why we didn't quite click,' admits Peter Crouch. 'Sometimes when teams win tournaments they don't always play well every game. I've seen lots of teams grind out results and start to perform in the latter stages, and I think that's what we were hoping to do. We had fantastic ability and players that could win games, and I think we disappointed ourselves a little bit, to be honest. We had good enough players to do better than we did.'

It was the third tournament at which Sven-Göran Eriksson had been the England manager, and every time he had led them to the last eight. Even though Eriksson was leaving after the World Cup, Paul Robinson insists he commanded the respect of the entire squad right to the end: 'I have a lot of time for Sven. He was brilliant, a great man manager, fantastic, a real gentleman and very knowledgeable on football. He had this fantastic ability and calmness to not let anything in his private life or any outside influences affect him on a day-to-day basis. Anything could be going on and he would be the same day to day. He would be honest, but he wouldn't get stressed or pressured and you would never see him worried about things. He had a great knack for dealing with things. He was always phlegmatic. He always got across well what he wanted to say and the way he was feeling. What he had to say was always constructive, and nine times out of ten it was positive, but he would also put right the wrongs. The respect was there to the end, because he treated you as grown adults.'

Even if the performances had been far from impressive, the England support in Germany had been fantastic. Thousands had travelled without tickets for the matches, but the presence of the fans' zones meant supporters could watch the games on big screens in designated towns and enjoy the experience of being with England at a major tournament. Back in Baden-Baden, Garibaldi's nightclub was celebrating England's progression to the last eight as well, with boss Tortora Carmine apparently having to order in more drinks and saying, 'The WAGs have been wonderful and are such great fun.'

Portugal stood between England and a semi-final place, the Portuguese having beaten the Netherlands 1–0 in a thoroughly bad-tempered second-round match in which the referee had shown the yellow card sixteen times, with four players sent off for second bookable offences. Maniche's early goal had been almost lost amid the mayhem. Barcelona's creative midfielder Deco had been one of those sent off, and his suspension for the quarter-final was of concern to coach Luiz Felipe Scolari, who had led Brazil to the title four years earlier. Gary Neville was fit to take his place at right-back for England after missing the three previous matches, as Eriksson stuck to the 4–1–4–1 formation – with Hargreaves sitting in front of the back four and Rooney up front on his own.

FIFA decided to close the roof on the stadium in Gelsenkirchen, and, with the stands close to the pitch, the noise reverberated around the stadium, creating an atmosphere that matched the grandeur of a World Cup quarter-final. After a cagey 45 minutes, England had to make a change at the start of the second half when Beckham hurt his ankle and was replaced by Tottenham's Aaron Lennon.

A teary England captain was holding an ice pack to his injury when, just after the hour, Wayne Rooney fought with Ricardo Carvalho and Armando Petit to regain possession of the ball on the halfway line – a tussle that ended with Rooney stamping on Carvalho's groin. This happened right in front of the referee, the Argentinian Horacio Elizondo, and Rooney's Manchester United teammate Cristiano Ronaldo was first on the scene, demanding a card. Rooney pushed Ronaldo away, but Elizondo sent the England player off for the stamp, and as Ronaldo wandered towards the touchline to get a drink, he winked at his bench. Afterwards Steven Gerrard was seething at Ronaldo's role in the red card: 'I think that sums him up as a person,' he said. 'I saw what Ronaldo did, and if it was one of my teammates I would be absolutely disgusted by him, because there's no need for that.'

Paul Robinson said that the red card, just as it had in St Etienne eight years earlier, brought out the best in the England team: 'It happened a distance away. I just saw a coming-together of players, and then you see the red card and your heart sinks. And then you look at the clock and how long there is to go, and you think, "Oh no." And then the grit and determination and competitor really, really comes out in you. And you think, "That's it, no one's getting past now. We're in this together. Knuckle down, dig in and if we're not going to win this then we're certainly not going to lose it. That's the attitude. We're not doing this again. We've been here too often. We're not going out now."'

Eriksson sacrificed Joe Cole and sent on Peter Crouch as England's lone forward. With temperatures now nudging 30°C, England held out valiantly and even created a couple of openings. Lampard's free kick was kept out by Ricardo in the Portuguese goal, and Lennon scuffed the rebound wide, while a deflected John Terry shot looped over the bar. At the other end, Hélder Postiga, whose equaliser at the same stage of the Euro 2004 tournament had taken the game into extra time, blazed over, and, just as in Lisbon two years earlier, it went to penalties.

Paul Robinson was happy with that: 'I had so much information. I had seen DVDs, reports, everything. When the individual stood up, I knew where I was going for each one. I had done my own research. I had a lot of people helping me, and I was delighted when it went to penalties, because we had gone down to ten men, we had held on and now this was my time to shine. I was so ready for it. I felt really, really confident.'

England had practised penalties assiduously throughout the tournament, but this was a different level of pressure altogether. If England were a horse, you would not have backed them. They had never won a penalty shoot-out at a World Cup and had gone out on penalties at Italia '90, Euro '96, France '98 and Euro 2004.

Portugal took the first kick, through Simão, and scored. Frank Lampard stepped up first for England. The midfielder had had a magnificent season for Chelsea as they retained the Premier League title, but he had not been at his best in Germany. He had missed a few chances that he would almost certainly have taken while wearing the blue of José Mourinho's team, and now he failed from the spot, Ricardo diving to his left to save a kick that was at a comfortable height for the keeper.

Viana then hit the post with Portugal's second kick, and Owen Hargreaves, who had comfortably been England's best player throughout the tournament, made it 1–1. A nervous-looking Petit shovelled Portugal's third kick wide, presenting England with the chance to go in front through Steven Gerrard, who, like Lampard, was a regular penalty taker for his club. But Gerrard put his kick in the same spot and at the same height as his midfield colleague, and Ricardo again made a straightforward save.

Standing by helplessly on the goal line, watching his colleagues, Paul Robinson was the last to know whether England had scored: 'You get to see them after everybody else, because you have a side-on view. The lads are all stood on the halfway line, so they can see which way the ball's going and which way the goalie's going, whereas I've got the side-on view, so I have to wait till it either hits the goalie, the net or misses. It's a little delayed reaction and a horrible situation.'

Postiga was fourth up for Portugal, and after beating David James in the shoot-out two years earlier, he now scored again, sending Robinson the wrong way. Liverpool's Jamie Carragher, a player who hardly ever missed in training, took England's fourth, and he succeeded again, confidently putting the ball away. But he hadn't waited for the whistle, and the referee forced him to re-take it. This time, Carragher went to the keeper's right and Ricardo got a strong hand on it and deflected the ball onto the bar and away to safety. All that meant that if the bête noire of English football, Cristiano Ronaldo, scored, then England were out.

Paul Robinson knew which way Ronaldo liked to go from the spot: 'Players change their mind as to where they are going to hit it, and as for Ronaldo's pen – well, every single bit of information I had said it would go high to my right, absolutely nailed on. So whichever number pen he took I was going high to my right for his. To be fair to him, he might have been clever enough to know that I might have had that information, so it's a game of double bluff. Ronaldo changed his way for the winning pen.' He certainly did, hitting it high to Robinson's left as the keeper took off in the other direction, trusting his research.

For the fifth time in sixteen years, England had gone out of a major tournament on penalties, and Frank Lampard's reaction sums up the feelings of the nation: 'It's so frustrating to go out on penalties again. That can happen to any team. It happened to Argentina the previous night against Germany. But the depressing feeling is that it has happened to England a few times now. The fact three of us missed a penalty means no individual is isolated for the blame, but that doesn't make it any easier for me. It's a horrible feeling to be one of those who missed a penalty, but those are moments when you stand up to be a man.'

'It's a horrible, horrible feeling,' says Paul Robinson. 'You see the lads on the halfway line, and the fans, and you realise it's done: the dream of reaching the World Cup final, of winning the World Cup, the hopes of everyone – the realisation of it all as you walk round the pitch. You see how upset the other lads were, and you're in shock for a bit.'

Steven Gerrard couldn't believe he had missed: 'I feel numb. I just can't get that miss out of my head. The way I hit a ball, I should score from the spot. I have taken 20 or 30 penalties in practice over the last month and probably scored 95 per cent of them. My strike wasn't accurate enough, and the ball didn't go where I wanted it to. It was the hardest game I have ever played, when we were down to ten men and the lads had nothing left. We did well just getting to penalties, and I thought we were going to do it this time. I'm just absolutely sick I didn't score my penalty. I'm gutted. I have never felt this bad as a footballer before.'

Paul Robinson was dragged off to have a drugs test by a UEFA delegate, whom he admits snapping at: 'The doctor comes in, and you try to have a wee. By the time I had gone back into the dressing room an hour later, the last of the medical team were having a shower. It was a very empty dressing room with bottles strewn around the floor, flips-flops, boots, a few leftovers. It was a horrible place to be on your own, [with] the realisation of what had happened and not knowing what the manager or the lads had said. You never quite get over it. I don't think the memories will ever leave you. I can immediately feel the disappointment talking about it to you now. A little lever switches in my brain.'

For all the talk of the golden generation, the World Cup in Germany was a big disappointment for an England team, full of real talent, who had travelled with a genuine chance. Gary Neville had taken over as captain when his friend David Beckham limped off in the second half in Gelsenkirchen. Neville did not try to hide from the reality: 'As a team, we haven't delivered. England have gone out of the World Cup in the quarter-finals again, and that is not good enough. There always has to be a scapegoat when England lose. When it settles down, people will look at the tournament as a whole and say we didn't perform as we could have done.'

The Sven-Göran Eriksson era had ended with some sort of uniformity: three major championships, three quarter-final exits – two of them on penalties to Portugal – and one defeat at the hands of the eventual winners. England had been consistent but not quite good enough, a seam that has run throughout its World Cup history with one obvious exception in 1966. Spot kicks decided the destination of the trophy in Germany as Italy beat France in Berlin, the denouement coming shortly after Zinedine Zidane had brought his illustrious career to an end in the most inauspicious way by headbutting Marco Materazzi.

The truth is that the 2006 World Cup was a massive let-down from England's point of view. Organisationally and logistically it was a big success: the idea of the fans' zones worked well, it was easy to move around the country and thousands of England supporters enjoyed being at a global sporting extravaganza that was so completely different from 1950, when England had first taken part. But there was never that frisson of excitement with Sven-Göran Eriksson's team of 2006, never that high provided by Beckham's winning penalty against Argentina four years earlier, Michael

Owen's sensational goal in France or David Platt's swivelled winner in Italy. It was a deeply unfulfilling month. As Steven Gerrard wrote in his autobiography, 'We went round Germany blowing our own trumpet and came home mute with embarrassment.'

Peter Crouch knows it: 'Anyone who was part of the Germany World Cup squad feels that there's some unfinished business there, and I would love to be one of those players who put it right in South Africa. I think we've got a fantastic squad, a fantastic chance and a great manager, and I only hope we do ourselves justice.'

England's World Cup song in 1982 – the first World Cup my generation of forty-somethings remembers England playing in – was called 'This Time (We'll Get It Right)'. The lyrics went:

> This time, more than any other time, this time,
> We're going to find a way,
> Find a way to get away,
> This time, getting it all together
>
> We'll get it right
> This time, get it right,
> This time

Maybe in South Africa they will. But if they don't, football being the drug it is in England, we will all be back for more as they aim for Brazil, in 2014.

BIBLIOGRAPHY

NEWSPAPERS/PERIODICALS

Coventry Evening Telegraph
Daily Express
Daily Mail
Daily Mirror
Daily Worker
El Sol (Mexico)
Empire News
FourFourTwo
Gazetta dello Sport (Italy)
L'Equipe (France)
New Statesman
News of the World
Soccer Digest
St Louis Post-Dispatch (US)
The Guardian
The Independent
The Sun
The Sunday Telegraph
The Sunday Times
The Times

BOOKS

Ball, Alan *Playing Extra Time* (Pan Books, London, 2007)

Bowler, Dave *Winning Isn't Everything . . . : A Biography of Sir Alf Ramsey* (Orion, London, 1998)

Charlton, Bobby *My England Years: The Autobiography* (Headline, London, 2008)

Eriksson, Sven-Göran *Sven-Göran Eriksson on Football* (Carlton Books, London, 2003)

Ferrier, Bob *Soccer Partnership: Billy Wright and Walter Winterbottom* (Heinemann, London, 1960)

Finney, Tom *Tom Finney: My Autobiography* (Headline, London, 2003)

Gerrard, Steven *Gerrard: My Autobiography* (Transworld, London, 2006)

Giller, Norman *Billy Wright: A Hero for All Seasons* (Robson Books, London, 2003)

Glanville, Brian *The Story of the World Cup* (Faber & Faber, London, revised edition 1997)

Collomosse, Andrew *The Lion of Vienna* (Sportsprint, Edinburgh, 1989)

Matthews, Stanley *The Way It Was: My Autobiography* (Headline, London, 2001)

Meisl, Willy *Soccer Revolution* (Phoenix Sports, London, 1953)

Powell, Jeff *Bobby Moore: The Life and Times of a Sporting Hero* (Robson Books, London, 2002)

Quelch, Tim *Never Had It So Good: Burnley's Incredible 1959/60 League Title Triumph* (Know The Score Books, Studley, 2009)

Robson, Bryan *Robbo: My Autobiography* (Hodder & Stoughton, London, 2006)

Davies, David with Henry Winter *FA Confidential: Sex, Drugs and Penalties* (Simon & Schuster, London, 2008)

WEBSITES

www.fifa.com
www.iachr.org
www.onthisfootballday.com

WORLD CUP FACTS AND FIGURES

ENGLAND'S WORLD CUP RECORD 1950–2006

1950   Coach: Walter Winterbottom. England went out at the first group stage.

1954   Coach: Walter Winterbottom. England lost to Uruguay 4–2 in the quarter-finals.

1958   Coach: Walter Winterbottom. England went out at the group stages after losing a play-off to the Soviet Union 1–0.

1962   Coach: Walter Winterbottom. England lost to Brazil 3–1 in the quarter-finals.

1966   Coach: Alf Ramsey. England beat West Germany 4–2 in the final, after extra time, to win the World Cup.

1970   Coach: Alf Ramsey. England lost to West Germany 3–2, after extra time, in the quarter-finals.

1982   Coach: Ron Greenwood. England went out at the second group stage.

1986   Coach: Bobby Robson. England lost to Argentina 2–1 in the quarter-finals.

1990   Coach: Bobby Robson. England lost to West Germany in the semi-finals 4–3 on penalties, after the match finished 1–1 following extra time.

1998   Coach: Glenn Hoddle. England lost to Argentina in the second round 4–3 on penalties, after the match finished 2–2 following extra time.

2002 Coach: Sven-Göran Eriksson. England lost 2–1 to Brazil in the quarter-finals.

2006 Coach: Sven-Göran Eriksson. England lost to Portugal in the quarter-finals 3–1 on penalties, after the match finished 0–0 following extra time.

PLAYERS IN ENGLAND WORLD CUP SQUADS 1950–2006

A'Court, Alan 1958
Adams, Tony 1998
Adamson, Jimmy 1962
Anderson, Stan 1962
Anderson, Viv 1982, 1986
Anderton, Darren 1998
Armfield, Jimmy 1962, 1966
Astle, Jeff 1970
Aston, John 1950
Baily, Eddie 1950
Bailey, Gary 1986
Ball, Alan 1966, 1970
Banks, Gordon 1966, 1970
Banks, Tommy 1958
Barnes, John 1986, 1990
Batty, David 1998
Beardsley, Peter 1986, 1990
Beasant, Dave 1990
Beckham, David 1998, 2002, 2006
Bell, Colin 1970
Bentley, Roy 1950
Bonetti, Peter 1966, 1970
Brabrook, Peter 1958
Bridge, Wayne 2002, 2006
Broadbent, Peter 1958
Broadis, Ivor 1954
Brooking, Trevor 1982

Brown, Wes 2002
Bull, Steve 1990
Burgin, Ted 1954
Butcher, Terry 1982, 1986, 1990
Butt, Nicky 2002
Byrne, Gerry 1966
Byrne, Roger 1954
Callaghan, Ian 1966
Campbell, Sol 1998, 2002, 2006
Carragher, Jamie 2006
Carrick, Michael 2006
Carson, Scott 2006
Charlton, Bobby 1958, 1962, 1966, 1970
Charlton, Jack 1966, 1970
Clamp, Eddie 1958
Clarke, Alan 1970
Clayton, Ronnie 1958
Clemence, Ray 1982
Cockburn, Henry 1950
Cohen, George 1966
Cole, Ashley 2002, 2006
Cole, Joe 2002, 2006
Connelly, John 1962, 1966
Cooper, Terry 1970
Coppell, Steve 1982
Corrigan, Joe 1982
Crouch, Peter 2006
Dickinson, Jimmy 1950, 1954
Ditchburn, Ted 1950
Dixon, Kerry 1986
Dorigo, Tony 1990
Douglas, Bryan 1958, 1962
Downing, Stewart 2006
Dyer, Kieron 2002
Eastham, George 1962, 1966

Eckersley, Bill 1950
Fenwick, Terry 1986
Ferdinand, Les 1998
Ferdinand, Rio 1998, 2002, 2006
Finney, Tom 1950, 1954, 1958
Flowers, Ron 1962, 1966
Flowers, Tim 1998
Foster, Steve 1982
Fowler, Robbie 2002
Francis, Trevor 1982
Gascoigne, Paul 1990
Gerrard, Steven 2006
Greaves, Jimmy 1962, 1966
Green, Ken 1954
Hargreaves, Owen 2002, 2006
Hateley, Mark 1986
Haynes, Johnny 1958, 1962
Heskey, Emile 2002
Hitchens, Gerry 1962
Hoddle, Glenn 1982, 1986
Hodge, Steve 1986, 1990
Hodgkinson, Alan 1962
Hopkinson, Edward 1958
Howe, Don 1958, 1962
Hughes, Emlyn 1970
Hughes, Laurie 1950
Hunt, Roger 1962, 1966
Hunter, Norman 1966, 1970
Hurst, Geoff 1966, 1970
Ince, Paul 1998
James, David 2002, 2006
Jenas, Jermaine 2006
Keegan, Kevin 1982
Keown, Martin 1998, 2002
Kevan, Derek 1958

Labone, Brian 1970
Lampard, Frank 2006
Le Saux, Graeme 1998
Lee, Franny 1970
Lee, Rob 1998
Lennon, Aaron 2006
Lineker, Gary 1986, 1990
Lofthouse, Nat 1954
Mannion, Wilf 1950
Mariner, Paul 1982
Martin, Alvin 1986
Martyn, Nigel 1998, 2002
Matthews, Stanley 1950, 1954
McDermott, Terry 1982
McDonald, Colin 1958
McGarry, Bill 1954
McMahon, Steve 1990
McManaman, Steve 1998
Merrick, Gil 1954
Merson, Paul 1998
Milburn, Jackie 1950
Mills, Danny 2002
Mills, Mick 1982
Moore, Bobby 1962, 1966, 1970
Mortensen, Stan 1950
Mullen, Jimmy 1950, 1954
Mullery, Alan 1970
Neal, Phil 1982
Neville, Gary 1998, 2006
Newton, Keith 1970
Nicholson, Bill 1950
Norman, Maurice 1958, 1962
Osgood, Peter 1970
Owen, Michael 1998, 2002, 2006
Owen, Syd 1954

Paine, Terry 1966
Parker, Paul 1990
Peacock, Alan 1962
Pearce, Stuart 1990
Peters, Martin 1966, 1970
Platt, David 1990
Quixall, Albert 1954
Ramsey, Alf 1950
Reid, Peter 1986
Rix, Graham 1982
Robinson, Paul 2006
Robson, Bobby 1958, 1962
Robson, Bryan 1982, 1986, 1990
Rooney, Wayne 2006
Sansom, Kenny 1982, 1986
Scholes, Paul 1998, 2002
Scott, Laurie 1950
Seaman, David 1998, 2002
Shearer, Alan 1998
Sheringham, Teddy 1998, 2002
Shilton, Peter 1982, 1986, 1990
Sillett, Peter 1958
Sinclair, Trevor 2002
Slater, Bill 1958
Smith, Bobby 1958
Southgate, Gareth 1998, 2002
Springett, Ron 1962, 1966
Staniforth, Ron 1954
Stepney, Alex 1970
Steven, Trevor 1986, 1990
Stevens, Gary A. 1986
Stevens, Gary M. 1986, 1990
Stiles, Nobby 1966, 1970
Swan, Peter 1962
Taylor, James 1950

Taylor, Tommy 1954
Terry, John 2006
Thompson, Phil 1982
Vassell, Darius 2002
Waddle, Chris 1986, 1990
Walcott, Theo 2006
Walker, Des 1990
Watson, Willie 1950
Webb, Neil 1990
Wilkins, Ray 1982, 1986
Williams, Bert 1950
Wilshaw, Dennis 1954
Wilson, Ray 1962, 1966
Withe, Peter 1982
Woodcock, Tony 1982
Woods, Chris 1986, 1990
Wright, Billy 1950, 1954, 1958
Wright, Mark 1990
Wright, Tommy 1970